ANCIENT SCIENCE AND DREAMS

Oneirology in Greco-Roman Antiquity

M. Andrew Holowchak

University Press of America,® Inc.
Lanham · New York · Oxford

University Press of America,® Inc.
4720 Boston Way
Lanham, Maryland 20706
UPA Acquisitions Department (301) 459-3366

12 Hid's Copse Rd.
Cumnor Hill, Oxford OX2 9JJ

Printed in the United States of America
British Library Cataloging in Publication Information Available

Library of Congress Cataloging-in-Publication Data

Holowchak, Mark.
Ancient science and dreams : oneirology in Greco-Roman antiquity / M. Andrew Holowchak.
p. cm
Includes bibliographical references and index.
1. Dreams—History. 2. Civilization, Greco-roman. I. Title.

BF1078 .H654 2001 154.6'3'0938—dc21 2001054039 CIP

ISBN 0-7618-2157-0 (pbk. : alk. paper)

™ The paper used in this publication meets the minimum requirements of American National Standard for Information Sciences—Permanence of Paper for Printed Library Materials, ANSI Z39.48—1984

Dedication

This book is dedicated to Professor Nicholas Jones, whose positive encouragement along the way made it possible to see this work through to completion.

> "For everything in a dream is more deep and strong and sharp and real than is ever its pale imitation in the unreal life which is ours when we go about awake and clothed with our artificial selves in this vague and dull-tinted artificial world."
>
> Mark Twain, "My Platonic Sweetheart"

Contents

Figures

Abbreviations for Greek and Latin Works

Greek Works

<u>Aeschylus:</u>
Ch.=Libation Bearers
Eu.=Eumenides
Pers.=Persians

<u>Aristotle:</u>
APo.=Posterior Analytics
De An.=On the Soul
EN=Nichomachean Ethics
GA=Generation of Animals
HA=History of Animals
Insomn.=On Dreams
Metaph.=Metaphysics
Sensu=On Sensation
Somn.Div.=Prophesy during Sleep
Somn.Vig.=On Sleep and Wakefulness

<u>Artemidorus:</u>
Oniroc.=Interpretation of Dreams

<u>Diogenes Laertius:</u>
Vit.=Lives of Philosophers

<u>Epicurus:</u>
Ep.Her.=Letter to Herodotus
Sent.Vat.=Vatican Sayings

<u>Epictetus:</u>
Diatr.=Discourses

<u>Euripides:</u>
Rh.=Rhesus

<u>Galen:</u>
Dign.=Diagnosis from Dreams
Exper.Med.=On Empirical Medicine
Hist.Phil.=History of Philosophy
Lib.Propr.=Idiosyncratic Books
Nat.Fac.=On the Natural Faculties
Meth.Med.=Therapeutic Method
Morb.Diff.=Classification of Diseases
San.Tuen.=On Hygiene
Sect.Intr.=On Sects for Beginners
Subf.Emp.=Outline of Empiricism
UP=Usefulness of Parts

<u>Herodotus:</u>
Hist.=Histories

<u>Hippocrates:</u>
Aër=Airs, Waters, Places

Aff.=On Illness
Aph.=Aphorisms
De Arte=Art of Medicine
Decent.=Decorum
Epid.=Epidemics
Flat.=Breaths
Int.=Internal Illnesses
Lex=Law
Morb.=On Disease
Morb.Sacr.=Sacred Disease
Nat.Hom.=The Nature of Man
Nat.Puer.=The Nature of Child
Prog.=Prognisis
Vict.=On Regimen
VM=Ancient Medicine

<u>Hesiod:</u>
Th.=Theogony

<u>Homer:</u>
Il.=Iliad
Od.=Odyssey

<u>Iamblichus:</u>
Myst.=Mysteries of Egypt

<u>Philo:</u>
Insomn.=Dreams

<u>Philostratus:</u>
Gymn.=Gymnastics

<u>Pindar:</u>
N.=Nemean Odes
O.=Olympian Odes

<u>Plato:</u>
Ap.=Apology
Chrm.=Charmides
Euthyphr.=Euthyphro
La.=Laches
Lg.=Laws
Phd.=Phaedo
Phdr.=Phaedrus
Phlb.=Philebus
Prm.=Parmenides
R.=Republic
Smp.=Symposium
Sph.=Sophist
Tht.=Theaetetus
Ti.=Timaeus

<u>Plotinus:</u>
Enn.=Enneads

<u>Plutarch:</u>
Mil.=Famous Soldier
Plac.Phil.=Opinions of Philosophers
Pyth.Or.=Pythian Dialogues

<u>Porphyry:</u>
Antr.Nym.=Cave of Nymphs

<u>Rufus of Ephasus:</u>
Quaes.Med.=Medical Questions

<u>Sextus Empiricus:</u>
M.=Against the Mathematicians

<u>Synesius:</u>
Insomn.=Dreams

<u>Xenophon:</u>
Cyr.=Cyropaedeia
Mem.=Memorabilia

Latin Works

Apuleius:
Pl.=On Plato

Augustine:
CD=City of God
Ep.=Letters
Imm.An.=Immortality of the Soul

Caesar:
Gal.=Gallic Wars

Cicero:
Acad.=On Academic Philosophy
Att.=Letter to Atticus
Brut.=Brutus
Div.=On Divination
Fam.=Letters to Close Friends
Fin.=On Ends
ND=On the Nature of the Gods

Clement:
Misc.=Miscellanea

Gregory the Great:
Dial.=Dialogues

Gregory of Nyssa:
Creat.Hom.=Origin of Man

Lucretius:
Nat.=The Nature of Things

Macrobius:
Somn.Scip.=Dream of Scipio

Pliny:
Nat.=Natural History

Quintus:
Inst.=Method of Oratory

Seneca:
Suas.=Persuasive Discourses

Suetonius:
Cal.=Caligula

Tacitus:
Ag.=Life of Agricola
Ann.=Annals

Tertullian:
De An.=On the Soul

Varro:
R.=On Agriculture

Other Abbreviation

D.L.=Diogenes Laertius

Dox.Gr.=Doxographi Graeci (H. Diels)

LSL=*Greek-English Lexicon* (Liddell, Scott, and Jones)

OLD=*Oxford Latin Dictionary*

Vorsokr.=Fragemente der Vorsokratiker (H. Diels)

Preface

In this undertaking, I analyze the ancient notion of the science of dreams, what I refer to as "oneirology", through Greco-Roman works from Classical Greece in the fifth century B. C. to the Roman Republic in the fourth century A. D. First, I examine empirical issues in ancient accounts. For example, were natural scientists, interpreters, and philosophers taking an honest and sober look at the content of dreams? Second, I analyze important nonempirical factors that went into their understanding of dreams. To what extent were ancient oneirologists uncritically accepting traditional ways of looking at dreams? Were some philosophical accounts generated by pure philosophic reflection, uncontaminated by empirical data, on the nature of dreams?

My assessment of ancient oneirology proceeds principally through two questions: "What was the nature of dreams to these ancient authors?" and "What functions did they perceive dreams to have?" Many of the problems concerning dreams that plagued these ancients—like ascertaining the correct interpretation of a dream or knowing that someone's report of a dream is true to the dream as it actually was dreamed—still haunt philosophers and scientists today.

Overall, I have selected some of the most important authors and significant oneirological works in antiquity. Yet, because my study covers some 900 years of Greek and Roman material, I cannot pretend to give readers anything other than a general feel of the social and intellectual climate during so large a span of time. In some cases, it is difficult enough to flesh out an author's views on dreams and have some measure of confidence in the accuracy of my reconstruction. For these reasons, I have adopted the policy of not trying to say too much to fill in gaps chronologically by hasty speculation on possible causal links between authors. Additionally, to give neglected works—like those of Plato, the Hippocratics, Lucretius, Galen, and Synesius—their full deserve, I have passed over other important authors, such as

Tertullian, Gregory of Nyssa, Augustine, and Macrobius, who may be more familiar to readers.

Concerning the secondary literature, like others before me, I have been influenced by E. R. Dodd's groundbreaking *Greeks and the Irrational* (1951). The fourth chapter of his work, devoted wholly to dreams, is a fine summary of the Greek attitude concerning dreams. A. H. M. Kessels' *Studies on the Dream in Greek Literature* (1978) gives a good reconstruction of the Classical and preClassical literary view of dreams in Greece. Claes Bloom's *Studies on the Dream Book of Artemidorus* is an older work (1936), yet one that contains sound historical and philosophical insights into Artemidorus' book of dreams and an excellent philological analysis of it. Roger Pack has also contributed significantly to an understanding of both Artemidorus the person and his *Onirocritica*. David Gallop has improved our understanding of Aristotle's thinking on dreams, especially with his translation and commentary of Aristotle's dream-related treatises (1990). Van Lieshout's *Greeks on Dreams* (1980) is a significant and excellent historical, philosophical, and philological contribution to an understanding of dreams in Greek antiquity. He deals with dreams in literature, philosopher's views on dreams, and the interpretation of dreams from Homer's time to Plato, handling such thinkers as Epicharmus, Democritus, Antiphon, and Heraclitus. More recently, Patricia Cox Miller (1994) has also contributed to our understanding of the significance of dreams in ancient times in her *Dreams in Late Antiquity*. The first half of the book especially offers valuable historical and sociological insights on the origins, interpretation, and functions of dreams from Homeric times to the Late Roman Empire. Ludwig Edelstein has certainly furthered our understanding of dreams in secular medicine as well as religious incubation through his essays on ancient medicine (1967) and collection of testimonies at healing sanctuaries (1945). C. A. Behr (1968) has a short, though somewhat dated essay on dreams in ancient Greco-Roman times in his translation of and commentary on Aelius Aristides' diary of dreams, *Sacred Tales*. Last, Steven Oberhelman's research on dreams in ancient Greco-Roman medicine must be acknowledged.

The secondary literature has certainly made a solid start of enhancing our understanding of the common as well as the uncommon perception of dreams in Greco-Roman society. What is wanting, however, is a critical and general account of oneirology *qua* science (in the broader, ancient sense of "science"). Thus, my book is an examination of what I take to be the three main components of ancient oneirology: accounts of the origins and formation of dreams, the art of interpretation through dreams, and the medical uses of dreams. This examination will sometimes merely take the form of reconstructing neglected ancient Greco-Roman accounts of dreams. Many ancient thinkers' views on dreams—Plato in *Timaeus*, Lucretius' *de Rerum Natura* (Book IV), and Synesius' *On Dreams*—to the best of my knowledge, have never fully been fleshed out. At other times, my intent is a critical evaluation of oneirology itself, especially when I turn to the science of prophecy through dreams (Cicero's *de Divinatione* and Artemidorus' *Onirocritica*) and the medical application of dreams in Part III. Consequently, my modest goal is to fill some of the gaps in the secondary literature.

Next, let me turn to the issue of terminology. The Greeks used several words for "dream—ὄναρ (n.), ὄνειρος (m.), ὄνειρον (n.), ὅραμα (n.), χρηματισμός (m.), ἐνύπνιον (n.), and φάντασμα (n.)—and a few terms for "interpreter of dreams"—ὀνειρόπολος (m.), ὀνειρόμαντις (f./m.), and ὀνειροκρίτης (m.). Of the words for "dream", ὄνειρος, ὅραμα, χρηματισμός, ἐνύπνιον, and φάντασμα took on specific meanings in at least two ancient accounts, those of Artemidorus and Macrobius: the first three terms being indicative of types of prophetic dreams and the final two referring to types of nonprophetic dreams. The ancient Greeks generally used ὄνειρος/ὄνειρον for any kind of prophetic dream, while ἐνύπνιον (literally, "something [seen] in sleep") was used to refer to a nonprophetic dream (whose cause was mostly thought to be internal and physiological). The Latin equivalent to ὄνειρος is *somnium* (n.), which is clearly related to the Latin word for sleep, *somnus* (m.). Macrobius also gives *visio* (f.) (=ὅραμα) and *oraculum* (n.) (=χρηματισμός) as particular kinds of prophetic dreams, and *insomnium* (n.) (=ἐνύπνιον) and *visum* (n.) (=φάντασμα) as kinds of nonprophetic dreams.

Throughout this work, I use the English terms "oneirocritic" to mean "interpreter of dreams", "oneirocriticism" to mean "interpretation through dreams" or "the art of interpretation through dreams", "oneiromancy" to mean "prophecy through dreams" or "the art of prophecy through dreams", "oneiric" to mean "of or pertaining to dreams", and "oneirology" to mean "science or study of dreams", loosely apprehended. All of these terms are established English words, though they may be unfamiliar to readers.

Next, the primary texts that I have used are as follows.

Homer: Monro and Allen's *Iliadis*, vols. i & ii and Allen's *Odysseae*, vols. i & ii
Plato: Burnet's *Platonis Opera*, vols. i-v;
Aristotle: Ross's *Parva Naturalia* and other Oxford texts on Aristotle for other works
Cicero: Pease's *de Divinatione*, vols. i and ii
Artemidorus: Pack's *Onirocriticon Libri V* and Kaiser's *Traumbuch*

Hippocrates, Galen, and Rufus: Littré's *Oeuvres Complètes D'Hippocrate,* Joly's *Hippocrate: Du Régime*, Kühn's *Galeni Opera Omnia*, Gartner's *Quaestiones Medicinales*, and Daremberg and Ruelle's *Oeuvres de Rufus d'Éphése*

Lucretius: Munro's *de Rerum Natura*, Ernout's *Lucrète: De Rerum Natura*, vols. i & ii and *Lucrète: De Rerum Natura: Livre Quatrième* and Bailey's *de Rerum Natura*, vols. i-iii

Synesius: Minge's *de Insomniis* (*PG, Tomus LXVI*) and Terzaghi's *Synesius Cyrenensis Opuscula*, vols. i & ii

For a more complete listing of ancient materials, see the bibliography section.

Last, unless otherwise specified, all translations are my own.

Acknowledgements

I would like to thank Jim Lennox, Mary Louise Gill, Nicholas Jones, Peter Machamer, James Allen, and Adolf Grünbaum for encouragement and helpful suggestions on an earlier draft of this project. Additionally, I would like to acknowledge all the "tireless" nocturnal investigators who have gone through the drudgery of extra daily sleep in an effort to disclose fully the nature of oneiric experience.

Introduction

Like many of us today, ancient Greeks and Romans took a lively interest in dreams. Whereas we tend to think that dreams can give us insight into our present or past affairs—such as early childhood traumata, emotional dispositions, or personal problems—the ancients counted on dreams especially for help in directing or for knowledge of their future affairs. Socrates, Plato relates in the *Crito*, resigned himself to his impending death because of the message of a handsome woman in a dream.[1] Philostratus tells of a retired Egyptian wrestler Mys, who was encouraged by a dream to compete again and given advice as to how to use the injury that had forced his retirement to his advantage.[2] Augustine mentions a Carthaginian doctor with gout who, about to be baptized, dreamed that demons in the guise of Negro youths forbade his baptism and trampled on his bad foot. Nevertheless, he went on to get baptized and, when he did, his gout left him forever.[3] Asclepius and Apollo (in one and the same form) were said to visit Aelius Aristides in a dream, bidding him to bathe in the local river as a means of expurgation.[4] St. Jerome dreamed that he was dragged before "the Judge", where everyone and everything was so bright and the Judge told him: "you are a follower of Cicero, and not of Christ". Afterward, he turned away from his beloved Cicero and reaffirmed his faith in Christ.[5] In short, just as many of us today count on science for knowledge of and guidance in our own affairs, many of the ancients believed they could gain some control over their lives through interpretation of prophetic dreams and the reading of other portents.

The ancient interest in dreams, both prophetic and nonprophetic, permeated and influenced Greco-Roman culture at all levels of society. Much of the drama of non-philosophical Often Greco-Roman literature (e.g., Homer's *Iliad* and *Odyssey*, Herodotus' *Histories*, Greek tragedy, Plutarch's *Lives*, Suetonius' *Caesars*, and Virgil's *Aeneid*) turned on prophetic dreams. This suggests that dreams were important in the lives of all Greeks and Romans. Interpreters of dreams thrived at the Greek agora and the Roman forum—especially at religious festivals. Homer, Herodotus, Arrian, and Plutarch tell us of military campaigns that were conducted or aborted because of an unfavorable interpretation. In medicine, dreams often determined a course of treatment in both established secular practice and at religious healing sanctuaries. Last, Aristippus, Aristotle, Theophrastus, and Chrysippus made dreams themselves objects of philosophical analysis—though many of these works do not survive—suggesting that dreams were considered to be phenomena worthy of serious investigative inquiry. The ancient Greek and Roman cultures were, it is fair to say, mightily under the sway of the various "meanings" of dreams.

It comes as no surprise, then, that there were many elaborate and rich accounts of different kinds or functions of dreams given by philosophers, interpreters of dreams, natural scientists, and physicians. The vast majority of these accounts preserve the notion, found in Homer, that some dreams are prophetic. Still, other accounts indicate that certain dreams can tell us about the current condition of our body or soul and, thus, seem quite modern.

Though early Greco-Roman oneirology was an undeniable mix of naturalism and supernaturalism, the overall Greco-Roman attitude toward dreams was surprisingly scientific—even by today's standards. First, from at least the fifth century B. C., dreams themselves became objects of scientific scrutiny. Philosophers and natural scientists gave accounts of the genesis and formation of dreams in keeping with prevailing views on natural science in antiquity. Next, interpreters of prophetic dreams developed rules and guidelines for distinguishing such dreams from nonprophetic dreams and for interpreting the former. They set down these rules and guidelines in elaborate nomological works on interpretation—of which, only Artemidorus' work survives completely. Last, dreams played an important role in ancient medicine. Many physicians urged that dreams should be employed for medical diagnosis and, in cases, argued effectively for such use, while religious healing sanctuaries used remedies that were supposedly given to supplicants by concerned gods in dreams.

From the picture I sketch, it should be obvious that there are stark differences between the Greco-Roman notion and our modern notion of science. To begin, ancient Greeks and Romans had no term comparable in meaning to our "science" today. The terms that they used had a wide variety of meanings. Greeks, for example, used terms such as ἐπιστήμη[6] (knowledge, understanding, art, scientific knowledge), φρόνησις[7] (perception, knowledge, practical wisdom), τέχνη[8] (art, skill, or craft), μνήμη or μνημοσύνη[9] (memory, remembrance, record), and ἐμπειρία[10] (experience, without knowledge of causes); Romans talked of *ars*[11] (art, skill, science), *scientia*[12] (science, understanding, knowledge, skill, expertise), *disciplina*[13] (knowledge, learning, teaching, system, method, science), and *doctrina*[14] (teaching, training, science, instruction, knowledge, learning), and *memoria*[15] (memory, recollection, history, record). Such terms were utilized by philosophers, orators, natural scientists, astrologers, craftsmen, interpreters of dreams, physicians, and a variety of other people. Consequently, our modern notion of "science" today is anachronistic, when applied to antiquity.

Now I turn to a brief overview of this book. Chapter one an account of some of the similarities and differences between ancient Greco-Roman and modern science. The remainder of the work is divided into three parts—each corresponding to one of the three main areas of scientific application of ancient oneirology. Part I examines naturalistic accounts of how dreams occur ("oneirogenesis") through a focus on works of Plato, Aristotle, and Lucretius. In Part II, I analyze the art of interpreting prophetic dreams ("oneirocriticism") by a study of works by Cicero, Artemidorus, and Synesius. Part III investigates dreams as diagnostic tools in secular medicine as well as their roles in religious healing sanctuaries. I summarize my findings in the final chapter. Throughout, I order the presentation in each section chronologically.

---

[1] *Cri*, 44a-c.

[2] *Gymn.* XXXXI (Robinson 1981, 226).

[3] *CD* XXII.

[4] Behr 1968, 226-227.

[5] *Ep.* XXII.30.

[6] E.g., Plato (*Sph.* 233c & *R.* 477b) and Aristotle (*APo.* 88b30, *EN* 1139b18, & *Metaph.* 981a2), and Hippocrates (*Lex* IV).

[7] E.g., Plato (*Phlb.* 63a & *Smp.* 209a), Aristotle (*EN* 1140a24, 1141b23, *GA* 753a12, & *HA* 608a15), and Xenophon (*Mem.* I.ii.10).

[8] E.g., Hesiod (*Th.* 496 & 929), Pindar (*N.* I.25), Herodotus (*Hist.* III.130), and Aristotle (*Metaph.* 981a2).

[9] E.g., Herodotus (*Hist.* IV.144), Plato (*Leg.* 741c), Aristotle (*Metaph.* 980b28), and Galen (*Sect.Intr.* II).

[10] E.g., Plato (*R.* 582b, *Leg.* 857c, & *Prm.* 137a), Galen (*Sect.Intr.* I), and Sextus Empiricus (*M.* VIII.191).

[11] E.g., Cicero (*Div.* I.2, 11-12, 34, II.14, 26, etc.), Tertullian (*de An.* XXXI), Tacitus (*Ann.* XII.61), and Lucretius (*Nat.* V. 1457).

[12] E.g., Cicero (*Div.* I.4, 24, II.30, 70, 100, etc.), Seneca (*Suas.* III.7), Pliny (*Nat.* II.141), Varro (*R.* II.i.2), and Quintus (*Inst.* I.iv.6).

[13] E.g., Cicero (*Div.* I.33, 91, II.10, 28, 74, 76, & 80), Apulius (*Pl.* I.8), Caesar (*Gal.* VI.xiii.11), and Plutarch (*Mil.* CLXXXVI).

[14] E.g., Lucretius (*Nat.* II.8), Pliny (*Nat.* XXXV.79), Suetonius (*Cal.* XXXIV.2), and Cicero (*Div.* II.70 & *Fam.* VI.xii.5).

[15] E.g., Tertullian (*de An.* 723), Tacitus (*Ag.* II.4), and Cicero (*Div.* I.2, 127, II.126, & *Brut.* XIV).

Chapter One
Science: Yesterday and Today

What Is Science?

Geneticists study the hereditary transmission of traits and diseases to gain a fuller understanding of human nature. Political statisticians, seeking causally relevant information, examine trends in voting populations to give them clues for campaigning strategies. Observational astronomers, guided by computer-aided technology, look back in time through telescopes to disclose the origin of the cosmos. Clinical psychologists use techniques to retrace associations in a patient's cognitive network in an effort to find early trauma that is etiologically linked to abnormal behavioral symptoms. Archeologists analyze remnants of tools at an ancient excavation site so as to piece together the manner of life for these long-lost people. Today, more than any other time in the history of the world, science is recognizably a great part of the lives of most people.

Yet what are the aims, principles, and methods of science? To what extent can science justify its claims? How do observation and experiment come into play? These questions and numerous others give us pause to ask, "What precisely is science?"

Doubtless, these questions are vital today, but they were just as engaging in antiquity, when science in its infancy struggled to define and justify itself. Thus, in writing an evaluative book on science and dreams in Greco-Roman antiquity, it is profitable, if not indispensable, to take a brief look at the birth and development of early science.

Science in Antiquity

Pre-Aristotelian Science

When we study the rudiments of early science, we come back to ancient Babylon, Egypt, and Greece. Yet as many prominent scholars of antiquity (e.g., Charles Kahn and G. E. R. Lloyd) have claimed, it is only with the Greeks that we find systematic attempts at associating scientific practice with a particular methodology. Real science begins with the Greeks.

For the ancients Greeks, science was an attempt to gain some sort of control over their lives and environment through turning a potentially hostile world into something familiar and accessible. Earliest Greek speculation, even mythopoetry like Hesiod's *Theogony*, was cosmological in scope. As the word "cosmos" suggests, Greek philosophers viewed the universe as an orderly system that was knowable through study and reason.

<u>Greek Monism</u>. The first attempts at systematic and rational understanding of the cosmos and the motion and change within it were monistic[1] and materialistic. The early Milesians in the sixth century B. C.—Thales, Anaximander, and Anaximenes—sought to reduce the flux of all visible phenomena to one sort of underlying, unchanging stuff. For Thales, this stuff was water. He also posited that all things are full of gods. Anaximander, who is believed to have been a younger contemporary of Thales, said that the underlying stuff was a boundless, indefinite sort of matter (*aperion*) out of which all things come and to which all things return by necessity. The third Milesian, Anaximenes, perhaps as a compromise between the boundless *apeiron* of Anaximander and the crude corporeality of Thales, stated that air was the primal stuff. Through rarefaction and condensation, air comprises all visible things. While fire was thought to be rarefied air, water, earth, and stone were air at increasingly greater levels of condensation.

Heraclitus of Ephasus (d. c. 480 B.C.) argued that the flux of observable phenomena is real and perhaps the only thing that is real. This flux he tended to identify with fire, a material element that is itself ever changing, yet ever the same. A wise person, for Heraclitus, was one whose soul was dry.

In stark contrast to Heraclitus and the early Milesians, Parmenides of Elea (c. 515 B.C. to c. 450 B.C.) maintained that rational reflection about the true nature of what is real imposes certain self-evident standards on this reality. In his poem *The Way of Being,* Parmenides asserted that "What-is is" and "What–is-not is not". What-is, his ultimate reality, is (1) one, (2) ungenerated, (3) indestructable, (4) eternal, and (5) unchangable. Thus, Parmenides was the first true rationalist.

Greek Pluralism. Other philosophers realized that the constant flux of things could more readily be explained by a less economical but more viable metaphysics—one that rejected monism.

Empedocles of Acragas (c. 493-c. 433 B.C.) asserted that the cosmos was a plenum and that there were four fundamental "roots" or underlying principles—fire, air, water, and earth—and two motive (perhaps material) forces—one that brings things together (Love) and one that tears things apart (Strife)—all of which work together in the eternal cycle of being.

Pythagoras of Samos (b. c. 570 B.C.) and his followers took scientific and philosophic practices and blended with them religious ritual, magic, and mysticism. Pythagoreans obeyed precepts like "Do not eat beans" and "Do not stir fires with iron". They also believed in the immortality of the soul. Much of this philosophic cult was a prescription for a way of life to purify the soul through a mathematical understanding of nature. Pythagoreans practiced science not for practical reasons, nor to quiet an innate curiosity. Science was a way of life in preparation for a proper life after death.

Anaxagoras of Clazomenae (c. 500-c. 428 B.C.) posited "there is a portion of everything in everything". Even the most uniformly fleshy piece of flesh of the smallest conceivable size has water, hair, tooth, bark, and all other things in it—though flesh predominates. Moreover, he maintained that there is no smallest part of matter. However small some bit of matter is cut, there is always another cut that can be made and this even smaller piece will have all things in it too. At the cosmic level, Mind moves all things, though in mechanical fashion.

Democritus of Abdera (c. 460-c. 370 B.C.) tackled the problem of change by asserting the existence of small, invisible, and unalterable uncuttables (ἄτομα). There are an infinite number of atoms of differing sizes and shapes that whirl about in the vortex of empty space. As they swirl, the come together to fashion visible objects and their parts.

Platonic Synthesis. Plato's (427-347 B.C.) thoughts on sameness and difference—the oneness and inalterability of reality, but the flux and plurality of visible things—are best spelled out in *Republic* VI-VII. Here Plato takes a fresh look at Parmenidean metaphysics, not by challenging any of Parmenides' assumptions on what is real, but through offering an explanation of reality, consistent with those principles, that does not *entirely* explain away visible phenomena. The results are his doctrine of the divided-line and his theory of forms.

In effect, *Republic* establishes a rationalist's compromise between Heraclitean, Pythagorean, and Parmenidean metaphysical principles. The difficulty is that this compromise is not much of an explanation of visible objects. Plato's reason for neglecting the visible world in *Republic* (and elsewhere) is that visible objects, being ever-changing, are not proper Parmenidean objects of knowledge, but rather are mere objects of opinion. Overall Plato, like Parmenides, draws a sharp line between objects of intellect and objects of sensation—and only the former are worthy of true philosophical investigation.

Nevertheless, Plato does grapple with a causal account of the world of visible things in a work entitled *Timaeus.* In keeping with the low regard Plato has of physical reality, he tells us, through the mouth of Timaeus, that he can do no more that provide a "likely story" (29d) when he tackles issues such as cosmic teleology, acoustics, harmonics, human physiology, and human psychopathology. Though these particular accounts are likely not his own, the overall teleological vision of *Timaeus* is uniquely Platonic.[2]

The cosmos had its origin due to a divine craftsman (δημιουργός), who employed two productive forces, Reason and Necessity, to put together the matter available for cosmic construction in the best possible manner (48a). At the cosmic level, the uniform and regular motions of the westward-moving sphere of the heavens and the eastward-moving circle of the ecliptic result in a helical movement of the Sun between the tropics (36b-d). At the subcosmic level, the materials out of which all things are constructed—fire, air, water, and earth—are explained by four even more basic geometric entities: the pyramid, the octahedron, the icosahedron, and the cube. These, in turn, are reduced to two basic triangles: the half-square and the half-equilateral (54a-55c). All of this occurs in the great "Receptacle of Becoming": space. Thus, in strict geometric fashion, the divine craftsman arranged the cosmos.

Aristotelian Science

In contrast to the relative poverty of earlier accounts, the finest attempt to standardize scientific practice and to distinguish between different manners of scientific investigation (broadly understood) into the nature of things exists in the Aristotelian corpus. Moreover, Aristotle gives us arguably the best depiction of science as it was actually practiced in Greco-Roman antiquity. G. E. R. Lloyd writes:

> Although groups of Hippocratic physicians, even in certain respects the Pythagorean communities, undertook empirical inquiries in particular fields, it was Aristotle—all are agreed—who was the first to institute a comprehensive programme of research covering the natural sciences as well as many other disciplines.[3]

And so, it is from Aristotle's philosophy of science that we find the best guidelines to enable us to answer the question: Were the ancient oneirologists doing science (at any level) consonant with their time?

Breakdown of Sciences. All investigation into the nature of things, for Aristotle, begins with human wonder. Between his *Nicomachean Ethics* (*EN*) and *Posterior Analytics* (*APo.*) Aristotle gives us a distinction between two types of investigation: *techne* and *episteme*. *Episteme*, he says at *EN* VI, is the faculty of affirming or denying matters of theoretical intelligence (διάνοια θεωρητική). It belongs to the realm of what is necessary (things ungenerated and indestructible like deity, the heavenly bodies, truths of mathematics and metaphysics, and general principles of the natural sciences). He also says that *episteme* is a necessary consequence of premises that are clearly known (1139b19-36 & 1140b40-42). This type of scientific knowledge, he adds in *APo.* I.2 occurs "when we know the cause on account of which the thing (to be explained) is so, that it is the cause of that thing, and that it could not have been otherwise" (71b9-12).

In contrast, *techne* subsists in the realm of contingent things (things neither ungenerated nor indestructible) that have their course of change in something other than themselves. It is the intellective faculty of affirming or denying that concerns manufactured things (διάνοια ποιητική). Its aims, concerning the production of something, are practical, and its end is the actual production of what one sets out to make. The reasoning here also aims at demonstration, but such "demonstrations" lack the certainty of those of *episteme*; the truth of the conclusions in technical affairs cannot be guaranteed by the premises because the premises themselves, involving changing things, are suspect (1140a1-23).

The distinction above loosely maps on to his tripartitioning of science given in *Topics*[4] (145a14-18 & 157a10-11) and *Metaphysics* (1025b18-26 & 1064a10-19). In these works, Aristotle mentions three kinds of *technai*: theoretical science (θεωρητικὴ τέχνη), political science (πολιτικὴ τέχνη), and productive science (ποιητικὴ τέχνη). The former, as the most esteemed branch, concerns ungenerated, indestructible, and unchanging things such as deity, principles of being, and heavenly bodies. We inquire into such divine matters not for any perceived reward or outcome, but for their own sake. The reasoning, involving premises whose truth is beyond question, is purely demonstrative. The subdisciplines of theoretical science are metaphysics or theology, mathematics, and natural science (psychology, geology, meteorology, physics, biology, etc.). Political science, in contrast, concerns contingent, human affairs (i.e., changeable things). It involves actions chosen because they are right actions and choiceworthy in themselves. Reasoning aligned with this art is nondemonstrative, for the premises from which we begin are fallible. The two subdisciplines of political science are political science, in the narrower sense of the science of the *polis*, and ethics. Last, productive science, like political science, concerns contingent and changing things. Yet the ends here are not right action, so to speak, but proper manufacture. Proper manufacture, unlike political deliberation, does not involve choice in action. The ends of manufacture themselves determine proper activity. Examples of subdisciplines are poetics, rhetoric, military strategy, domestic economy, and medicine.

Epistemology. At *Metaphysics* Α.1, Aristotle traces the path of the acquisition of knowledge from perception to *episteme* and *techne*. Knowledge begins with perceptions, perceptions lead to memory, and many memories of similar perceptions form experience (ἐμπειρία). From experience, we arrive at two kinds of scientific understanding: *episteme* and *techne*.

> And experience seems nearly the same as *episteme* and *techne*, and *episteme* and *techne* come about from experience. For experience fashioned *techne*, as Polus rightly says, *while lack of experience fashioned chance* (τύχη). And *techne* occurs whenever, from many ideas of experience, a single universal notion (ὑπόληψις) occurs from similar things. For having a notion that this thing cured Callias (who was sick with a certain illness) and Socrates and similarly many others, each in its own way, is a matter of experience. But having a notion that this thing cures all such men, designated as one class, who suffer from a certain illness—for example, the phlegmatic or choleric or those with burning fever—is a matter of *techne* (981a1-12).

We may gather much from this exceptionally dense piece of text. First, though they involve different objects, *techne* and *episteme* both involve an apprehension of what is universal; experience does not. Next, *techne* and *episteme* are built ultimately from an elaborate process of collecting and storing perceptions. The principles of both, then, are based upon some form of gathering particulars that is similar to enumerative induction.[5]

Yet Aristotle cautions, people with experience are more successful than people with rational understanding (λόγος) who have no experience. The reason he gives is "experience is an understanding (γνῶσις) of particulars, while *techne* is an understanding of what is universal, and all deeds and productions are concerned with particulars". Physicians, he adds, cure particular men, like Callias and Socrates, directly; *man*, in general, they cure only accidentally. Therefore, one who knows only what is universal and gives a rational account (λόγος) without experience, will often err in treatment.[6] For therapy, he says, concerns what is particular (981a13-23).

Nevertheless only craftsmen possess wisdom. Aristotle elaborates:

> Still, we think that knowing (τὸ εἰδέναι) and expertise (τὸ ἐπαΐειν) belong to *techne* rather than experience, and we suppose that technicians are wiser than men of experience, so that, for all men, wisdom attends upon knowing instead. And this is because some men (technicians) know the cause, while others (nontechnicians) do not. For men of experience know the fact (τὸ ὅτι), but they do not know the reason why (τὸ διότι); while others discover the reason why and the cause (τὴν αἴτιαν) (981a23-29).

The sign of knowledge, he asserts, is the ability to teach.[7] Because of this, in a sense, "*techne* is *episteme*, rather than experience". This is why theoretical science is the most esteemed (981b6-9).

Thus, for Aristotle, there are three levels of scientific investigation. First, *episteme* and only *episteme* is knowledge in the true sense of the word. Starting from true premises that involve many experiences of things invariable,[8] we gradually develop universal principles that are certain. From these, we syllogistically deduce true conclusions. Dealing with what is universal, *episteme* is teachable. *Episteme*, then, is pure theoretical science. Second, there is *techne*. *Techne*, like *episteme*, begins with premises ultimately derived from many experiences of things. Yet unlike *episteme*, these things, being items of manufacture, are variable.[9] Thus, its premises are, at best, likely to be true and its conclusions are suspect and void of certainty. Nevertheless *techne*, as productive science, involves causes (i.e., suspected causes, since its objects are variable) and is thus closer to real knowledge than experience. It, too, involving what is universal, is teachable. Last, experience is exclusively about particulars. Not involving what is universal, it is a knack for doing the right thing that is guided by a keen awareness of particular circumstances and past observations. Experience may be a useful guide to successful scientific practice, but it does not involve causes or what is universal and, thus, is not teachable.[10] Most importantly, with no regard for what is universal, consistency is not an issue: It is quite possible that what has once worked under a certain set of circumstances will not again work. This is scientific knack.

Scientific Explanation. Of the three forms of scientific investigation, only theoretical science, involving knowledge of causes, is true science for Aristotle. Knowledge of the cause, he says at *APo.*, takes shape as an explanatory demonstration (ἀποδείξις) in the form of a properly framed deductive syllogism (73a24). For the deduction to be of the right sort, the premises must be true, primary, and immediate as well as better known than, prior to, and explanatory of the conclusion (71b17-72a5).

Overall, the logic Aristotle lays out is categorical—that is, a logic of categories. Each sentence type has two categories, a subject and predicate category, and each sentence asserts or denies membership of one category in the other. In all, there are four possibilities: (1) A sentence can be universal in scope and affirmative; (2) a sentence can be universal in scope and negative, (3) a sentence can be particular in scope and affirmative, or (4) a sentence can be particular in scope and negative (see Figure 1.1).

	Universal	**Particular**
Affirmative	.All S are P.	Some S are P.
Negative	No S are P.	Some S are not P.

Figure 1.1. The four types of statements in Aristotle's logic of science.

These four kinds of categorical statements comprise the four different kinds of deductive-argument forms, called "figures" (see Figure 1.2)

Figure 1	**Figure 2**	**Figure 3**	**Figure 4**
M are P.	P are M.	M are P.	P are M.
S are M.	S are M.	M are S.	M are S.
S are P	S are P.	S are P.	S are P.

Figure 1.2. For each figure, the subject term and the predicate term are determined by the subject and predicate of the conclusion. The middle term is the term common to both premises. Premise one contains the premise with the predicate term, while premise two is that which has the subject term. Missing from each statement form is a quantifier (all, no, some, or some…not).

In all, there are 256 ways to construct a deductive argument—most of which are not valid.

In a proper scientific demonstration, the deduction must say more than *that* something is the case; it must tell *why* something is the case. For this, two conditions must be met. First, the middle term of the demonstrative syllogism, the term common to both premises, must be causal, not just descriptive. Second, the argument can only be laid out with universal and affirmative premises in the first figure. Aristotle sums, "If, then, it is something else and it is demonstrable, the cause must be a middle term, and it must be shown in the first figure, since what is being proved is universal and affirmative" (93a8-10).

To illustrate just how to form a correct demonstration, Aristotle has us consider two deductions: one of the fact (τὸ ὅτι) and one of the reason why (τὸ διότι). A deduction of the fact tells us merely that something is the case, but does not give us a proper explanation—one involving the cause. For instance, Aristotle has us consider a properly formed first-figure syllogism that shows the problem involved with deductions of the fact.

P1: All *things that do not twinkle* are *things that are near.*
P2: All *planets* are *things that do not twinkle.*
C: All *planets* are *things that are near.*

This suggests that *planets* are *things that are near* because they are *things that do not twinkle*. Yet, *not twinkling* is not a cause of *nearness*; it is nearness that causes them not to twinkle. The causal explanation is the other way around: *Planets* are *things that do not twinkle* because they are *things that are near*. In other words, the deduction of the fact is not demonstrative because it has the wrong middle term. In contrast, proper demonstration (the deduction of the reason why) is illustrated as follows:

P1: All *things that are near* are *things that do no twinkle.*
P2: All *planets* are *things that are near.*
C: All *planets* are *things that do not twinkle.*

Here, *nearness* is the reason why planets do not twinkle.

Ancient Medical Practice

Early Hippocratic Medicine. Early Greek secular medicine had begun to flourish in the late fifth-century B. C. Greek world through a group of doctors known as "Hippocratic" physicians. The extant writings[11] indicate that early Hippocratic medicine, like early oneirocriticism, met with great resistance in its effort to establish itself as science. Since many of these writings survive, we know much about ancient secular practice.

The Hippocratic author of *The Art of Medicine* states, "First, I would define medicine as the complete removal of the distress of the sick, the alleviation of the more violent diseases, and the refusal to take up cases in which the disease has already won the mastery, since we know that everything is not possible in medicine".[12] Here we find a pledge on behalf of this physician to aid those in distress, but only insofar as cure still seems possible through craft. The implication is that too many failures of difficult cases can give a physician and the art a bad name. *Prognosis* I advises that a physician's reputation will be enhanced by telling a patient about the past and future state of the illness in addition to its present condition.[13] *The Oath* and *Precepts* VI indicate a commitment toward scientific integrity and an ethical code of practitioners. *Decorum* and *The Canon* indicate a bond of physicians through medical secrecy in the "mysteries of science", which suggests a connection to the religious mystery cults of the fifth century B. C.

Most secular doctors were private practitioners who learned their art through apprenticeship, [14] not formal schooling—though schools did exist in Cnidus and Cos by the fifth century B. C. To gain a clientele, medical practitioners often had to be itinerant,[15] but some of the most skilful physicians found employment in their own state. Physicians' methods were anything but antediluvian, even by today's standards. These included surgery, cautery, blood-letting, purgative drugs, and, especially, regimen (diet and exercise) designed to restore a balance of the material elements within a patient's body.

Earliest Hippocratic practice was factional, and two methodological strains—one that was rational and one that was empirical—were manifest early on. The rational approach was etiological—seeking knowledge through a hunt for causes guided by *a priori* principles such as the principle of opposition,[16] the principle of analogy,[17] and the principle of composition.[18] Causal understanding could only come about by ruling out false causes, thereby contributing to a richer understanding of etiology of illness.[19] Rationalism was influenced mightily by philosophers such as Empedocles, Democritus, Aristotle, and the Stoics. The empirical approach, in contrast, was based principally on past observations, the reports of other physicians, and even some creative experimentation.[20] Detailed methodological observation was indispensable in developing empirical medicine. Empirical physicians drew from a vast array of sources in an effort to combat disease, but they always insisted upon remaining free from the constraints of dogma.

Yet as was the case with ancient oneirocritics' success at interpreting dreams, what secured a physician's reputation, at bottom, was his perceived ability to cure patients and predict the course of illness. From the causal perspective, an understanding that so many internal and external factors are at play must have frustrated physicians—especially since the slightest omission of causal detail could easily lead to misdiagnosis and the wrong prescription for treatment. Thus, the author of *Epidemics* warns that cure is difficult and often the best a physician can hope for is to do no harm.[21] *Ancient Medicine* cautions that the many failures of medicine should not count against its scientific status, since, over the years of investigation, great discoveries have been made.[22] The authors of *The Art of Medicine* and *On Prognosis* flatly advise physicians not to take up hopeless cases.[23] While those looking for causal understanding probably explained away failure through the complex web of causes that went into etiological understanding of illness, empiricists fell back on their science of semiotics through memory and observation. Both took umbrage in critics' lack of understanding of the difficulties and complexities of their art.

All of this shows unambiguously that secular medical practice was looked upon with some suspicion and mistrust. Yet in spite of the skepticism secular physicians often encountered, superstition and mysticism were to an unexpected degree absent from their practice.

Religious Healing Sanctuaries. In contrast to secular medicine, numerous healing sanctuaries—dedicated to beneficent healing gods such as the Greek god Asclepius and the Egyptian god Serapis—sprang up in Greece, Egypt, Italy, Asia Minor and elsewhere, and were commonplace throughout Greco-Roman antiquity, even in early Christian times. Suppliants would go to a sanctuary where a healing god was said to effect cure—often in miraculous fashion. Extant testimonies of miraculous or magical cures in antiquity, being too numerous to dismiss with a wave of the hand, invite examination and explanation.

Dreams, as I show fully in chapter 10, were an indispensable part of treatment at such religious sanctuaries in a practice known today as "incubation". When the ill traveled to a religious sanctuary, after a meager votive offering, they would go to sleep in a special room, the *abaton*, where a healing deity was said to visit them in sleep. This deity would then assist the supplicant through either suggesting a cure, usually carried out subsequently by attendants or physicians at the sanctuary, or administering a cure. As testimonies indicate, remedies ranged from plausible to incredible. Like secular medicine, incubation thrived in Greco-Roman times as early as the fifth century B. C.

Reason Versus Knack. By the second century A. D., we get a clear picture of the factionalism within the science of medicine through the works of Galen. The primary tension, as Galen sees it, is between rationalist practitioners (referred to as "Dogmatics" or "Dogmatists") and empiricists. This, of course, is the same division that we saw in early Hippocratic practice, only by the time of Galen, the tension is more pronounced. The three Galenic treatises from which I draw are *Sects for Beginners*, *Outline of Empiricism*, and *On Medical Experience*.[24]

The most telling observation Galen gives is that rationalist and empiricist medical *practices* are virtually indistinguishable. For instance, let us consider how Galen depicts a physician from each school deals with memory loss. A rationalist may argue that memory loss is the result of swelling of the cerebral membrane and any kind of motion is bad for a swollen membrane, so no one should talk to one with memory loss. In contrast, an empiricist would merely note that since all observed cases of speaking to a patient with memory loss worsened his condition, no one should talk to one with memory loss.[25] The main difference between these conflicting schools is the manner in which remedies are found and not the remedies. He elaborates:

> And, to speak quite generally, the dogmatics and the empiricists draw on the same medicines for the same affections. What they disagree about is the way these remedies are discovered. For, in the case of the same manifest bodily symptoms, the dogmatics derive from them an indication of the cause, and, on the basis of this cause, they find a treatment, whereas the empiricists are reminded by them of what they have observed often to happen in the same way.[26]

Following Aristotle's epistemology at *Metaphysics* A.1, whereas empiricists are guided solely by their collections of past experience, rationalists strive for a causal understanding of such experiences—they strive to be able to formulate general principles to guide medical practice. Empiricists aim to remove symptoms; rationalists aim to treat the cause of the symptoms.

For empiricists, experiences are formed in different ways. Some are spontaneous visual perceptions that occur by chance (e.g., when someone ill drinks cold water and feels better) or by nature (e.g., when someone ill breaks into a spontaneous sweat and feels better). Some are extemporaneous, as when someone is led on by a dream to try some remedy and, when he does, he feels better. Others are imitative, as when something has been observed to work in a certain manner, though the number of observations is not compelling, and the physician imitates what he has observed.[27] Each of these can be the result of one's own perception, a report of a perception, or a type of analogical reasoning that guides novel cases, *epilogismos*.[28]

Experiences are then collected according to similarity into theorems such as (1) what always happens, (2) what usually happens, (3) what happens as often as it does not, and (4) what rarely happens. The empirical principles guiding empirical practice are "Similar remedies for similar affections" and "If a remedy proves ineffective after some time, try its contrary".[29]

Rationalist medicine, in contrast, is a search for causes of illness. Manner of procedure is through indication—a rational method that allows inference from symptom as observed sign to unobserved underlying cause. According to Galen, rationalists speak of three types of indication. In order to establish α as the cause of τ, a rationalist physician needs to know (1) primary indications (the nature of the human body), (2) secondary indications (e.g., the strength of the patient, his nature, and his age), and (3) tertiary indications or auxiliary factors that causally play a less direct role (e.g., climate, waters, occupation, foods, and habits).[30] This web of causes is intricate and physicians must know how to factor in all indications in order to achieve diagnostic and therapeutic success.

Against rationalist physicians, empiricists argue that other craftspersons—helmsmen, farmers, wine-growers, and others—practice their crafts remarkably well without a knowledge of causes.[31] Additionally, since the methods for diagnosis and treatment of diseases are the same for empiricists and rationalists, adding a causal explanation is superfluous. Moreover, rationalists themselves disagree wildly on their conclusions regarding causes. While empiricists and rationalists alike agree that vinegar aids digestion, one rationalist asserts that this is due to its warmth, while another contends that this is due to its capacity to pulverize food. Therefore, empiricists contend, the method of indication is unavailing.[32]

Against empirical medicine, rationalists claim that the alphabet, geometry, and music are founded on reason, not experience. Additionally, they note that observation is insufficient to guide treatment, since there must be a means of separating symptoms into different kinds and judging how their observed order impacts illness. Furthermore, since the storehouse of circumstances surrounding any single case is unimaginably large, reason is necessary for disentangling the many supposed etiological factors and ascertaining true causal relevance. Otherwise, investigation is arbitrary.[33]

Science Today

Two Main Approaches

In contemporary philosophy of science, there have been two main views: the logical approach and the historical approach. According to the former, science is recognizable by a unique method and the language it employs. According to the latter, science has no unique logic or language, but is driven by cultural considerations at any one given time in its practice.

The logical approach, logical positivism, had its roots in the empirical thoughts of philosophers such as Bacon, Locke, Hume, and Mill. Formally, positivism began with philosophers and scientists from Vienna and Berlin in the twentieth century. Thinkers such as Popper, Carnap, and Hempel sought to demarcate sharply the practice of science, which was essentially empirical, from other nonempirical disciplines like philosophy, religion, or pseudo-science. They developed a language of science that distinguished between observational and theoretical (nonobservational) entities in scientific parlance. They also sought to differentiate sharply between the discovery and justification of theories, only the latter of which was part of true scientific practice. For instance, Karl Hempel, in his well-known deductive-nomological (D-N) or covering-law model of scientific explanation, argues that proper explanation takes the form of a deductive argument, illustrated as follows:

$$\begin{array}{l} \mathbf{C_1,\ldots, C_m} \\ \underline{\mathbf{L_1,\ldots, L_n}} \\ \mathbf{E} \end{array}$$

where $\mathbf{C_1,\ldots, C_m}$ indicate the circumstances surrounding the event to be explained, $\mathbf{L_1,\ldots, L_n}$ represent the laws invoked, and E is the explanandum. The D-N model is eerily Aristotelian in certain respects in that proper explanation, first, must take the form of a special kind of deductive argument and, second, must be causal. Thus, for positivists, the apparent progress of science over the years is easily explained: Science builds upon prior understanding with new discoveries and with refinements of prior ones.

Within the last fifty years of the twentieth century, positivism came under attack by thinkers who opted for an historical approach to the practice of science. Thomas Kühn was one of the most celebrated critics of positivism with his *Structure of Scientific Revolutions* in 1962. Kühn argues that science is not progressive, but revolutionary and problem-solving. As the problems of one time or culture are not the same as those of another, so too do the problems of sciences differ within different scientific communities over time. Within a scientific community there are periods of normal science in which a paradigm, like Ptolemaic geocentrism, becomes established and remains unchallenged. When internal problems or anomalies surface and challenge a dominant paradigm to a considerable degree, a scientific revolution ensues. A new paradigm, having its own language and incommensurable with the old one, replaces the old. Thus, for Kühn and other like-minded historicists, the error of positivists comes precisely in their refusal to examine closely the practice of science in their "discovery" of the logic of science. There is for historicists no logic of science.

While both views contribute something to our understanding of science, each is extreme and simplistic. The positivist tradition, in an attempt to explain the success of science, has neatly ascribed a language and logic to science by largely ignoring the actual practice of science. In contrast, the historical approach reduces science to a problem-solving enterprise that promises us no understanding of reality qua reality and gives no account of progress in science.

Science and Understanding

Cultural Relativism. The ancient Greek philosopher Protagoras is claimed to have said, "Man is the measure of all things: of things that are, that they are, of things that are not, that they are not". This, in its simplest articulation, is the gist of relativism.

For the cultural relativist, the cannons of reason are believed to vary from society to society over time and truth is dictated by one's social group at a particular time, not any appeal to an independently existing reality. Scientific explanation for relativists is a matter of solving problems that occur within a given scientific community. Such problems are soluble by employing only those concepts of a community, or establishing coherence with other acceptable claims within that community. This makes scientific communication between different scientific communities (e.g., Ptolemaists and Copernicans) impossible. For relativists, the choice between models of reality is nonrational and the advances of science are illusory. The most decisive objection to any sort of relativism is that relativism, to make any sense at all, must be proposed in a nonrelativist manner and, thus, is self-defeating.

Scientific Realism. Scientific realism is roughly the view that the objects exist independently of us and that scientific investigation can go some way toward disclosing the nature of these things. Philosophers and scientists have posited the existence of universals, material objects, scientific laws, numbers, and even propositions in an effort to explain visible reality. For the realist, truth may be a correspondence of words with things in the world or a matter of logical consistency of statements in a framework of accepted truths. Realists explain the advances of science by the assumption that science is progressing and gaining a more complete understanding of the nature of things. A large problem for realists is the theory-dependence of scientific statements. As Pierre Duhem has shown, any attempt to refute a scientific hypothesis involves auxiliary hypotheses within a deductive system whose truth is merely assumed within the deductive system. In consequence, what might appear to be a refutation of a hypothesis is best construed as an inconsistency among the hypothesis and the conjunction of auxiliary hypotheses. Therefore, systems of scientific realists may tell us more about individual philosophers or their scientific community than the nature of reality.

Scientific Empiricism. Following the tradition of Aristotle, Bacon, Hobbes, Locke, and Hume, empiricism is the view that all knowledge fundamentally relies on experience. David Hume has argued that to say "α is the cause of τ" requires that we establish a *necessary connection* between the two events, when all that we are entitled to say from experience is that we have observed their constant conjuction in the past. No amount of observation, it is obvious, can establish a necessary connection. Likewise, reason is unavailing, since no argument can provide a guarantee that the future must be like the past. Our attitude concerning the perceived order of visible things must consequently be skeptical.

It is plain to see that canonical empiricism is not a form of realism in any interesting sense. At worst, those who take only sense data as true or metaphysically fundamental find themselves mired in the inescapable solipsism of phenomenalism. At best, empiricists admit to the existence of an external reality about which they can have no true understanding whatsoever. In between, there are a host of other problems: the assumption that observations themselves are not theory-laden, the possibility of a priori knowledge, and the relationship of theory to observation, to name a few. Overall, philosophical explanation today in the empiricist mold is no hunt for causes, but generally a matter of empirical adequacy.

Summary

I have included this brief prefatory sketch in this chapter to illustrate the following points:

- There was no clear demarcation of early science from other cultural influences—like philosophy, religion, and mythology—and there seems to be no such demarcation of science and culture today.
- Early accounts of how science ought to be practiced, like the account Aristotle gives at *APo.* or the methodologies underpinning the ongoing debate between empiricists and rationalists in ancient medicine, are sophisticated even by today's normative standards and have modern-day implications. (Cf. the disagreement between realists and nonrealists today, the impact of Aristotle on positivism, or the tension between Behavioral and nonBehavioral psychologists.)
- Last, the considerable disagreement among critics of science concerning the nature and practice of contemporary science should caution us before we undertake hasty critical appraisal of ancient scientific practice by today's "standards". Critical evaluation of ancient science by current standards must be tempered by the understanding that consensus of opinion does not exist among experts for modern-day science.

Consequently, the general *modus operandi* of this undertaking will be to appraise ancient oneirology by the ideals of Aristotelian philosophy of science or by conformity with ancient medical practice.

---

[1] Implying that there is some primary reality (1) that underlies all change or (2) that is something out of which all things come.

[2] Mourelatos 1991, 12-13.

[3] Lloyd 1979, 201.

[4] See Owens (1991) for a spirited comparison of this tripartitioning to a modern notion of pure and applied sciences.

[5] *EN* VI.6 adds that *nous* is then responsible for an intuitive grasp of these inductively generated principles and recognition of their inviolability. Though here and both at 1141b2-3and 1142a26-31, he suggests that we utilize *nous*, strictly speaking, only to grasp those first principles of *episteme*, not *techne*. I take him to mean by this, not that we do not use *nous* for the principles of *techne*, but that the link between *nous* and *episteme* is special in that only the objects of *episteme* conduce toward true knowledge.

[6] Though rational understanding ultimately must appeal to collections of experiences, not every case of rational understanding needs to do so. Aristotle is thinking here of one who comes to know that something universally applies (i.e., being taught something), without having had any experience of it. We

may be suspicious of Aristotle's suggestion that this is a genuine case of understanding the *logos*.

[7] Both *episteme* and *techne* involve reasoning (λόγος), and so, unlike matters of experience, both are teachable (1139b25-27).

[8] The objects of theology, mathematics, and physics. The latter change when construed as particulars, but not when understood universally.

[9] We may take political science to be a type of *techne*, though its aims are practical, not productive.

[10] Though empirical practice is not rational, that does not mean that it is not in some sense scientific. For remember, experience fashions *techne*, and empirical practitioners are, when it comes to practice, superior to those who know the cause but who are without experience.

[11] E.g., *de Arte*.

[12] *De Arte* II.

[13] Perhaps, as G. E. R. Lloyd states, a means of showing medicine to be a science greater than divination (1991, 255).

[14] *VM* III.

[15] *Aër*.

[16] Opposites cure opposites (e.g., *Flat.* I.33-34).

[17] What is bad in waking life is a symbol of bad things in dreams (*Prog.* XXV). E.g., a flower wilting in a dream signifies ill because a wilting flower in waking life is a bad thing.

[18] All things are caused by hot, cold, wet, and dry within each person (*Morb.Sacr.* XXI).

[19] For instance, the same effect can be the result of different causes (*Acut.* XI). The post-hoc fallacy is even referred to at *de Arte* XXI. There are also internal (*Nat.Hom.* IX, *Vict.* I.2, and *Aff.* I) and external causes (*Aër* II & XI, *Nat.Hom.* IX, *Aph.* I & III.5, *Morb.Sacr.* XVI, and *Epid.*) are to be considered.

[20] E.g., *Prog.* II, *Epid.* (esp. I.23), *Nat.Puer.*, and *VM* I.2.

[21] *Epid.* III sc. 9 sr. 1, cs. 5 sr. 2, & XI.

[22] *VM* XI-XII.

[23] *De Arte* III & *Prog.* I.

[24] Translation from Walzer and Frede througout this section.

[25] *Exper.Med.* XXV.

[26] *Sect.Intr.* IV.

[27] *Subf.Emp.* II.

[28] *Subf.Emp.* II-III.

[29] *Subf.Emp.* IX.

[30] *Sect.Intr.* III-V.

[31] *Exper.Med.* IX.

[32] *Exper.Med.* XI & XIII.

[33] *Exper.Med.* III-VII.

Part I
Naturalistic Oneirology

Introduction

The earliest surviving depiction of dreams in Greco-Roman antiquity is in Homer's *Iliad* and *Odyssey*. In the main, Homer depicts dreams as visual presentations, where a personage relates a message to the sleeper. Such presentations are most often divinely sent. For instance, at *Il.* II.56 Agamemnon relates to a council of elders, "A divine dream came to me in sleep (θεῖός μοι ἐνύπνιον ἦλθεν ὄνειρος)" and *Od.* XX.87 reads, "A divine being also sent evil dreams to me (ἐμοὶ καὶ ὀνείρατ' ἐπέσσευεν κακὰ δαίμων)". Homer and all of Greco-Roman antiquity after him consistently talk of "seeing" a dream (ὄναρ ἰδεῖν, ὁρᾶν ὄψιν, visum esse in somnis, etc.), not of "having" a dream, as we are inclined to say today. Additionally, sometimes the dream is said to visit the dreamer and stand over him.[1] Sometimes it even leaves behind a token as proof of its actuality.[2]

The episodes involving dreams and dreaming in Homer's two works show that the early Greek depiction of dreams is supernatural—that is, characterized by divine or eidolic figures.[3] According to this view, a dream is a real appearance by some deity or *eidolon* that important figures see in sleep. Its function is to convey significant information to sleepers about the future in a relatively straightforward manner,[4] or advise sleepers on some action to perform or eschew. Hermes' nocturnal visit to Priam (*Il.* XXIV.677-688) in order to conduct him away from the Achaeans and Athena's appearing to Nausicaa in sleep as a dear friend of hers (*Od.* VI.13-50) are examples of an appearance of a deity. The fashioning and sending of an *eidolon* to Penelope at *Od.* IV.795-842 in the likeness of her sister, since the likeness is specifically called an *eidolon*, and the oneiric visit of Patroclus' soul at *Il.* XXIII.62-108 (also called an *eidolon*) are examples of the appearance of an *eidolon*. Thus understood, Homer's picture of dreams continues a line of ancient thinking found in Mesopotamian tablets, Egyptian Papyri, and Semitic texts in which significant dreams are a type of reality not fully distinguishable from waking reality.[5] With due concession to Homer's literary intentions in his works, the view I have sketched above was likely the general Greek view of dreams in Homeric or, at least, pre-early Archaic times.[6]

The early Archaic Greek view of dreams thrived in Greek antiquity immediately following Homer—especially in dreams at religious healing sanctuaries (see chapter ten) and certain of the dreams or references to them in Herodotus,[7] Pindar,[8] the tragedians,[9] and Plato.[10] Yet after Homer, there began a growing dissatisfaction with supernatural accounts of phenomena. Philosophy and natural science emerged and took root, and natural scientists sought explanations of being and change in the nature of things themselves, not through the direct agency of some deity. The gods were still perceived to be involved in natural affairs, though their precise causal role came increasingly to be seen as less direct or, at least, less perceptible.

Dreams themselves became part of philosophic and scientific investigation as early as the sixth century B. C., with the philosopher Heraclitus. By the fifth century B. C., Greeks began giving naturalistic accounts and characterizations of dreams that critically involved a changed notion of "soul". After Homer, the soul began to be perceived as complex and functionally diverse. More significantly, it became substantive and agentive.

According to the view popularized by E. R. Dodds, the main reason for this substantive soul was the infiltration of Orphic-Pythagorean religious mysticism and cultism into Greek society. This heightened sense of religiosity had the effect of hypostatizing the soul and setting the "soul and body at odds". Instead of being simply the life or breath of the body, as it was for Homer, after Homer, the soul was perceived to be its "reluctant prisoner".

Whereas the Homeric soul was relatively featureless and uninvolved in their formation, by the fifth century and well into the Late Roman Empire, nearly all Greco-Roman oneirologists believe that the soul has many functions and that it is ineliminably involved in the genesis and formation of dreams. The Theban Pindar writes that, while our bodies sleep, often a divine image of life remains active, indicating to us future joy or adversity.[11] Xenophon, in the early fourth century B. C., tells us that our souls become freest in sleep and enjoy insight into future events, thus, showing their own divine nature.[12] The Hippocratic author of *Regimen* says, at around 400 B. C., that the soul liberates itself during sleep and performs all of the functions of both body and soul.[13] The Stoic Posidonius believed that in one type of dream the soul leaves the body and harmonizes with immortal souls stamped with truth.[14] Neoplatonist Philo of Alexandria, early in the first century A. D., relates that sometimes the frenzied soul in sleep sets itself in motion and foretells what is to be.[15] In the late fourth century A. D., Synesius writes of the sleeping soul that ascends to the superior region where it converse with gods and stars.[16]

In general, post-Homeric Greco-Roman oneirologists recognized two sorts of dreams involving the soul (hereafter, "psychogenetic" dreams): (1) psychoenstatic dreams, where (a) a psychic or bodily impression or (a) a divine or *eidolic* message appears to the soul of a dreamer, and (2) psychoecstatic dreams, where the soul of a dreamer leaves the body to gain divine or true information from the otherworld.[17] Thus, whereas the early Archaic approach was one that is chiefly interested in outcomes—whether the message of a dream, interpreted aright, will turn out true or not—the view shortly thereafter combined this interest in outcomes with a keen focus on the psychic origin of dreams. Among those whom I discuss in this book—Plato, Aristotle, Lucretius, the Stoics, the Hippocratic author of *Dreams*, Galen, and Synesius—all unambiguously articulate an interest in both oneiric prophecy and the psychogenesis of dreams. Tertullian,[18] Macrobius,[19] Gregory of Nyssa,[20] and Iamblichus[21] are prominent examples of post-Homeric thinkers not examined. The interest in the prophetic power of certain dreams, as underscored by Homer, never waned throughout Greco-Roman antiquity.

In this section, I look at and critically analyze naturalistic oneirology. In chapter two, I essay to reconstruct from limited material a naturalistic account of dreams in a relatively late work in the Platonic corpus, *Timaeus*. Turning to Aristotle in chapter three, I focus chiefly on two treatises in his *Parva Naturalia*: *On Sleep and Wakefulness*, and *On Dreams*. Finally, in chapter four, I flesh out Lucretius' naturalistic account of oneirogenesis from Book IV of his monograph, *de Rerum Natura*.

---

[1] A fine example is the baneful dream (οὖλος ὄνειρος) of *Il.* II.5-84. Zeus talks to the dream itself, which he is sending to Agamemnon, instructing it to convey a deceptive message to the Achaean king. The dream left, arrived at the hut of the king, then stood over his head to deliver the message.

[2] E.g., Pindar's *O.* XIII.65-82. See van Lieshout 1980, 21-23 and Dodds 1951, 105-106.

[3] *Il.* XXII.199-202, where Achilles' pursuit of Hector is compared to a dream in which one cannot catch what one chases, may be an exception. *Od.* XIX.535-570 also seems an exception because of its allegorical nature. Yet allegorical dreams were no less divinely sent in Homeric or pre-Homeric times in other cultures. Consider Jacob's dream of a ladder (*Genesis* XXVIII) in the Hebrew tradition or Gilgamesh's dream of a sky bolt in the Mesopotamian tradition that forewarned of the coming of Enkidu (*Gilgamesh*, Tablet I, *SBV* v). Dodds says that Homer's figure in dreams is a "god, or a ghost, or a pre-existing dream messenger, or an 'image' (εἴδωλον) created especially for the occasion". He cites *Il.*II.5-84 as an example of a dream messenger and *Il.*XXIII.62-108 as an instance of a ghost (1951, 104 & 122). Also, it is likely best to take the οὖλος ὄνειρος at *Il.*II.5-84 as an εἴδωλον fashioned by the gods similar to *Od.*IV.795-842 or a divinity. Moreover, Homer uses εἴδωλον and ψυχή interchangeably at *Il.*XXIII.62-108 and *Od.*XI.204-222. So Patroclus, though he is being kept out of Hades, is as much an εἴδωλον as the other εἴδωλα in Hades.

[4] These relatively unambiguous messages in Homer's two epics gave way to dreams of a mostly allegorical nature in post-Homeric literature, especially tragedy. Kessels (1978, 175) argues that the similarity between the Homeric dreams and those of the Epidaurean temple cures of incubation suggests that the former had cultic significant—perhaps even for royal families in Homeric times.

[5] See Dodds 1951, 102-104; Kessels 1970, 389-391; Van de Castle 1994, 47-57; Vieyra 1959, 89-98; Sauneron 1959, 17-63; Messer 1918, 10, 38; Gallop 1990, 3-4; Björk 1946, 308-311; and Oberhelman 1993, 124-125. For a comparison of the dream in Homer's two epics, see Messer 1918, especially pp. 47-48, and Kessels 1978, especially pp. 148-150.

[6] For a slightly different account, see Kessels 1978. My own account here draws plentifully from the fine insights of Kessels.

[7] *Hist.* I.34, 38-45, II.139, 141, V.55-56, & VII.12-19, 47.

[8] *O.* XIII.61-83, *P.* IV.156-168.

[9] E.g., Aeschylus' *Eu.* 94 ff., Euripides' *Rh.* 780 ff.

[10] *Cri.* 44a-c, *Phd.* 60e-61b.

[11] Fr. 116B (131S.).

[12] *Cyr.* VIII.7.21.

[13] *Insomn.* lxxxi.

[14] Cicero's *Div.* I.64.

[15] *Insomn.* I.i.2, II.i.2.

[16] *Insomn.* 1317a-b (Migne pagination).

[17] This depiction captures the general climate of fifth-century-B.C. Greek thinking on dreams until Christian times and the inception of demon-sent dreams (in the Christian sense of "demon"). Demon-sent dreams were otherworldly in origin, yet were mostly believed to convey false or deceptive information. In *de Anima*, Tertullian writes: "The first type of dream we have declared to emanate from the devil, even though such dreams are sometimes true and favorable to us. But when they deliberately set out to delude us with false appearances...they betray themselves as vain, deceitful, wild, licentious, and foul. This is not surprising, if we suppose that the images of what underlies are also the reality (*res*) of those things" (XLVII.1). See XLVII.2-4 for his account of three other kinds of dreams.

[18] *An.* XLVII.1-4.

[19] *Somn.Scip.* I.iii.1-13.

[20] *Creat.Hom.* XIII.

[21] *Myst.* III.2-3.

Chapter Two
Teleological Naturalism in Plato's *Timaeus*

Introduction

The coming to be of the visible world—which is dependent upon the eternal, intelligible forms and eternal being—is the subject of Plato's *Timaeus*. The work has two references to dreams, 45d-46a and 70d-72d, which have been mostly overlooked by experts on the dialogue and by those working on dreams in antiquity. From these it is possible to reconstruct one of the earliest psychogenetic accounts of dreams. The foremost aim of this chapter will be to effect such a reconstruction, insofar as this is possible. However, before turning attention to this work, first let me say something about the philosopher and the place of *Timaeus* in the Platonic corpus.

Plato, in the many extant works that he has left behind, tells us very little about himself. His earliest biographers, Apuleius (second century A. D.) and Diogenes Laertius (third century A. D.) tell us that he was born in 427 B. C., during the Peloponnesian War, from a long line of distinguished Athenians. Living during the decline of Athenian imperialism, Plato must have known well uncertainty, intrigue, conspiracy, and hardship.

In 387 B. C., Plato traveled to Italy and met Archytas of Tarentus, a Pythagorean philosopher, and Dion, the brother-in-law of the tyrant of Syracuse named Dionysius. Here he was certainly influenced by the Pythagorean love of mathematics and its application to real-world explanation as well as Pythagorean mysticism. He would return in 367 B. C. and 361 B. C., where he would try unsuccessfully to educate

Dionysius II (successor of Dionysius) in philosophy and implement the principles of political justice outlined in *Republic*.

Shortly after the first trip to Italy, Plato founded his Academy in Athens, where he taught and published most of his works. In 367 B. C., Aristotle joined the Academy and remained there until Plato's death in 347 B. C. Other prominent influences on Plato were the philosophers Heraclitus and Parmenides, both of whom contributed immensely to the development of Plato's metaphysics and epistemology.

Scholars generally group Plato's dialogues into three periods—each of which is indicative of progress or change in his thinking. In his early works, Plato's focus is to give us a picture of the historical Socrates, who searches the gathering places in Athens for knowledge of virtue. Plato's manner of exposition in these early works is Socratic. Therefore, elenctic dialogue, a method of cross-examination through short question and answer, is the preferred literary device.[1] In the middle works, Plato, through Socrates, moves beyond ethics toward a whole range of philosophic issues from epistemology and education to politics and the possibility of life after death. No longer is a virtuous education mere intellectual training, as it is for the early dialogues; Plato now gives an account of human living that takes into consideration our appetites, feelings, and spirit. Last, in the latest group of Plato's dialogues, Socrates, when he is actually present, has a relatively insignificant role to play. In addition, Plato is often grappling with difficulties in the views expressed in the middle works. Some of these ideas, he even seems to be rejecting outright. *Timaeus*, a work that concerns the origin of the visible world, belongs to this last grouping. I turn now to some introductory comment on this dialogue.

The setting for *Timaeus* is Athens, during the Panathenaea.[2] Socrates and Critias[3] of Athens are entertaining Timaeus of Locri, who is said to be an esteemed politician, philosopher, and astronomer (20a & 27a), and Hermocrates of Syracuse, a prominent figure in Sicilian politics. We find early on that the men, on the previous day, had been discussing political matters (17b)—the very matters that make up the early books of *Republic*—and the beginning of the *Timaeus* is a recapitulation of that discussion (17b-19a). The main body of *Timaeus*, given by Timaeus himself, is thus a sequel to those affairs covered in *Republic* (20b).

Structure of *Timaeus*

Timaeus' "banquet of words" to describe the coming to be of the visible, physical world (οὐρανός) begins at 27c and continues until the work ends (92c). Since the world has come about from a material model of perfect and eternal, intelligible being, it is merely a material likeness of intelligible perfection. Thus, any account of it will itself only be at best an approximation of truth (29c-d).

Timaeus' account of visible things involves the interplay of two causal principles, Reason (νοῦς) and Necessity (ἀνάγκη), at different levels of coming to be. Since Plato mentions dreams in two different sections of the work—one, where the influence of Reason is obvious (70d-72d), and another, where Necessity seems to be the predominant constructive power (45d-46a)—I need to say something concerning the composition of the work as a whole.

According to Timaeus, the physical world began when Reason, being the superior force, persuaded Necessity to fashion the greatest part of generated things toward what is best. Necessity then molded the primal chaos, a material soup of elements, into a copy of what is eternally and unalterably real, and, given the matter available, it aimed to make the best likeness. Hereafter Timaeus discusses the construction of the world from two levels: from top-down, a god's-eye perspective, where the works of Reason were directly at play and most noticeable (29d-47e & 69a-92c); from bottom-up, where Reason put Necessity, the wandering or errant cause (πλανώμενα αἰτία), to work for the majority of coming-to-be things (47e-69a).

From 29d-47e, Timaeus tells us that creation unfolded by means of a *Demiourgos*, a divine craftsman whose being is as eternal as the forms and who fashioned the ordered, sensible world out of what was before visibly discordant and random. The *Demiourgos* used as a model an intelligible, living creature (ζῷον), of which all other living creatures[4] are living parts (29d-30c). This creature, as a model for the cosmos as a whole, is reality in the highest degree. The sensible world—being a copy of true, intelligible being (29b) and having been put together in the best possible manner—was then given intelligence (30a-b). Since it needed to possess the sundry forms that intelligence does in the eternally living creature, the earth, all the creatures that dwell on or around it, and the heavenly gods were created (39e-40c).

Section 47e-69a gives us the bottom-up perspective. Here Reason persuaded Necessity to fashion the greatest part of things in the best possible manner (48a). Understanding space as the receptacle (ὑποδοχή) of all becoming (48e-49a), Necessity then imposed geometric form on the primal chaos of inchoate matter (53c-55c).

The final section deals with the parts of the body and soul (69a-73a), the substances of the body (like bone and flesh) (73b-76e), growth and diminution (80d-81e), diseases of the body and soul (81e-87ba), and other such things.

Dreams at 45d-46a

At 44d, Timaeus begins a discussion of how, in all probability, humans were created. First, he talks of the head as a "spherical body" in which the revolutions of the immortal soul are confined (44d-45b). From 45b to 46a, he gives a physiological account of the eyes and how vision occurs—offering what appears to be a general explanation for sleep and dreams (both being intimately associated with vision) from 45d-46a. It is to this account that I now turn.

In sleep, the pure fire (πῦρ εἰλικρινές) or visual flow (τὸ τῆς ὄψεως ῥεῦμα), which issues out into ambient air during the day and enables us to see things by mixing itself with the light of day[5] (45b-d), is cut off when night comes. The visual flow now mixes with what is unlike itself and, consequently, is changed or extinguished because the nocturnal air has no fire.[6] Soon the eyelids shut, and the power of this fire is thereby enclosed. The internal fire now disperses and evens out the internal motions (τὰς ἐντος κινήσεις), thereby causing tranquility[7] (45d-46a).

Concerning dreams, Timaeus says:

> And when the quiet is profound, a sleep with few dreams falls upon us. But when certain stronger [internal] motions lag behind and remain in their places (τόποις[8]), these motions bring about internal appearances. These are similar in quality and number [to the κινήσεις] and are remembered [by us] when we are awake as having been outside of us (τοιαῦτα καὶ τοσαῦτα παρέσχοντο ἀφομοιωθέντα ἐντὸς ἔξω τε ἐγερθεῖσιν ἀπομνημονευόμενα φαντάσματα[9]) (45e-46a).

The Motions Behind the Images

Though the reference to dreams from 45e to 46a is short, it is compendious. It may not allow one to flesh out an account of dreams for Timaeus, still it is rich enough to generate some fruitful speculation about what such an account might be like. Yet before I begin such an account, it is critical first to clear up one issue: What are the internal motions mentioned at 45e that give rise to oneiric images?

Timaeus talks of the effects of certain disruptive motions from 42e to 44d, and this is a good place to begin an investigation. Here Timaeus describes the initial disturbance that occurred in the circuits (περιόδοι[10]) of newly incarnate souls in the divine craftsman's act of the creation of humans. Such newborn souls experienced six motions that interfered with the natural circular motions within as they were bombarded by the continual ebb and flow of nutritive intake and the objects of sensation. These were movements up and down, right and left, and forward and backward (43a-b). With no one circuit acting as governor in these first humans, these newly incarnate souls were unregulated by reason and, thus, highly unstable (44a). This description, Timaeus says, not only applies to the first generation of people but also to every newborn baby's soul. Through maturation and education, the sensual and nutritive bombardment lessens and the several circuits are corrected, and the developing person begins to become rational (44b).

This passage anticipates a second account of vision that is given from 46c to 47c. Here Timaeus states that the power of sight was given to us by the gods to enable us to see the circuits of intelligence in the heavens and thereby gain an understanding of the revolutions (περιφοραί) of our own intelligence through the notions of number, time, the nature of the world, and, in general, the study of philosophy (47a-b). In looking toward and contemplating the heavens, we quell certain wandering motions (πεπλανημέναι[11]) and reproduce the perfect circuits of the god in ourselves (47c). This account of vision deals with causes (αἴτιαι) in the most straightforwardly teleological sense, not auxiliary or proximate causes (συναίτιαι), where the influence of the final cause may be imperceptible or difficult to discern (46c). The implication is clear: The account of dreams from 45b to 46a, dealing with phenomena only at the physiological level, is one that refers only to auxiliary causes.[12] It is noteworthy that, in the account of vision from 46c to 47c, dreams and dreaming are not at all mentioned.

Most importantly for our purposes, the wandering motions that disturb the circuits of the noncontemplative soul at 47c bear a stark resemblance to the violent motions that cause disorder in the settled revolutions in the bodies of infants mentioned at 43a-b. In the former, the wandering motions work against reason and the circuits of the harmonious soul; the latter case depicts violent motions that dominate an infant's life. With due respect for simplicity, there is no reason not to identify these two motions. Might not the internal motions that give rise to dreams (45e) be the same?

By linking dreaming so closely to vision, Plato must have known that oneiric images most often correspond closely to waking, visual phenomena. If we understand the wandering internal motions that give rise to dreams to be "untamed" sensual (mostly visual) perceptions or remnants of perception[13] that are identical to those at 43a-b and 47c, then the puzzle is solved.

During the day (or just prior to night), the visual flow that emanates from the eyes returns likenesses of the sensory objects to the perceiver. In some cases, those sensual remnants that have not reached the soul before sleep, but wander through the body as motions, are seen as dreams when eventually they do reach the soul. In other cases, either those matters with which the soul is preoccupied prior to sleep or bodily disturbances from within are the kinetic images of dreams. All such motions are characteristic of a soul that is unsettled by reason. Taylor proposes something similar in his commentary. He writes:

> The explanation of dreams which follows shows that the motions referred to are, in the first instance, local motions of various kinds in the eye itself..., but since, as we shall learn later on, sensation depends on stimulation of the brain, we may fairly suppose all sorts of internal disturbances in the organism as a whole to be included.[14]

This approach puts a premium on vision in the formation of all dreams. But this emphasis is not exaggeration; it is textually grounded. As we saw above, it is no accident that the physiological account of dreams from 45d to 46a directly follows the physiological account of vision (45b-d).

If this is so, the six violent motions of 43a-b, the wandering motions of 47c, and the stray internal motions that generate dreams at 45e all describe exactly the same kinds of motions, mostly the result of sensation. The earliest account depicts the chaotic, sensual bombardment of a soul ungoverned by reason in infants (and, no doubt, those whose intellective faculty is undeveloped or greatly underdeveloped). The accounts at 45e and 47c characterize any soul (presumably, one that is adult and nondefective) where reason to some extent governs. Here some of the internal motions move in their proper (circular) route; others stray. Together these passages suggest an inverse relationship between the power of reason and the number of the internal, disruptive motions: the greater the intellective capacity, the fewer noncircular internal motions to disturb the intellective soul. Moreover, it would seem that dreams too, forming out of these disturbing or wandering motions, run contrary to reason. The lesser the intellect, the more disturbing internal motions and, consequently, the greater the number of dreams.[15]

Dreams at 70d-72d

Later, when Timaeus returns to the top-down perspective where Reason is most directly active and most visible, Plato gives a more elaborate account of dreaming (70d-72d). Now I turn towards a reconstruction of Plato's account of dreams in *Timaeus*.

In sleep, when understanding is fettered, the appetitive soul (τὸ ἐπιθυμητικόν), stationed between the midriff and the navel and as far away as possible from the seat of counsel and the most authoritative part of the soul,[16] receives impulses from the intellective soul (τὸ λογιστικόν) (70d-71a). Having both bitterness and sweetness in its nature, the liver[17] receives contrary impulses. When it receives impulses of a base sort, it thrives in its bitterness and becomes wrinkled and rough. Feeling pains and woes, it gives back frightening images to the intellect (71b-c). At other times, it receives impulses of a different sort and gives back contrary images (τἀναντία φαντάσματα). Thriving in gentleness and well-being, it becomes smooth, like a mirror, and returns more pleasant images—involving past, present, or future goods or evils—to the intellective soul. In this way, Timaeus states, the *Demiourgos* has foreordained the power of prophecy in humans, especially those of a base nature or those whose reasoning is disengaged (71c-d). Unlike Homer's account, there is no direct activity of the god involving dreams; the *Demiourgos* has merely fashioned humans so that they have a capacity for knowing the truth that requires cooperation between the intellective and appetitive souls.

True dreams can only be interpreted by one of sound mind, not by one in a state of frenzy (72a). Hence, he says, arose the custom of setting up interpreters of dreams (72b).

Squaring 45d-46a and 70d-72d

The immediate problem is the relation between this account and the one offered earlier from 45d to 46a. On the one hand, it might just be that Timaeus believes that these are accounts occurring at different levels of explanation in the formation of distinct kinds of dreams: the earlier account being one at the physiological level and dealing indirectly with Reason by mentioning only auxiliary or proximate causes (for bitter dreams?); the later giving a god's-eye, teleological account, where the activity of Reason is easily evident (for mild dreams?). If so, perhaps there is nothing further to say. On the other hand, might there not be a temporal relationship between the two accounts? If so, then a closer look at these two passages just might heighten our understanding of how Reason directs Necessity for the best possible end throughout the entire formation of dreams and give us a fuller understanding of the function of dreams for Timaeus.

From 71b to 71d, Timaeus mentions two types of messages sent to the liver (and two corresponding dreams that subsequently occur): terrifying messages and those that are mild and inspiring. Are both of these dreams meaningful or true? In other words, do the frightful messages also convey significant information—ominous warnings or signs of what was, is, or will be? If so, then one possible relationship between 45d-46a and 70d-72d is this: The latter deals exclusively (and teleologically) with two species of true dreams, while the former is an account of all other (empty) dreams at the physiological level. However, if nightmares have nothing to do with past, present, or future goods or evils, then the precise relationship between these two seemingly different accounts becomes unclear.

Archer-Hind and Taylor[18] see no difficulty. They believe that the two accounts are two explanations for two different types of dreams: significant dreams from 70d to 72d (which comprise true dreams and nightmares) and insignificant dreams from 45d to 46a. While 45d-46a gives a general account of most dreams, insignificant dreams, 70d-72d exclusively tells how significant dreams occur. In other words, Timaeus' nightmares are a species of significant dreams also, messages sent to warn the dreamer of impending evil. Of these, Archer-Hind writes: "[T]he pains and nausea [of the liver] would cause evil dreams, which served as portents and deterents".[19]

Van Lieshout expresses the contrary view. He states that the account from 70d to 72d is both one of prophesying through dreams and those "without any revealing value", though he says nothing about how it relates to 45d-46a.[20]

The text of 71c-d does not seem to support Archer-Hind and Taylor. Here Timaeus states:

> And, on the other hand, when some mild inspiration from the intellect depicts opposite presentations, it relieves the bitterness.

> Not having a power either for moving or for touching a nature opposite itself, but using the innate sweetness of the liver on the liver and directing matters so that all is straight and smooth and free, it makes gentle and happy (ἵλεων τε καὶ εὐήμερον) the part of the soul settled around the liver, which has a modest nocturnal pastime of practicing divination during sleep (ἔν τε τῇ νυκτὶ διαγωγὴν ἔχουσαν μετρίαν μαντείᾳ χρωμένην καθ' ὕπνον), since it does not partake of reason and deliberation.

Archer-Hind himself acknowledges that the τε from ἔν τε τῇ νυκτὶ merely couples ἔχουσαν with the ἵλεων τε καὶ εὐήμερον directly preceding it. If this is so, and this seems to be the most grammatically sound reading, then it establishes the link of divination with gentleness and happiness alone, and makes it improbable that nightmares are divinely sent or true.

The solution to the difficulty concerning the relationship of the two passages, I suggest, is that the physiological account of vision and dreams from 45b to 46a is an earlier stage in the formation of all dreams. The picture we arrive at, then, looks something like this. First, 45b-46a establishes vision as the *sine qua non* of dreaming; without it, there can be no internal motions and dreams would not occur. Consequently, there is not and need not be anything ostensibly teleological about the explanation here. The text from 70d to 72d then describes how the movements set up by vision ultimately give rise to all of the images of dreams—those caused by decaying visual presentations, by internal bodily disturbances, or by psychological concerns. These motions, during sleep, arrive at the intellective soul, housed in the brain, where they incite oneiric messages to be conveyed to that part of the appetitive soul stationed in the liver.[21] The working of the intellective soul at this stage manifestly involves the final cause; Necessity now subserves the authority of Reason. In all, the intellective soul functions like a coordinating center for dreams. When "divinely inspired", it breathes gentleness on the liver, causing it to smooth out and send back true dreams. At all other times, it sends fearful messages to wrinkle the liver and reflect back nightmares to the intellect.

Two Plausible Models

A problem quickly emerges. This reconstruction assumes that there are only two dreams: true dreams and nightmares. Yet it seems incredible that Timaeus would believe that there are no other kinds of dreams.

Perhaps Timaeus mentions only these because they come about through the cooperation of both the intellective and appetitive souls. Might there not be a third type of dream, wholly disconnected from the agency of the appetitive soul, that is linked to the spirited soul? Here Plato is silent. Yet his silence concerning the spirited soul (or dreams bearing thumic characteristics) makes it likely that the motions to and from the liver are not at all influenced by the spirited soul.

There is a second problem with Timaeus' account. Of all the faculties, why would the intellective soul send frightening or alarming messages to the liver, if these serve no function (such as to warn the dreamer of impending disaster)? Of true dreams, prophetic messages pose no difficulty, for it is easy to see how these may prove advantageous to the dreamer. Since the intellective soul initiates frightening dreams also, they must be of some functional significance for the dreamer. Yet as we have seen, 71c-d suggests otherwise.

There is another difficulty in attempting to reconcile 45b-46a and 70d-72d. For 45d-46a states that the visual flow during sleep acts to smooth out the wandering motions within. This suggests that the visual flow works, in the best possible way, to try to make dreaming impossible so as to promote peaceful sleep. That the visual flow or internal fire should work to prevent the occurrence of dreams is sensible when dreams are frightening, but what sense can we make of this when the divinely inspired intellective soul intends to send true dreams? We cannot assume that a peaceful, dreamless sleep is preferable to having sleep with true dreams—especially those of the prophetic sort.

These difficulties can be solved by distinguishing between four kinds of motions, not all of which need to be qualitatively distinguishable, and four different stages in the formation of dreams in the *Timaeus*. First, there are the movements set up in the eyes that begin the whole process. Second, there are subsidiary movements—such as psychological movements (caused by worries, distress, etc.) or physical movements (caused by unusual, internal physical conditions like arrhythmia)—that arise from these and make their way to the brain, the location of the intellective soul, as the raw material for dreams. Some of these subsidiary movements are violent; others are smooth. Third, the intellect directs both movements to the liver to be fashioned into the images of the two types of dreams. Last, the liver returns these messages to the intellective soul, as a mirror reflecting back images, though in the "language" of the liver.

Now if we posit that the visual flow operates just in the earlier stages of formation of dreams and attempts to level out and disperse motions before they arrive at the intellective soul (stage two), then (1) the visual flow either functions directly and selectively under the guidance of intellect or (2) it acts according to Necessity to reduce arbitrarily the number of movements that reach the intellective soul. On either account, the internal motions referred to at 45e, since they include those motions that cause true dreams *as well as* frightful ones, cannot then be identical to the six motions of 43a-b and the wandering motions of 47c, because the latter are merely disruptive and act contrary to the best interests of the immortal, intellective soul.

If the visual flow works selectively under the auspices of Reason to favor those motions that convey true information, the gentler and smoother motions, then it is likely that the final cause directly enters the picture at stage two; only stage one is explicable by the activity of Necessity.[22] The visual flow, then, functions exclusively or chiefly to level out the disruptive motions before they reach the intellect. In those whose intellective faculty reigns supreme, dreams, especially frightening ones, occur only infrequently and the motions responsible for true dreams, of necessity being undisturbed (or nearly so) by the visual flow, may move relatively unimpeded to the intellect, whenever present. In those whose intellects are underdeveloped, the total confusion by the swarm of movements, caused chiefly by the superabundance of violent motions, prevents the internal fire from having any perceivably calming effect. According to this "selection hypothesis", nightmares occur often for dullards and reprobates, and the likelihood of having a true dream for such ones is thereby greatly diminished.

On the other hand, if the visual flow works to level out motions without regard to type (nonselectively), then it is likely that the final cause is not directly at play in stage two, but perhaps only in stages three or four. According to this account, the visual flow functions according to the dictates of Necessity, instead of what is best. It strives to level out *both* smooth and violent motions, and the intellective soul then creates dreams from what, if anything, remains of the motions. Again, on such a model, it is the disposition or character of sleepers that determines the frequency of true dreams and nightmares. Those who have cultivated reason would have many more smooth motions than violent ones and, thus, many more true dreams.

Both of the models sketched above reconcile the two accounts of dreams in the *Timaeus* equally as well.

Concluding Remarks

The following conclusions may be drawn for the account of dreams given in *Timaeus*.

- Timaeus explicitly specifies only two types of dreams: those inspiring fear, nightmares, and those inspiring gentleness, true dreams.
- The account at 45d-46a is probably an earlier, physiological stage in the genesis of all dreams, while 70d-72d explains teleologically how the intellective soul gives rise to fearful and true dreams later on.
- Vision itself plays an indispensable role in dreaming, being ultimately what is responsible for all of the motions that generate dreams.
- The intellective soul, through interaction with the appetitive soul in the liver, plays a vital role in the formation of *all* dreams, not just true ones (as in *Republic*).
- Last, the character of dreamers determines the proportion of true dreams to nightmares: Dullards have few true dreams, while those who have honed their intellect have many more true dreams.

---

[1] *Euthyphr.*, *La.*, and *Chrm.* fall into this category of works.

[2] A religious festival held annually in honor of the goddess Athena.

[3] 20e-21a suggests that this Critias is the grandfather of the Critias who was one of the thirty tyrants and who is featured in the Platonic dialogue bearing his name (20e-21a).

[4] Presumably, the Forms.

[5] Cf. *Tht.* 156d-e and 182a. In addition to the light of day and visual flow, there is a third type of "fire" involved in seeing. At 67c, Plato calls the color of the external object "a flame (φλόξ) streaming off every body, having particles proportioned to those of the visual current, so as to yield sensation" (Cornford translation 1937, 152). See also Archer-Hind (1973, 156-157) and Taylor (1929, 277-282).

[6] Aristotle challenges the credibility of this nocturnal extinction at *Sens.* 437b11-24. Here he argues that, according to Plato, by comparing the light that issues from the eye to the light from a lantern at night, vision should be possible during the night.

[7] Taylor in his commentary offers the helpful analogy of a wave recoiling and obliterating small, local eddies (1929, 282).

[8] Taylor thinks that these τόποι are regions such as the eye and the sensory centers, where "differential motions" linger (Ibid, 283).

[9] As others have duly noted, the text here is ambiguous. Rivaud, taking ἀφομοιωθέντα with both ἐντός and ἔξω, translates: "...[images]

semblables à des objets intérieurs ou extérieurs et dont nous conservons souvenance au réveil" (1963, 163). He is certainly following Martin who translates: "...images semblables à des objets soit intérieurs, soit extérieurs, et dont le souvenir se conserve aprés le réveil" (1976, 125). I am following Archer-Hind (1973, 159), Taylor (1929, 44), and Cornford (1937, 153) who take ἀφομοιωθέντα only with ἐντός. For instance, Taylor translates: "...images are formed within and remembered without on waking...". Cornford adds that the last bit of Greek here probably means "when we have emerged in the waking world", though it is consistent with seeing the images outside of us whenever we recall the dream, something he does not rule out entirely (1937, 153).

[10] The Hippocratic author of *Insomn.* (see chapter seven) uses this same word to refer to three groupings of fire-made circuits (περιόδοι) in each human body (I.x).

[11] Cf. 48a, where Plato refers to Necessity as an αἰτία πλανώμενα.

[12] See also his introductory remark at 47e, where he begins to discuss the works of Necessity.

[13] Φαντάσματα and internal κινήσεις are also essential to Aristotle's account of dreams (see chapter three).

[14] Taylor 1929, 283.

[15] Cf. *Ap.* 40d, where Socrates says that should death be a dreamless sleep, it would be an unspeakable gain.

[16] The immortal soul, which is identified as the intellective soul, resides in the head (44d-45b). The two parts of the mortal soul, the spirited soul and the appetitive soul, are situated in the breast and the trunk (between the midriff and the navel), respectively. Therefore, the neck and the midriff function as boundaries for the three areas of the soul (69d-e). As depicted, the appetitive soul, being basest, is as far away from the intellective soul as the god could arrange it, for the sake of the intellect's peace (70e) and because of the appetitive soul's lack of rational apprehension (71a).

[17] In the Hippocratic work *Int.,* excess bile in the liver is stated as the cause of derangement and nightmares (XLVIII). *Morb.Sac.* XVII-XVIII explains that bile causes one to be hot-headed and this, in turn brings about bad dreams.

[18] Taylor 1929, 505.

[19] Archer-Hind 1973, 265.

[20] Van Lieshout 1980, 122.

[21] I am assuming here something like a selection process for all of the numerous movements in the intellective soul or a mechanism that weeds out many of these movements. Cf. Lucretius' *Nat.* IV.781-817.

[22] Of course, this need not imply that further discrimination does not occur later in the intellective soul.

Chapter Three
Aristotle's Oneirological Materialism

Introduction

Whereas dreams and the generative processes underlying them are not the chief or exclusive focus of any one of Plato's works, Aristotle devotes two treatises to these topics, *On Dreams* and *On Prophecy during Sleep*, and a third treatise to sleep, *On Sleep and Wakefulness*. These are the subjects of this chapter.

A long-time pupil of Plato's Academy, Aristotle had a keen and omnivorous passion for learning and understanding that looked beyond Plato's rationalism for answers. A compiler, an observer, and sometimes even an experimenter, Aristotle wrote on physiology, biology, psychology, meteorology, and physics as well as logic, metaphysics, philosophy of science, ethics, politics, and art. Of the many works that we know Aristotle composed, today only about one-fifth, roughly 30, works survive.

Diogenes Laertius tells us that Aristotle was born in Stagira (Thrace), when Plato was 43 years of age (384 B. C.). His father Nicomachus was physician to current Macedonian king, Amyntas.

At 17 years of age, upon the death of his father, Aristotle joined the Academy, where he would remain for 20 years until the death of Plato. From 347 to 343 B. C., he moved to Ionia, where he married and met his friend and successor Theophrastus. In 343 B. C., he moved to Macedonia to tutor Alexander the Great, son of King Philip.

From 335 to 323 B. C., Aristotle went to Athens to found his own school, the Lyceum. The Lyceum, mirroring Aristotle's own omnivoracity for learning, enjoyed considerable status in its day and probably resembled a modern-day university. Alexander himself reputedly donated the extraordinary sum of 800 talents[1] to its development and upkeep. Aristotle and his followers researched numerous projects, one such undertaking being the study of the 158 most important Greek constitutions.[2] At the Lyceum, he probably expounded upon scientific and philosophic matters in the morning to a general audience, while engaging smaller, learned audiences with more intractable concerns in the afternoon.

Aristotle's treatise on sleep and two treatises on dreams are collected in his *Parva Naturalia.* In these works, Aristotle does not analyze dreams themselves—that is, oneiric content—instead, like Plato in *Timaeus*, his focus is oneirogenesis. Ultimately his explanation of the origin of dreams, fashioned in terms of the material conditions of sleep, is entirely naturalistic. In all, these treatises are perhaps the most thorough examination of the topic in all of Greco-Roman antiquity.

Despite the focus on the underlying material processes responsible for dreams in the *Parva Naturalia*, Aristotle does have something to say concerning the many functions that dreams have both in these works and through passing remarks on dreams in different treatises. For Aristotle, dreams reveal emotional and moral dispositions and even the physical health of the body. In addition, *On Prophecy during Sleep*, as its title suggests, is devoted exclusively to the issue of prophetic revelation through dreams.

In what follows, focussing mostly on his treatises, *On Sleep and Wakefulness* and *On Dreams*, I take a closer look at Aristotle's thoughts on the formation, universality, and functions of dreams.

Three Crucial Propositions

In *On Dreams*, Aristotle says that he will seek out that faculty of the soul to which dreams appear. First he considers sensation (αἴσθησις). He argues that, since the senses are inoperative in sleep, it cannot be by sensation that we dream (458b1-9).

Next he considers opinion (δόξα). When someone approaches, we say both that what approaches is a man and that he is good-looking. Yet we cannot form an opinion that the man is good-looking without sensation. Yet the senses are idle in sleep, and opinion cannot function without sensation. Consequently, we must as well eliminate the opinionative part of the soul (458b10-26).

Nevertheless, judging of some sort is what the soul actually does in sleep. For in sleep, he says, we dream that what comes toward us is both a horse and beautiful. Yet any kind of judgment requires something to judge—a perception. We can only say of a horse that it is beautiful when we have a perception of the horse (458b10-14). He concludes, "Indeed this much is clear: The same faculty by which we are deceived in illness when awake also brings about a dream (πάθος[3]) in sleep". This is the imaginative part of the soul[4] (τὸ φανταστικὸν τῆς ψυχῆς). Therefore, dreaming "does not occur without seeing and without perceiving something" (458b27-32). This connection of dream and perception, especially vision, is entirely in keeping with the account Plato gives from 45b to 46a of *Timaeus*.

But how can this be if the senses are idle in sleep? Aristotle acknowledges that, though it is true that the senses do not work in sleep, it is not true that we experience nothing sensory in sleep (458b30-459a6). Though the senses no longer function in sleep, certain affections borne of them that are set up by the reception of the sensory stimuli when the senses were functioning while awake, persist throughout the body (459a25-27).

Aristotle proposes the following. The affections that exist potentially in the soul when someone is awake become more noticeable as perceptual remnants or stimulatory motions during sleep.[5] Though they exist in wakefulness as well, they go unheeded, and remain like a small fire next to a great one. With sleep, the particular senses become inactive and the link between perception and intellection is severed. In *On Prophecy during Sleep*, he states:

> For the motions (κινήσεις) occurring during the day, if they are not very great and powerful, pass unnoticed along side of the greater waking motions. But in sleep, the opposite takes place. For [then] even what is small seems to be great (463a8-11).

Next, the stimulatory motions move to the heart, the ἀρχή of sensation, since the blood tends to gather there during sleep.[6] With few or no sensory impressions being received during sleep, the heart more easily attends to the slighter omnipresent remnants of prior sensory impressions—the residual perceptual motions (460b27-461a9, 461b11-13, & 463a8-22).

This is the first of three crucial propositions upon which Aristotle's theory of dreams is structured. Formally stated:

> S_1: When the external objects that cause sensory impressions are removed, their sensory impressions (αἰσθήματα) remain perceptible[7] (460b1-3).

For just as inanimate moving objects do not cease to move when they are no longer in contact with their moving cause, so too sensory impressions do not end with the removal of their external cause.

Aristotle offers several observations in support of S_1—visual experiments so simple that anyone can perform them (though not all are correct observations). He argues that when we shift our gaze to the dark after we have stared at a bright object, we see nothing in the dark because the motions excited by the light still subsist in our eyes. Also, when we look at the sun and then shut our eyes, we still see an image of the sun in the same line in which it previously appeared to us. Its color, at first the same, soon decays to red then to purple then to black before it vanishes completely. Again, when we look at an object of any color for a long time and then suddenly shift our attention to another object, this second object seems to take on the color of the first. Last, fixing our gaze upon a moving object (like a river) for a long time, we seem to see stationary objects in motion as well (459a27-b20). Since what is true of vision must also be true of the four other particular senses, these observations show that when the appropriate sensory organ no longer receives an object of sensation, an affection persists in that organ.

The second proposition may be stated as follows:

> S_2: We are easily deceived about sense perceptions when under the sway of the emotions (460b3-4).

An amorous person, even with scant or specious visual evidence, sees his beloved in another object. Likewise, a coward takes any small resemblance of an enemy as a sign of that enemy. Here the point is implicitly that dreamers—with their senses inoperative and, consequently, their critical faculties impaired—are in a similar state to any person under the sway of emotion. In other words, dreamers are easily fooled by what they see in sleep. The deeper the emotional sway that the dreamer has toward a particular object, the less resemblance an oneiric image need have to that object to be mistaken for it by the dreamer (460b3-9).

We may add a third claim to these, which I derive in part from his treatise *On Sleep and Wakefulness*:

> S_3: In sleep, both the particular senses and their common or master sense[8] are shut off, and thereby the faculty of judgment is impaired.[9]

For dreams would not occur were it not for the cessation or relaxation of certain capacities of the soul. If the senses were operative in sleep, though the images responsible for dreams would still exist, they would be imperceptible. Like a great fire next to a small one, the sensory impressions would drown out the residual ones. So with the cessation of certain capacities of the soul, we gain a capacity for an internal awareness we would not have had were we constantly in the waking state[10] (455a29-b2, 460b16-18, and 461b5-8).

Implications of These Propositions

From this triad of propositions, let us try to make some sense of Aristotle's account of dreams. S_1 and S_3 give us reason to believe that dreamers can do no other than assume that their oneiric images are true. For, during sleep, if sensory remnants remain when sensation is shut off and judgment is impaired, then the images seen in sleep are just as real to dreamers as waking-life impressions are to those who are awake.

On the Soul provides additional support for this. First, in terms of their composition, Aristotle gives us every reason to think that oneiric images, though sensory remnants, are indistinguishable from the more direct images of sensation. In other words, like sensory impressions, images in dreams comprise special sensibles (e.g., color and, to a lesser extent, sound, flavor, etc.), incidental sensibles (e.g., that the white object is the son of Darius), and common sensibles (movement, rest, figure, number, and size). *On the Soul* also says that the special sensory organs (sight, hearing, taste, etc.) are the *sole arbiters* of the truth or reality of the special objects they receive about which they cannot or, at least, are most unlikely to err (418a11-15, 428b17-27). But with the special senses in repose during sleep, they cannot contribute to any judgment at all. So presumably either judgment is not involved with remnants of the special sensibles while dreaming or, if it is, it merely assumes the reality of what it "perceives" in such cases, since *phantasia*, the faculty responsible for dreams, is at work here and not the special senses. Regarding the other, more complex objects of sensation—the incidental and the common sensibles (movement, rest, number, figure, size)—one can go awry with these simply because these are formed by a combination of thoughts (430b26-32) and, thus, the faculty of judgment is necessary. Yet judgment in the area of the incidental sensibles and common sensibles must rely crucially on the input of the special senses to come to the correct decision.[11] However, in sleep, the senses are altogether idle and unable to pass or assist judgment.

Does *phantasia* itself pass judgment while we dream? Aristotle intimates that *phantasia* is a faculty that involves judging, though he never quite clearly spells out just what he means by this (428a1-4). He also tells us that the images of this faculty of the soul are mostly false (428a12). Later, however, he adds that sometimes—when the soul is clouded by illness, emotion or sleep—we act in accordance with the images of *phantasia* (429a5-9). Though 428a1-4 intimates that *phantasia* is a faculty that can judge, simple reflection on the nature of dreams makes it difficult to believe that Aristotle did think that judging of any kind actually does occur while we dream—at least for the great majority of dreams.[12] Therefore, though *phantasia* has a capacity to judge each dream, we must assume that it actually does so only in a few instances. If, then, no judging occurs in the overwhelming majority of dreams, following 429a5-9, it is plausible that dreamers simply accept the images of dreams as real during sleep.

By itself, S_2—that we are easily deceived when under the sway of emotions—seems to be a cognitive rule for understanding either ambiguous and unclear dreams or remnants of dreams. With sleepers likened to those under the sway of emotion, it follows that dreamers are likely to mistake uncertain oneiric images for objects with which they have some emotional investment in waking life, for better or worse. If this is correct, then dreams, episodes of dreams, or oneiric figures in them must often be constructions by the dreamer from the uncertain, faint, or ambiguous perceptual remnants that present themselves to the dreamer. For any such dream, the unclear manifest dream is only relevant insofar as it influences the construction of the dream's narrative as dreamers believe it to have occurred. Since the construction occurs in accordance with the emotional dispositions of dreamers, it is likely that dreamers who are especially overcome by emotions would have a disproportionately large number of reported dreams that manifest these affections[13]—assuming, of course, there are no underlying physical constraints.

Let me pause here to summarize. First, dreamers must (in some sense) take any manifest dream as real while asleep, regardless of the absurdity of its content. Second, if a dream is ambiguous, faint, or unclear, dreamers are likely to "see" images in it as things with which they are emotionally involved, if there is at least some slight resemblance.

Formation of Dreams

Overall, the omnipresent residual motions left behind from sensation form a succession of images. These residual impressions are so related that, first, if they go undisturbed, they move toward the heart in an orderly way and, second, if one perishes, another will quickly take its place. Concerning the former, when the purer, hotter blood is separated from the less pure and colder blood, as is best, stimulatory motions traverse the blood relatively unperturbed and the heart receives clear impressions. This is how dreams occur in healthy people. Regarding perishability, Aristotle asserts that the sensory motions behave with respect to each other like artificial frogs, weighted by salt, that pop up to the surface of a pond when the salt has dissolved.[14] Moreover, just as the frogs cannot make an appearance at the surface of the pond until the salt has sufficiently dissolved, "in this manner, the stimulatory motions exist in us potentially, but are actualized when what holds them in check is relaxed" (461b11-17).

When the heart receives the stimulatory remnants that form a quasi-impression of, say, Coriscus, this quasi-impression is much like the actual impression received when the senses were activated and "it is true to say that this is like Coriscus, though it is not Coriscus" (461b22-25). When there is any disturbance in the flow of these stimulatory motions during sleeping, the result is either a distorted image or no image at all. For though one can see an impression of oneself in a clear and tranquil liquid, when the liquid is noticeably disturbed, either a distorted impression or no discernible impression occurs (461a14-24). Obviously, the blood through which oneiric images flow is just such a liquid for Aristotle.

Aristotle also compares stimulatory movements to clouds or small eddies in a river. Like clouds, the slightest disturbance affects the shape of the motions and quickly what one takes to be a person can become a centaur. Yet like eddies in a stream, these motions are continuous—though sometimes the pattern formed by them, because of some perturbation, is disturbed and altered (461a8-12 and 461b18-22).

By comparing dreams with artificial frogs, cloud-shapes, and eddies, Aristotle makes some attempt to account for the movement in and coherence and drama of certain dreams. The residual stimulatory motions, when traversing the blood to the heart in a relatively undisturbed manner, may present themselves to the dreamer in such rapid succession that the total effect is somewhat comparable to seeing a movie[15] today from a video cassette.

With the analogy of a clear and undisturbed liquid, one sees plainly the type of relationship that exists between the stimulatory motions and the external objects ultimately responsible for them. Just as a tranquil pond is true to the image of an object near its surface, when the stimulatory motions are left to wander to the heart undisturbed, they present to it an image similar to the object externally responsible for it. Yet Aristotle also says that the residual perceptions are like clouds which first appear one way and then another. This shows the frailty of sensory impressions. When sleepers have a surfeit of food or drink within themselves and an in ordinate amount of insanguinous matter coursing through their bloodstream (or they are in some other insalubrious condition that disturbs the even flow of their blood), the sensory images within are corrupted.

Aristotle concludes that "a dream is a certain presentation (φάντασμα...τι)[16] that occurs during sleep" (462a16). This, he believes, is sufficient to rule out the phantoms (εἴδωλα) of youngsters, madmen, and drunkards. However, since he observes that some people actually take in some sensations while sleeping,[17] he qualifies the definition in this way, "Insofar as one sleeps, the presentation that results from the movement of sensory impressions, whenever it exists during sleeping, is a dream" (462a17-32).

Dreams and Pathology

A close inspection of Aristotle's account shows that dreams for him have a link with the pathological. Aristotle likens sleep itself, though it has a restorative function, to epilepsy (and other similar diseases), childhood, fatigue, dwarfishness, melancholy, bigheadedness, vein-constrictedness, and drunkenness (456b29-457a35). Sleep is likened to each of these conditions, conditions of a less-than-perfect organism, because sleep, though essential for proper human functioning, is itself an unstable and imperfect state. After all, every sleeper is potentially awake and wakefulness excites perception and allows people to exercise reason—a condition best suited to human existence.

Since sleep itself is a less-than-perfect state for an organism, it follows that dreams, being phenomena occurring in sleep that are intimately conjoined to sensation, are a less-than-perfect way of perceiving. With the senses shut off and the critical faculty impaired, sleepers have no capacity to judge what they dream. Thus sleepers perceive that a human-headed centaur is real, and an image of mighty Titormus[18] as emaciated becomes plausible.

Since corrupt and incomprehensible images often take on a reality congruent with the emotional dispositions of dreamers, those inflamed by love, Aristotle says, see their beloved in anyone else who bears even a faint resemblance to their beloved. Likewise, a coward sees his enemy in an image in a dream that only feebly resembles him. Thus, oneiric reports of dreamers are often constructions from ambiguous or distorted images in accordance with dreamers' emotional dispositions. It follows that lovers will "see" and report dreams of their beloved in a manner disproportionately greater than the actual oneiric images of their beloved. The stade runner on the night before a competition may "see" any sustained movement in a dream as his participation in the 600-foot race. Sleepers' reports of dreams, then, can give an indication of their particular emotional state (or emotionally charged interests) or psychological wellbeing at any given time. This discovery has nothing to do with the meaning or function of dreams; it is an accidental characteristic of some dreams brought about by the material conditions of sleep and a person's psychological state at the time of a dream.

Universality of Dreams

Let me next turn to my second issue: the extent to which other living organisms dream. At *Generation of Animals* V.1, Aristotle states that, because of the unalterable link between dreaming and perceiving (especially dreaming and seeing), of living organisms, only animals can dream (779a2-4).

Of those animals that dream, humans dream the most. In *History of Animals* IV.10 Aristotle writes, "Of all animals, humans are most given to dreaming". Then he surprisingly adds, "Children and infants do not dream, but in most cases dreaming comes on at the age of four or five years". In certain exceptional cases, some humans go through the whole of their lives without dreaming. Of these, some take to dreaming later in life and this usually forebodes bodily decay—resulting in death for some and in debilitation for others (537b13-20).

It is worth emphasizing that Aristotle does not state that certain people *fail to remember* their dreams but that certain people *have* no dreams. This is difficult to reconcile with an account of dreams being caused by and composed of perceptual remnants, which all people have. We can salvage this apparent inconsistency if we assume, for Aristotle, that these exceptional people either (1) do not sleep at all, (2) have no relaxation of their critical faculties during sleep, or (3) have perceptual remnants but fail to recognize or remember these motions. Of these, the one and two are easily dismissed. First, since sleep is the necessary biological counterpart to wakefulness and stands toward it as potential to actual, all people must sleep. Second, Aristotle states flatly that sleep essentially involves a relaxation of the critical faculties. We are left, then, with only the third option. Yet this too is suspicious, for Aristotle makes no mention in these cases that the problem is one of poor recall or memory.

A solution to this difficulty comes at the end of his final chapter of his treatise *On Dreams* and at *History of Animals*. At *H A* IV.10, Aristotle discusses those who never seen a dream in their life and compares them both to children and to those who have fallen asleep just after eating. Of these, some end their lives never having dreamed. Others, when far advanced in age, first dream.

> One must believe that the cause of the nonoccurrence [of dreams in these people] is something similar [to the cause of the nonoccurrence of dreams in those who fall asleep after eating and in children], since dreams do not occur to either of the latter two. Nature has put those who do not dream together in such a way that much evaporation occurs toward the upward part of their body. This evaporation, when it is carried down again, effects a dollop of movement. It is reasonable that, in such people, no dream (φάντασμα) appears. But when they advance in years, it is not unusual that a dream should appear [to them]. For when there is a change due to age or experience (πάθος), it is necessary that the opposite of what has previously happened occurs (462b3-12).

In short, some people do not dream simply because their bodily constitution, like the bodily constitution of a child, is constantly so much disturbed by the evaporation of hot matter upward that they cannot see any images.

Still, this is problematic. To see why, let us liken the bodily constitution of a nondreamer to the surface of a greatly agitated bed of water. Even in a greatly agitated bed of water some things are visible—though what is seen, reflected violently, is most often unrecognizable. Why, then, do nondreamers see nothing in sleep? I think that Aristotle would concede that they must see something, but that what they see at any moment in sleep is so distorted it bears no resemblance to visible reality and, therefore, cannot be considered an oneiric image. If this is correct, at least part of what it means for someone to have a dream for Aristotle is that that person experiences clearly delineated perceptual objects in sleep or, at least, something that somewhat resembles a clearly delineated perceptual object.

About the prevalence of dreaming in other animals, at *HA* IV.10 Aristotle says the following:

> And furthermore not only do men appear to dream, but also horses and dogs and oxen, and even sheep and goats and the whole genus of viviparous quadrupeds. And dogs show [that they dream] by barking [in sleep] (536b27-30).

He adds that ovipara may not dream, though they do sleep (536b30-32).

Aristotle has nothing to say about the occurrence of dreaming in other animals.[19]

"Functions" of Dreams

Let me now turn to the third issue: the different functions of dreams.

Throughout his corpus, Aristotle refers to three functions of dreams: Some dreams signify our bodily health; some tell of our moral state; and others foretell events.

Concerning dreams relating to our physical health, Aristotle recognizes that sometimes the disposition of one's body becomes manifest in dreams. Such dreams are physical indications of the health of a particular person's body that are translated by the soul into dreams.[20] In *On Dreams*, Aristotle says that dreams make small motions appear large. From a tiny drop of phlegm someone might dream of honey and sweet juices. From slight sounds one might dream of thunder.[21] Other dreams, because of the internal physical disturbances that cause them, indicate incipient illness. Slight bodily disturbances are redoubled by the sleeper and take the form of a dream that is a sign of illness (463a8-20). Consequently, if the underlying material conditions are aberrant and unnatural, the dreams to which these give rise often reflect these anomalies.

Moreover, if certain people have bodily dispositions, afflictions, or disturbances that mimic the conditions that promote sleep and thereby cause disturbed dreams or a lack of dreaming, in contrast, we may assume that others, say well-proportioned and robust adults, are disposed to exceptionally clear and vivid dreams. Aristotle says just this at 461a26-29.

Concerning moral dreams, in chapter xxx of the *Problems*, perhaps a spurious work, Aristotle (or a later peripatetic) observes a connection between what we think about while awake and oneiric content. Better people have better dreams because they tend to think about better things; those of an inferior moral status have worse dreams (957a26-32).[22] Here, as with Plato, we notice that the soul itself has a critical role in the formation of certain dreams. In other words, it is possible for dreamers to betray their moral status not only by their biased reporting of ambiguous, faint, or unclear dreams[23] (*On Dreams* 460b3-9), but also because certain disturbing motions of the soul sometimes themselves become dreams.

Last, Aristotle acknowledges that some dreams are even genuinely prophetic. In *On Prophecy during Sleep*, he states that there are certain extravagant dreams, whose origin is not in the dreamer, that are fulfilled by future events. These he provisionally dismisses as coincidental at 463b1-23, only to reexamine the issue beginning at 464a1. Here he grudgingly concedes that certain abnormal humans have a nature that enables them to take in and see the images of things yet to be.[24]

Now let me turn to the formation of Aristotle's thoughts on dreaming. In agreement with the ancient Greek notion that dreams are chiefly visual phenomena, Aristotle was bound to explain the formation of dreams in a manner that conforms to his own thoughts on sensation and other psychic phenomena in important treatises like *On Sensation* and *On the Soul*. Interestingly enough, there is much in his oneirology that is the direct result of experience. At 459a23-28 of *On Dreams*, Aristotle states flatly that his oneirogenetic account is mostly based upon a study of the circumstances attending sleep (Τι δ' ἐστὶ τὸ ἐνύπνιον καὶ πῶς γίνεται, ἐκ τῶν περὶ τὸν ὕπνον συμβαινόντων μαλιστ' ἂν θεωρήσαιμεν). In particular, we have seen that he supports his "first crucial proposition" concerning dreams—When sensation has stopped, the affections in the sensory organs persist—by an appeal to visual experiments (459b2-24). In addition, his references to the different functions of dreams strongly suggest that he is drawing from other sources when referring to these: Plato for moral dreams, Hippocratic physicians for physically revelatory dreams, and the overall fourth-century B. C. milieu in antiquity for prophetic dreams. This too is in keeping with ancient empiricism.[25]

Concluding Remarks

In summary, since not all dreams for Aristotle are meaningful or functionally significant in the same way for all human beings, it is implausible that Aristotle ascribed a purpose to dreams for proper human functioning. All dreams, except prophetic ones, are explicable wholly in naturalistic terms, mostly relating to the material conditions of sleep. The naturalistic language he employs to describe the process of the formation of dreams has much in common with the language Plato uses in *Timaeus*. However, whereas Plato was equally interested in both dreams and their formation, in the *Parva Naturalia* Aristotle's focus is on the latter. Nevertheless, Aristotle's account here is one of the most complete and sober in Greco-Roman antiquity.

---

[1] One-day's wage for the average working man was one drachma. One talent was equivalent to 6000 drachmae. If we assume the average working man's wage is today $100 per day, then the contribution was roughly $480,000,000!

[2] Only one, *The Athenian Constitution,* survives.

[3] Consistent with his usage throughout the *Parva Naturalia*, πάθος may refer to a secondary motion, residual sensation, emotion, or even a dream, as it does here.

[4] *Phantasia* or imagination. *Phantasia* also plays an important role in dreaming for the Cyrenaian bishop Synesius (see chapter seven). For more on *phantasia* in Aristotle, see *de An.* III.3 (427b29-429a9).

[5] These, for instance, he refers to as αἱ κινήσεις αἱ ἀπὸ τῶν αἰσθημάτων γινόμεναι (460b29), αἱ ἐνοῦσαι κινήσεις (461b12), and κινήσεις φανταστικαί (462a9). In contrast, τὸ ἐνύπνιον is τὸ φάντασμα τὸ ἀπὸ τῆς κινήσεως τῶν αἰσθημάτων (462a30). Recall that Plato calls the material causes of dreams κινήσεις. E.g., αἱ ἐντὸς κινήσεις (*Ti.* 46a).

[6] Sleep, then, is a chilling of sorts, of which an explanation comes at 457b10-458a10. Here Aristotle proposes a few accounts of how sleep can chill while its causes are themselves hot. The rising vapor from what remains after digestion moves to the head where it is cooled and gathered into phlegm (cold and most), then sent down to chill the hot, which has unnaturally collected around the heart. Cf. the Hippocratic work *Flat.*, where the author describes sleep as a chilling and slowing of the blood and dreams as certain fancies that linger on (XV.12-19). See also the Hippocratic works *Morb.Sac.* XVII-XVIII and *Int.* XlVIII. At *de An.* II.1 (412a24-26), Aristotle says that sleep and waking are like the unexercised and the exercised possession of knowledge.

[7] See also *de An.* III.2 (425b24-26).

[8] At 455a13-b2, Aristotle argues that it would be silly to think that all the senses simultaneously shut off with sleep, without some sort of common cause. A more plausible alternative, he posits, is the shutting down of τὸ κυρίον τῶν ἄλλων πάντων αἰσθητηρίον, which, in turn, causes the particular senses to shut down.

[9] In *Creat.Hom.*, Gregory of Nyssa says that, with sleep, there is a reversal in the order of the supremacy of the soul's faculties. When awake, the mind reigns supreme, followed by sensation and nutrition. During sleep, nutrition reigns, since rest is necessary for the diffusion of nutriment (XIII.3), while the activity of the senses and mind is quieted, though not extinguished (XIII.5 & 7). Aristotle says something similar here, since he believes that sleep generally follows the taking in of nutriment (456b17-29) and, at *EN* I.13, he adds that the vegetative part of the irrational soul seems to function most in sleep (1102b3-10). Cf. Plato, *Ti.* 45d-e, and Lucretius, *Nat.* IV.758-765 & 916-959.

[10] Henri Bergson (1914; 28, 33, & 51) has argued that dreams help give us an internal awareness that is limited by waking life. For Bergson, consciousness delimits the immense flow of unconscious thinking by focussing thinking. Waking thought is like the point of a pyramid: Only a small aspect of our past experiences is visible.

[11] This occurs in a hierarchical manner. For instance, at 460b20-27 of *Insomn.*, Aristotle considers someone who crosses his fingers and then tries to decide how many objects lie before him. He states counterfactually, "If there were tough alone, we would decide that the two are one". Yet we do not judge thus "for sight is more authoritative than touch". So a correct judgment is passed because of an *unequal* input of the senses.

[12] *Insomn.* 462a3-8 refers to certain dreams in which we are aware of the falsity of oneiric images due to our awareness that we are asleep *while we are asleep* ("lucid dreaming" today).

[13] *Pr.* XXX.14 tells us that oneiric content is cognitively, volitionally, and morally influenced. He states that we dream of things that occupy our minds

before sleeping. Therefore, wishes, thoughts, and even the character of the sleeper impact a dream's content (957a22-33).

[14] These frogs were children's toys, made of cork and covered with enough salt to make them sink in water. When the salt dissolved, the frog would pop up to the surface of the water (Meseguer 1961, 18). Any physical condition of the types Aristotle lists at 456b29-457a34 can disturb sleep and affect dreaming.

[15] Though one of questionable thematic unity.

[16] Aristotle calls a dream a *phantasma*, but it is clear that not every *phantasma* is a dream (458b18-26). Nussbaum (1978, 221-269) and Schofield (1978, 103-132) argue that the view that *phantasma* for Aristotle is some sort of image is too narrow. Dreams, however, are particularly problematic, since their link with vision is obvious in Aristotle as well as in Greco-Roman antiquity in general. Plato and the Stoics also call a dream *phantasma* (*Ti.* 46a & Diogenes Laertius' *Vit.* VII.50).

[17] Aristotle does allow that some people still do take in external impressions through the sensory organs while sleeping. He states, "It happens also that some perceive, in a certain way, sounds and light and flavor and touch [when asleep]—though feebly and, as it were, remotely". In this way, he argues, wakefulness is present in some sense while sleep is present in the ordinary sense. Because the presence of wakefulness here, he concludes that these people cannot be said to be dreaming (462a19-29).

[18] Titormus was a famous strongman from Aetolia, whose strength, according to Aelian, was said to exceed even the great Milo of Croton (Robinson 1981, 88).

[19] He does, however, have much to say concerning sleep in other animals at *HA* IV.10.

[20] The diagnostic dreams of secular medicine (see chapter eight).

[21] Here Aristotle anticipates much of the research into the physical causes of dreams done especially in the last 100 years. It is well established that external physical disturbances occurring during REM sleep are often symbolically incorporated into the narrative of a dream.

[22] See also *EN* (1102a34-b11), where Aristotle states that there may be a connection between oneiric content and a dreamer's moral status.

[23] What Freud dubbed "secondary revision".

[24] See Holowchak 1996, 418-422.

[25] Galen's *Subf.Emp.* VIII.

Chapter Four
Lucretius Ivory-White "Images" of Night

Introduction

In his work *de Rerum Natura*, the Roman poet Lucretius launches perhaps the most rigorous attack against predictive dreams and their divine causes, both of which were rife in Greco-Roman antiquity. He puts forth in this poem a naturalistic account of dreaming that wholly excludes either mediate or immediate interaction with gods through dreams and leaves no room for dreams portending future events. Moreover, he never mentions the medical applications of dreams, such as diagnostic dreams in secular medicine and dreams in the religious practice of incubation, and—unlike Plato,[1] Aristotle,[2] Cicero,[3] and Artemidorus[4]—he has nothing significant to say about how dreams relate to one's moral or social standing.

Like Aristotle in the three treatises on sleep and dreams *in Parva Naturalia* and Plato in *Timaeus*, Lucretius' focus is on how dreams come about, not on what dreams mean. Following the Epicurean tradition, his treatment of dreams indicates that they are wholly void of prophetic significance and of little if any practical significance. Dreams, he says, do no more than mirror our daily preoccupations. For Lucretius, all dreams pass through the gate of ivory and all must be understood psychogenetically.

Of the poet himself, little is known, other than that he lived in the early part of the first century B. C. Nonetheless, speculation on Lucretius abounds, from the notion, popularized by Tennyson, that his death came by being driven mad after taking a philter to the baseless view that he was mad while composing the work, though lucid enough at certain times to see it through to its present state. It is profitless to pursue such matters with the paucity of reliable evidence that bears on them. Let me then turn my attention to the poem itself and his account of dreams within.

Structure of *de Rerum Natura*

De Rerum Natura aims primarily to relate the principles of Epicurean atomism to its audience in poetic form. Lucretius writes as a missionary whose primary aim is to free people's minds from the anxieties[5] caused by religion (especially divine retribution and intervention), the fear of death, and the false notion that there are no limits to our desires. Such anxieties cloud our souls and creep into our dreams, so that, while asleep, we even seem to see those who are dead (I.127-135). The remedy is a thorough dose of the principles of Epicurean physics and epistemology.

The poem itself is quite long and there seems to be general agreement on the overall plan, though great disagreement concerning substructure. Written in six books, it is readily broken down into three parts. The first and second books give the physical foundations of atomism. Books three and four deal with the two divisions of the corporeal soul—*anima*, which is responsible for sensation, and *animus*, which is the seat of emotion and thinking—and Lucretius discusses dreams from IV.722 to IV.1036. The final two books examine the world (*mundus*), comprising the heavens and the earth. To gain a better understanding of Lucretius' account of dreams, we must probe a little further into his physical universe.

Following Epicurus and Parmenides, Lucretius argues that things that come into being cannot do so from nothing (I.146-214) and things that perish are unable to pass away into nothing (I.215-264). At I.265-328, he sets out to prove that there must be invisible bodies of matter from which visible bodies come to be and into which they pass away (I.265-328). In addition, arguing that motion would be impossible without emptiness, he posits infinite void (*inane*) in and around things[6] (I.329-417, 951-1007). Bodies, he avers, are known to all of us through our *communis sensus*, but atoms cannot be perceived by the senses, but are known to exist by the rational faculty of the *animus*[7] (I.418-425). These invisible bodies—being solid, indivisible, and indestructible atoms (*corpora*[8]) (I.483-634)—are infinite in number (I.1008-1051) and have an extraordinarily large variety of shapes[9] (*figurae*) (II.333-380, 478-521). They move by their own weight downward (II.184-215) at equal velocity through the void[10] (II.142-164, 225-242). When they spontaneously slip slightly from their downward course and collide with other such bodies, they form more complex, perceptible bodies (II.216-293). Moreover, through the movement of the atoms, every body which comprises them is itself moved (II.80-141). Ultimately all change and all perceptible bodies are explicable through the clashing, movements, arrangement, position, and shapes of imperceptible bodies falling and swerving in the void (II.865-930 & 991-1022).

Formation of Dreams

As I mention earlier, Lucretius' treatment of dreams in Book IV is primarily an excursion into the formation of dreams by examining the processes believed to underlie them. Consistent with Epicurus' thinking on the subject,[11] dreams have no divine character and are not at all prophetic for Lucretius; they originate from the influx of certain "images", whose nature is discussed in depth from IV.26-215.

Perceptible bodies, as concretions of atoms, because of vibrations deep within them, continually discharge extremely fine atoms (*corpora*) from their surfaces in every direction. These atoms, having a certain coaffection with each other, convey likenesses (*effigias*) or tenuous figures of their objects (*simulacra*)[12] to percipient beings (IV.42-65). These *simulacra* travel with extraordinary rapidity—as fast as water reflects the images of stars on a clear night (IV.176-229)[13] So many *simulacra* stream off objects at all times, carrying with them all the air between themselves and the percipient body, that we do not see each individual *simulacrum*, but rather we seem to see the actual things responsible for them. In all, Lucretius notes that the situation is analogous to being struck by a cool wind: We do not feel each particle of wind as cool, but the total effect gives such an impression (IV.239-264).

For Lucretius, a *simulacrum* is generated in three ways: by being withdrawn from its object and transmitting a likeness of that object, by being withdrawn from an object and combining with one or more other *simulacra* to create a new *simulacrum*, and by spontaneous production in the air[14] (IV.129-142, 732-743). The first way accounts for the *simulacra* of vision and, therefore, corresponds to the *anima*; the latter two are the fantastic *simulacra* of dreams and correspond to the *animus*.[15]

Concerning the difference between these *simulacra* of dreams and visual ones, he writes: "To be sure, these *simulacra* [of dreams] are much thinner in texture than those that fill the eyes and induce vision". So thin are they that they enter the body through the pores[16] during sleep (IV.728-731), yet they have such an impact that one alone can stir the *animus* by a single blow (*ictu una*)[17] (IV.745-748).

During wakefulness, human flesh is bombarded continually by repeated pounding (*crebro ictu*) of air from outside (IV.934), while from within inhaled air takes a toll on the body (IV.937-938).

Ultimately, these beats (*plagae*) (IV.940) effect a breaking down of the *anima*[18] (IV.932-961). The senses and remembering become inoperable (IV.762-765), though the intellect of the *animus* remains awake (*mens animi*) (IV.758). The force of the *anima* is dispersed throughout the limbs.[19] Part of the *anima*, being cast out, disappears and part withdraws and is thrust into the depths of the body[20] (IV.916-918). "Therefore, when the motions are changed, sensation retires deep within" (IV.949). With nothing to support the limbs, the body languishes as the eyelids and arms droop.[21] Sleep follows and the *simulacra* that enter through the pores are perceived as a dream (IV.950-953).

The process that brings about sleep is a step towards death.[22] Throughout the normal course of a day, *anima* is affected like it is when one is wounded (III.168-176), one has epilepsy (III.487-509), or one is paralyzed (III.526-547). The body is so beaten throughout the day that the orderings of the principles of the body and *animus* are disturbed: Atoms of the *anima* disperse and withdraw within the body, and also are expelled outward.[23] Lucretius reminds us at IV.923-924, however, that should the whole *anima* be expelled, death would fall upon us. In all, *anima* and sensation, when one sleeps, behave like fire that is hidden beneath much ash; when awakened, *anima* is like the moribund fire rekindled to strength (IV.925-928).

Dreams and the Function of Sleep

Clearly, sleep for Lucretius is a retreat from the diurnal beating that the body takes. Yet more than this, sleep comes about to enable the body to recover (somehow) from this beating. In sleep, the senses retire and memory fades as some atoms of *anima* disperse, some withdraw, while others are expelled. The overall effect, in some unspecified manner, must be restorative.[24] However, in sleep, we still breathe and still are lambasted by air and *simulacra* through our pores, though probably to a lesser extent. Just how sleep is restorative while this still is going on is something Lucretius does not address, though the answer, if one exists, must lie in the concentration, dispersion, and expulsion of atoms of *anima* during sleep.

The real difficulty in this account is how *anima* revives itself or is revived to resume proper sensory functioning. There is, of course, the problem of how the part that has retreated and condensed can return and spread itself throughout the body and as well as that of how the part that has dispersed can readjust to allow sensation to continue. For it is possible to imagine that those atoms of *anima* that have dispersed or retired within will resume their former status when the body has recovered, perhaps through the behest of *mens animi*. The stickiest problem is with the part that has completely left the body. For it is not easy to see how just those atoms that have left the body will enter back.

Lucretius discusses the nature of *anima* and its relation to *animus* from III.94 to III.416 and this is the place to search for a possible solution. We learn at III.136-144 that *anima* and *animus* are in close union and together make a single entity, even though *animus* abides in the region of the breast and *anima* is dispersed through the whole body. At III.161-176, he explains that both *animus* and *anima* are corporeal, since both are seen to interact with body—for instance, when rousing the body from sleep. Yet since both are so easily stirred, they must be composed of extraordinarily small, slight, and round atoms or seeds (*semina*) (III.186-188, 199-200, 203-205). These seed are so slight that, when death overcomes someone and *animus* and *anima* have parted, no difference in appearance or in weight is perceivable in the corpse (III.208-215). III.128 tells us that *anima* is composed of heat and a vital wind. However there is no heat without air, so *anima* must comprise air too (III.231-236). Still, heat, vital wind, and air are not enough to enable sensation to occur. There must be, Lucretius argues, something even finer, an unnamed fourth ingredient,[25] "which first distributes sense-producing movements throughout the limbs" (III.237-245). This unnamed ingredient, as *anima animae*, lies hidden deep within (III.273-275). Being set in motion, it moves heat, then the "blind power of wind", and finally air. As a consequence, in feeling pain or pleasure, first the blood is agitated, then flesh stirs, and, last, bone and marrow are moved (III.246-251).

Lucretius next relates that all four types of these atoms act as if together they are one body (III.265). Later, we learn that if the nature of *anima* is torn asunder or if the *anima* is somehow severed from *animus*, the dissolution of the entire body ensues (III.323-336). With this description of the intimate interrelationship between *animus* and *anima*, one sees plainly how sleep is a condition akin to death.

Given the nature of *anima* and *animus* and the intimate way in which the four types of atoms of *anima* intermingle, what happens during sleep when part of the *anima* becomes concentrated and recesses, part of it disperses, and part leaves the body? Is there somehow a segregation of the four types of atoms in the body or is it merely a matter of a deviation from the normal, functional distribution or arrangement of the four types of atoms of *anima*? Since sensory dysfunction or incapacitation occurs at sleep and either of these two accounts would result in this, both are plausible. Yet on either account, how do the atoms of *anima* get back to their normal distribution and arrangement in the body to allow for wakefulness and sensation? Is it *animus*, considered as a part of *anima*, that is responsible for somehow recalling and reordering the atoms of *anima* through motions of its own? If not, then do the atoms of *anima* themselves have some capacity to return and regroup themselves?

In addition, what of the atoms that have left the body during sleep? Where do these reside during sleep and how do they return? Schrijvers thinks that Lucretius may have believed that these are retrieved during respiration. He cites the use of the words *reconflari* ("to be rekindled", when comparing *anima* at sleep to a moribund fire) at IV.927 and *reflatur* ("it is blown out", with reference to the air of our breaths) at IV.938, and adds that respiration for Lucretius is the nutrition of *anima.*[26] Yet do we retrieve precisely those atoms that have left the body during sleep or merely atoms of a similar kind? If the former is the case, then the atoms that have left us during sleep must somehow remain nearby until they can mysteriously reenter or be recalled at waking. What is worse, this presupposes a perfectly efficient "mechanism" for such a recall. A more plausible alternative is that we recall atoms of a similar kind, readily available from the air we breathe, through respiration. If so, then the real problem does not concern those atoms that have left the body, but instead those that have dispersed and concentrated within the body during sleep. How are these atoms of *anima* reordered for normal human, wakeful functioning? The difficulty with either account is that *respiration is a cause of both sleeping and waking.* Respiration functions then both in a degenerative and a restorative manner, and it seems unlikely that this is what Lucretius had in mind.

We get some way toward a solution to the problems at hand at III.396-416. Lucretius states here that *animus* is more responsible for clinging to life than *anima* (III.396-397). *Animus*, in fact, continually keeps *anima* from passing outside of the body (III.398-401). As when limbs are severed, when part of *anima* is harmed, destroyed, or removed, people continue to live as long as *animus* remains unharmed (III.402-407). The relationship of *animus* to *anima* is similar to that of pupil to eye. Injure the eye and, so long as the pupil remains unharmed, there is still sight; injure the pupil and sight is immediately gone (III.408-416). Now given that *anima* is nonfunctional in sleep (IV.916-961) and that *mens animi* remains vigilant during sleep (IV.758), it seems reasonable to conclude that *animus*, concentrated in the breast, is what recalls and reorganizes atoms of *anima*. Just how it does this, however, remains a mystery.

Coherence of and Movement in Dreams

There is a third problem directly related to the formation of dreams. Given the tenuity of *simulacra* and the two different, fantastic ways in which images of dreams are formed, one clearly apprehends why dreams are confused and disordered. Yet it is difficult to discern why any dreams, especially lengthy ones, should have a consistent story-line, a logically progressive sequence of events, or anything at all sensible and nongrotesque about them, which many dreams certainly do have. Concerning this difficulty, McCurdy writes:

> It is perfectly in keeping with Lucretius' theory that absurdities such as centaurs should crop up in the process; by chance-collisions various atomic patterns may fuse together into one strange form even before they appear to the dreamer. It is a much more serious problem how it happens that the dream-image so often conforms to the character of the dreamer and takes its place in a logical, or at least dramatically coherent, sequence.[27]

The problem is magnified by the types of *simulacra* that make up dreams. Recall at IV.129-142 and 732-743 that these *simulacra*, being formed either spontaneously in the air or by combinations of *simulacra*, differ from those of vision, which are generated by a continual stream of *simulacra* from objects.[28]

Lucretius notices this problem and even attempts a solution. From IV.779 to IV.817,[29] he looks at how images in dreams are brought to *animus* (IV.779-787, 802-817) and how movement in dreams occurs (IV.788-801). Concerning the first, he considers whether, at the bidding of the will, the desired *simulacra* immediately come to the sleeper from wherever they may chance to be. He writes:

> And in these matters, many things are asked and many things must be cleared up by us, if we seek to explain things intelligibly. First, it is asked how, when a whim has come to us, *animus* immediately thinks of that very thing. Or do the *simulacra* keep a watch on our will and does the image occur to us as soon as we want—whether we wish for the sea, the earth, finally the sky? Gatherings of men, a procession, feasts, wars; does nature create and prepare all of these at our bidding, especially when the *animus* of others in the same region and place thinks about things quite different?[30] (IV.779-787).

Leaving this matter temporarily unresolved, he moves to consider another, related matter: the apparent movement of figures in dreams. Why, he asks, do we see the images of *simulacra* move about with coherence and fluidity? He says (sardonically) that they, being trained to be able to perform their games at nighttime, overflow with art and wander about (IV.788-793).

His answer to this second problem immediately follows. Just as reason can distinguish many smaller moments of time at any one moment of time, at each moment, great numbers of multifarious and swiftly moving *simulacra* are present and at hand. When one perishes, another takes its place in a different posture and the prior *simulacrum* seems to have moved[31] (IV.794-801).

At IV.802-817, we get our solution to the problem, raised at IV.779-787, of how *animus* procures the images of dreams. Because of their thinness, *animus* can only see those *simulacra* that it strains (*contendit*) (IV.802) or has prepared itself (IV.804) to see; all others perish. In addition, *animus* expects to see what would naturally follow each perceptual image in waking life (IV.806). Just as we cannot see fine things unless we strain ourselves to see them (IV.807-810) or we do not notice plain things unless we turn our attention to them (IV.811-813), we do not see the images of dreams unless we sharply attend to them (IV.814-815). Finally, he says puzzlingly that we draw the greatest consequences from small signs in sleep and involve ourselves in deceit (IV.816-817). Similar to what Aristotle says in his treatise *On Dreams*, lines IV.816-817 suggest for Lucretius that dreams are constructions of dreamers.

The process of dreaming, then, looks something like this for Lucretius. Many images are present in *animus* at any one time. During sleep, *animus* attends to one of them to the neglect of the others. When this one flits away, from the numerous images at our disposal in our psychic reservoir, *animus* attends to another that bears some likeness to what we would expect to follow the first in waking reality. For instance, if the first image is one of preparing for a kill while on a hunt for boars, the second selected by or presented to *animus* might be an image of a kill. When no such similar images are readily available, an image of a different kind rises before us and there is a radical shift in oneiric content: What was once a woman becomes a man; one face or age is now another[32] (IV.818-822).

Let me now say more concerning lines IV.816-817. These intimate that there is more to dreaming than merely seeing a succession of images flit about during sleep. The Latin reads: *deinde adopinamur de signis maxima parvis ac nos in fraudem induimus frustraminis ipsi.*[33] *Adopinari* is the Latin equivalent to προσδοχάζεσθαι, which has the sense of importing into judgment an element beyond sensation,[34] while its prefix, *ad-*, marks a tendency to accomplish the action indicated by the verb, in the sense of something being brought before imagination.[35]

IV.816-817 tells us that dreaming for Lucretius cannot be reduced to a succession of images culled or presented before *animus* in accordance with waking-life expectation (IV.806). *Adopinari* at IV.816 tells us quite clearly that opinion or judgment of some sort must be involved in the oneeiric process. Dreams, then, are *constructed*, since we sometimes end up deceived: We judge that we see something different from the actual raw data of the dream (IV.817).

Selection Model of Dreams

Just how are dreams constructed for Lucretius? I outline briefly a plausible model, the "selection" model, whose constraints are the following:

> S_1: Since the senses, memory, and *anima* in general are inoperable in sleep (IV.762-765 & 916-961) and *mens animi* remains wakeful (IV.758), it is *mens animi* that is crucially involved in the formation of dreams.
>
> S_2: *Animus* must prepare itself and strain to see the fine, plain images responsible for dreams. As it focusses on one, all others perish (IV.807-813). (The intensity of focus is probably related to ability to remember upon waking.)
>
> S_3: Having selected or received the first image, *animus* quickly culls or receives the next from what is readily available in the reservoir of images pursuant to waking-life expectations (IV.806). If a reasonable successor is unavailable, it culls or receives the best possible successor from the readily available stock (IV.818-822).
>
> S_4: Opinion or judgment of some sort adds to the process and thereby makes each dream a construction (IV.816-817).

First, there is a rough theme or idea that begins the whole oneiric process. This may be something one was mulling over prior to sleep, some sensory remnant, or any such thing that remains in *animus* just prior to the dream.[36] Thereafter, *mens animi* selects an image similar to what one would expect to follow in waking life, then selects successive images in a similar fashion from those in the reservoir of available images. After the first image is culled, another which reasonably follows the first is chosen, then another, and so on. Here the initiating theme or idea is *not* something that remains in *animus* and guides the selection process throughout, as the meaning or theme of each dream. It merely begins the selection of images. *Animus*, guided only by the image prior to the one presently preoccupying it, makes sure that at each stage an adequate image is culled so that the dream occurs roughly in a logically progressive manner. Since the initiating theme does not guide but only initiates the succession of images, the final image, on such a model, would probably be at variance with the initiating theme in most dreams. As such, there is nothing teleological about this model.[37]

Opinion likely comes into play in the following way: *Mens animi* passes judgment on the successive oneiric images immediately after they play themselves out during sleep.[38] In this sense, we build false opinions and deceive ourselves simply because we extrapolate beyond the raw succession of images seen in sleep. A dream on this model is not just a succession of images; it is a succession of images plus the judgment of opinion immediately upon waking.

Overall, the selection model seems to me to make the best sense of the constraints on the formation of dreams that Lucretius elaborates and I have enumerated above.[39] Let me now turn from the formation of dreams toward oneiric content.

Lucretius on Oneiric Content

Unlike Aristotle, Lucretius did not ignore oneiric content while looking at the processes underlying dreams. He gives evidence of being an astute observer of oneiric content. Consistent with his construction hypothesis, Lucretius notes that we dream about our deeds and thoughts of the day. Barristers dream of law, generals dream of fighting battles, and sailors dream of waging war with the wind (IV.962-969).

Furthermore, animals too dream of what has preoccupied them during the day. Stout horses sweat and seem to exert themselves in sleep. Pack dogs whine and draw up their noses and paws as if they are on the hunt for beasts. Birds also suddenly flee, awakened from sleep, as if pursued by birds of prey (IV.991-1010).

Great mean perform great deeds in sleep. Kings fight and are taken in battle. Others cry out as if being gnawed by the bite of a lion or panther (IV.1011-19). Many meet with death in their dreams. Some see themselves tumbling or falling from a steep precipice (IV.1020-1023). A thirsty dreamer gulps down nearly an entire stream of water (IV.1024-1025). Clean people imagine that they lift their garments to urinate, only to find, on waking, that their Babylonian coverlets are soaked (IV.1026-1029). Pubescent youths defile their raiment with semen because they see beautiful females in sleep (IV.1030-1036). Overall, these examples tend to get baser and, thus, they may be a humorous poke at the Stoics and their notion of divinely portentous dreams.[40] Nevertheless, they attest to an acuteness of observation and suggest that Lucretius must have been greatly fascinated by the psychological subtleties of oneiric expression.

All of these examples are entirely in keeping with the continuity hypothesis in today's psychological literature on dreams. Tersely expressed, it states that dreams, like mirrors, reflect our waking personality.[41] Many others, such as a thirsty person's dream of gulping down nearly an entire stream, smack of the wish-fulfillment thesis made famous by Freud in his 1900 monograph *The Interpretation of Dreams*.[42] However, in contrast to most modern-day psychological accounts of dreams, Lucretius gives no indication that dreams are of any great significance or utility, psychologically or otherwise, for humans or other animals that dream. They reveal no internal secrets and disclose no hidden truths.[43] This, I believe, makes Lucretius' account of dreams quite unique in Greco-Roman antiquity.

Dreams in *de Rerum Natura*

In this section, I propose to address briefly how Lucretius' account of dreaming in Book IV figures into the overall plan of *de Rerum Natura.*

This is difficult, given the complex nature of Book IV, especially lines 858-end. After discussing *simulacra* (IV.26-215), sensation (IV.216-721), and mental perception (IV.722-821) and giving vent to antiteleological sentiments at IV.823-857, Lucretius tackles nutrition (IV.858-876), locomotion (IV.877-906), sleep (IV.907-961), dreams (IV.962-1036), and sexual desire (IV.1037-1287). Precisely how do dreams fit in with these other four topics and Lucretius' aim of freeing people from the anxieties associated with religion, their false views of desires, and the fear of death?

First, all of the issues from IV.858-1287 are vital, in the literal sense of the word, in that they concern important bodily functions that critically involve the soul. Here Lucretius is likely objecting to teleological or functional explanations by philosophers, natural scientists, and religious zealots prior to and during his time. What Lucretius professes to show is that even the most important human functions can be fully explicated by the nonteleological principles of Epicurean physics and a perfect understanding of these physical principles is a panacea for the ills caused by the fear of death and the beguiling tenets of religion. Dreams, being neither god-sent nor prophetic, have nothing teleological about them for Lucretius; they are explainable completely by the influx of *simulacra* and certain simple mechanisms.

References to dreams elsewhere in the poem indicate that dreams are themselves enormously responsible for much of our religious fervor and folly as well as our belief in an afterlife. First, at I.127-135, Lucretius explains how seeming to see those who have died in dreams contributes to the belief that such people have not really died, but rather have moved on to another lif. Another very relevant piece of text is V.1161-1203. Here Lucretius gives an explanation of how dreams have contributed to religious excitement and false views of the gods.

The significance of this text to dreams cannot be understated, and so I examine it closely below.

Lucretius says that it is not difficult to put into words why altars fill the cities, new shrines are constantly being built, religious rituals are performed, and people throng to religious festivals. His explanation takes us to two accounts of the activities of the gods.

First, the races of men, he explains, used to see large, powerful, and beautiful figures both in wakefulness and especially in sleep. Observing that they seemed to move and speak in proportion to their appearance and that there was some consistency in their appearance, the ancients attributed sensation, the ability to perform miraculous deeds without fatigue, and even everlasting life to them. And because these figures seemed to perform dangerous and impossible tasks without fear of dying, men deemed them happy. Thus, the ancient picture of the gods, beings uninvolved in the affairs of men, was generated. In such a manner, men truly learned of the gods through dreams.[44]

Yet this true picture of the gods was soon distorted. Since men could not apprehend the causes of celestial and atmospheric phenomena, they claimed that these must be the doings of the gods. Soon the gods were incorrectly perceived to interfere in the affairs of mortals. Lucretius laments: "O unhappy human beings, you attributed such actions to the gods and assigned bitter wrath to them!" It is not piety, he adds, to cover one's head, turn toward stones, approach altars, prostrate oneself upon the ground, sprinkle altars with sacrificial blood, and link vow to vow; rather piety consists in being able to regard all things with a mind at peace. In a word, Lucretius tells us at V.1161-1203 that an incorrect perception of dreams themselves was greatly responsible for much of the anxiety in his time.

Since dreams were in large part responsible for much of the rampant irrationalism and unhappiness of his day, it follows that Lucretius' account of dreams at IV.962-1036 is part of the overall Epicurean, ataractic cure. Once again, a grasp of Epicurean physics is an appropriate rationalistic therapy for those who live both in blind observance of senseless religious rituals and under the sway of emotions. Correct understanding of how things really work leads to peace of mind and the utmost pleasure one can hope to attain.

Concluding Remarks

In conclusion, consistent with the principles of Epicurean atomism, Lucretius states that all dreams have the same origin and same account. For him, there is only one kind of dream, the false or insignificant dream, and its explanation is entirely naturalistic and void of prophetic (or any kind of) significance.

Still, Lucretius' account of dreams in Book IV plays and important role in the work as a whole. Since dreams themselves have been instrumental in generating the view of an afterlife and fostering false views about the gods, a proper naturalistic understanding of them can only conduce towards peace of mind.

---

[1] *R.* IX 571d-572b & *Ti.* 71e-72b.
[2] *Pr.* XXX.14 (957a22-33).
[3] *Div.* I.60 & 121.
[4] *Oneiroc.* IV.proem.
[5] The Epicurean notion of ἀταραξία.
[6] At I.969-983, he asks his readers to proceed to the most remote region of space and cast outward a *volatile telum.* The shaft, he says, will either pass beyond the imagined boundary into empty space or fix itself into something beyond the "boundary". In either event, what was perceived to be a limit proves to be no limit.
[7] The argument here is that the *communis sensus* affirms the existence of perceptible bodies. We reason from perceptible phenomena to the existence of certain imperceptible, primary existents and their attributes and behavior. As with the Stoics, all inferences begin with the assumed validity of sensory experience and end with an appeal to it.
[8] Since Lucretius uses *corpora* sometimes to mean both the simplest, irreducible bodies and other times to mean perceptible bodies (e.g., I. 483), I shall translate instances of the former as "atoms" or "imperceptible bodies" and instances of the latter as "bodies" or "perceptible bodies" throughout.
[9] The number of tokens of each shape being infinite (II.522-568).
[10] Lucretius believes that heavier bodies fall more quickly only when falling through some medium, since it is only by virtue of the resistance of the medium that differently weighted bodies fall at different rates. Since the void offers no resistance, the rate of fall is the same for all bodies (II.225-242).
[11] *Sent.Vat.* #24.
[12] The Latin equivalent for Epicurus' term εἴδωλα.
[13] Asmis believes that the speed of eidolic movement from an object to a percipient subject for Lucretius and Epicurus varies inversely to the number of collisions of its constituent atoms (1984, 110-111). This is a sensible suggestion, but it lacks textual support.
[14] Consequently, the various false images of dreams, like Centaurs and Cerberus-like faces, occur (IV.722-735). Book IV.129-142 tells us that those formed spontaneously in the air constantly change their appearance in the manner of clouds. Cf. Aristotle's *Insomn.* 461b18-25 where he too likens oneiric images to clouds.
[15] These correspond to Epicurus' σύστασις, though his account is certainly less clear. Epicurus acknowledges one type of σύστασις as a confusion of images, then mentions that there are other ways by which εἴδωλα can be fashioned. This is perhaps a reference to their spontaneous formation.
[16] Here Lucretius strays from Epicurus (*Ep.Her.* §49-52), who posits that the εἴδωλα that stir the *animus*, like those of a dream, do not enter through the

pores.

[17] This is not to say that one *simulacrum* alone can effect an oneiric image.

[18] The words *plaga* and *ictus* suggest that the overall effect is very violent. Both mean "blow" and "stroke" as well as "wound", "cut", and "stab", while *plaga* has a general sense of "injury" or "disaster". Lucretius gives us an account of *ictus* at II.944-962. A blow greater than the body can withstand ultimately breaks up the vital motions of *anima* and scatters it out through the pores. Death follows. When the blow is not lethal, the vital motions prevail, stilling the prodigious disorders and rekindling sensation.

[19] Epicurus says that it is by virtue of its being enclosed within the body that *anima* has sensation, for the body has given *anima* this capacity and thereby acquires some ability to sense itself (*Ep.Her.* §64).

[20] IV.944-949 & 959-961 make it clear that *anima* is affected in three ways, not two. The former states that part of *anima* is cast out (*pars...eiciatur*), part withdraws and retires (*pars abdita cedat*), and part is dispersed throughout the limbs and is not able either to be united in itself or suffer reciprocal motion (*pars...distracta per artus non queat esse coniuncta inter se neque motu mutua fungi*). The latter says, "For the same reason, the recession of *anima* becomes deeper, and, being cast outside, it is more ample (*foras eiectus largior eius*), and, inside, it is more divided and separated within itself". It helps to understand that *anima* is by nature not localized (like the *animus* in the breast [III.136-140, 548-550]), but distributed throughout the whole of the body (III.143-144). So, when Lucretius tells us that *anima* is so dispersed that it is unable to partake of its sensual duties, we must understand a thorough and dysfunctional dispersion. Again, with some part of *anima* retiring deep within, perhaps the sensitive part, there follows an unusual, dysfunctional concentration of its constituent atoms, probably toward the center of the body. Ernout (1916_1, 38 fn.1) states incorrectly that Lucretius' account here is "exactement l'enseignement de son maître" at *Ep.Her.* §66. Here Epicurus tells us that *anima* has both rational and irrational parts—the former, dispersed throughout the body; the latter, concentrated in the region of the chest. In sleep, the smooth and round atoms of the irrational part of *anima* are confined or dispersed (ἐγκατεχομένων ἢ διαθοπουμένων) and afterward collide through impacts (εἶτα συμπιπτόντων τοῖς ἐπερεισμοῖς). Epicurus says nothing about any atoms being cast outside of the body.

[21] The taking in of food effects the body similarly, though to a greater extent (IV.954-958). Aristotle, in *Somn.Vig.*, makes even more of the link between eating and sleeping. At one point, he says of sleep: "[T]his affection [sleep] occurs from the vaporous uprising due to food" (456b17-19). Yet sleep for Aristotle is a natural recession of hot matter toward the center of the body that occurs most often, not exclusively after eating (457b1-3). Other conditions that have the effect of digestion also conduce toward sleep, such as fatigue, youth, epilepsy, dwarfishness, and bigheadedness (456b34-457a26).

[22] Conversely, at III.919-930, Lucretius likens death to an everlasting sleep. Cf. Philo's *Insomn.* I.xxiii.151 and Augustine's *Ep.* #159.

[23] As strange as it may seem, Lucretius' statement of the diurnal beating

that one's body takes has a parallel today. Research on free radicals, molecules with an unpaired electron in their outer orbital within the body, suggests that even the very act of breathing may cause deterioration of membrane lipids and alterations in enzyme activity that can lead to and exacerbate various disease processes (Kanter 1994, 205-215).

[24] Aristotle, too, believed that sleep is restorative. Sleep rests the primary sense organ, the organ of sensation, and thereby conserves it (*Somn.Vig.* 458a26-33). See also Augustine (*Imm.An.* §14), Clement (*Misc.* IV.22 & V.9), and Gregory of Nyssa (*Creat.Hom.* XIII.2)

[25] Epicurus believed ψυχή was composed of θερμός, πνεῦμα, and some third finer, nameless ingredient. He does not mention any airy component (*Ep.Her.* §63).

[26] Schrijvers 1976, 247.

[27] McCurdy 1946, 227.

[28] Asmis (1984, 137), citing IV.129-142 and 739-743, argues that we could easily imagine, if we sometimes allow images of dreams to be the result of streams, that two streams merge in midair and then continuously flow to the sleeper to form a compound image of, say, a centaur. Yet she does not address how such an account deals with such images *sustained* over any amount of time. Such intermingling of streams would have to be very precise over some period of time for any sustained image of a centaur to appear. Aristotle's account of oneiric images as residual sensations in *Insomn.* avoids this problem.

[29] I follow Bailey who, it seems to me, has cleared up much of the confusion concerning this section of text. For instance, following Lachmann in noting that the section beginning at IV.818 seems to be connected with the passage ending at IV.776, Munro writes that the passage in between, IV.794-817, is obviously a subsequent addition to surmount difficulties concerning the immediate mental apprehension of whatever *animus* desires. He states, "The poet is evidently embarrassed by the prodigious difficulties which this theory of mental apprehension involves and struggles hard to solve them: not content with the preceding paragraph, he has tried to better this argument in this one" (1886 vol. ii, 262). The tendency, here, is to regard IV.794-817 as supplemental to or in competition with the hypothesis of IV.779-793. McCurdy (1946, 227), for instance, sees them as competitive hypotheses. Bailey's understanding of the text does not require that IV.794-817 is a subsequent addition. He believes that Lucretius is looking at *two different problems* from IV.779-817: mental apprehension of images in dreams and the apparent movement of these images. The former is entertained from IV.779-787; the latter, from IV.788-793. IV.794-817, then, offers solutions to both of these problems (1947, 1273-1275). Asmis (1981) offers a fine summary of attempts to deal with this text. She also offers an alternative reading that involves transposing lines IV.768-776 between IV.815 & 816. Bailey's reading, however, seems the most economical.

[30] Cf. Cicero, *ND* I.108, where Academic Cotta discusses the likelihood of the Epicurean account of procession of images in waking and sleep to his interlocutor, Vellius the Epicurean.

[31] This is similar to Aristotle's analogy of artificial frogs that successively

pop up in a pond when the salt that weighs them down is sufficiently dissolved (*Insomn.* 461b11-17).

[32] Asmis argues that in all such cases of radical shift, the "mind *does not* (my emphasis) make an effort to sustain the image of a single individual" (1984, 122). Lucretius' examples here do not bear this out. Were there a complete dearth of effort to sustain a single individual, the succession of images would be wholly arbitrary. The types of shifts here suggest a *slight* lapse of attention or, better yet, the unavailability of prior images and the culling of what is most similar to them from what is readily available.

[33] IV.816-817 is reminiscent of IV.379-468, where Lucretius deals with false judgments the mind makes from sensory data, exculpating the senses and the sensory images from any "wrongdoing". In all such cases, as with dreams (IV.453-461), the falsity lies not in the images before *animus*, but in the opinions of the mind (*opinatus animi*) (IV.462-466).

[34] Bailey 1947, 1278.

[35] Ernout 1916_2, 112.

[36] This makes best sense of the examples of dreams Lucretius gives from IV.962-1036, being in keeping with our daily preoccupations. Asmis believes that the "effort or preparation of the mind" in sleep, following our diurnal preoccupations, "is not necessarily a deliberate act" (1984, 123).

[37] IV.806 and Lucretius' general aversion toward teleology of any sort (e.g.: IV.823-857, V.146-169, & 419-421) makes it implausible that the initiating theme or *mens animi* guides selection throughout.

[38] Similar to Freud's notion of secondary revision.

[39] Havelock Ellis has a contemporary account of dreaming that is similar in many respects. Concerning the generation of oneiric images, he writes: "There is, then, at the basis of dreaming a seemingly spontaneous procession of dream imagery which is always undergoing transformation into something different, yet not wholly different, from that which went before. It seems a mechanical flow of images, regulated by associations of resemblance, which sleeping consciousness recognizes without either controlling or introducing foreign elements" (1922, 27).

[40] See Bailey 1947 (1295-1296) and Furley 1966 & 1977 (3-4).

[41] As opposed to the compensatory hypothesis, made famous by Jung, which states that dreams, functioning to compensate for defects of our waking-life personality, are in some sense opposite to our waking personalities. See Van de Castle 1994, 250-253.

[42] That dreams are generated by an unconscious wish and that oneiric content is just the (mostly disguised) fulfillment of that wish (Freud 1993, 119).

[43] In other words, the wish-fulfillment nature of some dreams is mere coincidence.

[44] Cf. Sextus' *M.* IX.25 and Cicero's *ND* I.46.

Part II
Oneirocriticism

Introduction

Through evidence of the existence of interpreters of dreams, such as Antiphon the Athenian in the fifth century B. C. and Aristander of Telmessus in the fourth century B. C., and various references to interpreters of dreams in the literary and historiographic traditions, we know that interpreters[1] of enigmatic kinds of prophetic dreams thrived at various levels of Greek society no later than the fifth century B. C. These early interpreters, later called "oneirocritics", offered guidance and apotropaic[2] advice for kings and common-folk alike and were generally regarded as craftsmen who were every bit as skilled in their art as, say, a smith or a physician was in his. Just as physicians observed and cataloged the onset and progression of diseases and astronomers observed and catalogued the position of the sun, moon, and planets over time, so too did interpreters of dreams listen to and catalog the various reports of dreams and their outcomes.

Though not everyone in ancient Greco-Roman times believed in prophecy through dreams, it probably took little to satisfy those who did. Clever oneirocritics, like today's palm-readers and psychic advisors, could survive and even flourish in their art by interpreting dreams in a highly ambiguous manner[3] or by merely sometimes hitting the mark.[4]

In this section, I analyze prophecy through dreams as science. First, in chapter five, I look at the debate over oneiromancy (prophecy through dreams) as sketched in Cicero's Academically styled treatise—*de Divinatione.* I undertake a philosophical critique of both the methods outlined in Book I for a science of oneiromancy (and prophecy in general) and the arguments against such a science in Book II. The sixth chapter examines the only existing complete book on oneirocriticism from Greco-Roman antiquity: Artemidorus' *Onirocritica.* In this chapter, I give a sketch of the *Onirocritica*, describe Artemidorus' methods of interpretation, and outline the empirical program behind his methods. Afterward, I evaluate Artemidorus' work both from his own objectives, stated in the proem of Book I (and reiterated elsewhere concerning the scientific validity of oneirocriticism), and from the practice of secular medicine prior to and during Artemidorus' time. In the final chapter of this part, chapter seven, I look at the best example of a Neoplatonic study of dreams: Synesius' *Dreams.* Here I look for a systematic treatment of dreams in this divinely inspired, loose collection of intriguing insights on dreams.

---

[1] E.g., called θυμομάντεις, ὀνειρομάντεις, and κριταί by Aeschylus (*Pers.* 224 & *Ch.* 33 & 37) and, in the tradition of Homer, οἱ ὀνειροπόλοι by Herodotus (*Hist.* I.107, 108, 128, & V.56). See van Lieshout for a fine compilation of such sources (1980, 165-181).

[2] From ἀποτροπή, which means "an averting of evil".

[3] Like the famous response of the oracle at Delphi to the king of Lydia, Croesus, as told by Herodotus. The latter had asked the oracle whether or not he should go to war against Cyrus of Persia and was told that if he should begin battle against Persia, he would destroy a great empire. He went to war and, subsequently, his army was annihilated by the Persians. Thus the prophecy came true because a great empire, Lydia, was destroyed (*Hist.* I.53). Yet had he defeated Cyrus and the Persians, he would have destroyed a great empire as well.

[4] It is a well-established psychological fact today that people easily forgive false prophets and forget false prophecies if at least once in a while the "seer" makes a true prediction. One has only to consider the many predictions of the "seers" in the tabloids that are sold at any supermarket toward the beginning of a new year. Almost all of these prove to be false at the close of the year, yet this has little affect on both the perceived credibility of the "seers" and the purchasing behavior of those who believe in them.

Chapter Five
Stoic Oneiromancy in Cicero's *de Divinatione*

Introduction

By the first century B. C., we have unambiguous evidence that interpreters of dreams and all forms of prophecy were coming under fire in Greco-Roman culture: Cicero's work *de Divinatione*.

De Divinatione is a lengthy treatise that rigorously debates the legitimacy of ancient methods of prophecy, called "divination", in its many guises.[1] In addition, this treatise is philosophically valuable because it calls into question the empirical methods used by prophets that enabled them to predict certain future events from portents. I restrict my analysis to those sections of the work concerning dreams. Before turning to the work, however, let me say something about Cicero himself.

Cicero was born in 106 B. C. at Arpinium. As a young man, he studied philosophy, literature, poetry, politics, and rhetoric, and began a successful forensic career in 81 B. C. From 79 to 77 B. C., he went to Athens for reasons of health and studied under Antiochus of the Old Academy. He then traveled to Rhodes to study under the Stoic Posidonius. At the same time, he was educated in oratory by a handful of experts, most notably Molo. After a few years of travel, he began a political career back in Rome that involved rapid advancement from quaestor in 75 B. C. to consul in 63 B. C. He was exiled from 58 to 57 B. C., due to his part in the suppression of a conspiracy involving Catiline. Shortly after his return from exile, he withdrew from public life and turned full attention to writing. Cicero was assassinated on December 7, 43 B. C., by condemnation of Mark Antony.

Toward the very end of his life, when Cicero was shut off from the Senate and forum, his works show an unquestionable shift from political matters to philosophy. Astonishingly, the bulk of these philosophical works—*Academics*, *Tusculan Disputations*, *On Divination*, *On Fate*, *On Friendship*, *On Ends*, *On Duties*, and *On the Nature of the Gods*—were composed within just two years, from 45 to 44 B. C. The philosophical strain of his thinking is Greek in that it shows a reverence for development of character through the cultivation of virtue.

Regarding his merits as a philosopher, opinions vary. Cicero himself admits that his philosophical ideas are not his own, but those of the Greeks.[2] In Romanizing Greek philosophy, he oversimplifies it, often to the point of corruption. Nonetheless, he is an important source for thinkers whose views would have otherwise been lost to us.

His philosophical style is a blend of substance and rhetoric: He addresses weighty issues in a rhetorically eloquent manner. For Cicero, both philosophy and oratory are important tools for persuasion. From philosophy, he draws content; from oratory, ornament.

His philosophical style in *de Divinatione* is in the manner of the of skepticism of the New Academy,[3] where all reasonable philosophical pronouncements were examined, both pro and con, in an effort to find the truth. For Academic skeptics, there was not truth to be found. Instead, they settled for suspension of judgment, which then lead to equanimity, not confusion. Regarding how a wise person was to act, Academic skepticism was not paralytic. Instead of "what is certain", which was the Stoic guide for action, Academic skeptics based action on "what is probable". In final analysis, wisdom was the suspension of judgment on all matters admitting of doubt and adopting probability as a guide for action.[4]

Let me now briefly turn to the work as a whole. In Book I, Marcus Cicero's brother Quintus defends the Stoic view of divination,[5] which was prevalent among thinkers during Cicero's days, as the two walk around the Lyceum at Marcus' Tusculan villa. Here Quintus outlines a program designed to rebuke those who would say that there can be no science of the various means of prophecy. Relating this to dreams, covered from I.39 to I.65, this program is an attempt to exonerate prophecy through dreams (oneiromancy) by, among other things, suggesting a method according to which a skilled oneirocritic can distinguish prophetic from nonprophetic dreams. In the second book, while the two are seated in the bibliotheca of the Lyceum, Cicero himself attacks the Stoic view of divination.[6] He covers dreams from II.119 to II.147. Consistent with the Academic format, Book II presents a series of arguments against the Stoic view and demands that, if the various mantic arts are to be considered sciences, like other sciences they must explain through an appeal to causes. In short, the debate in *de Divinatione* is a reflection of the tension between reason (λόγος) and experience (ἐμπειρία) that pervades much of Greco-Roman medicine.

Stoic Account in Book I

Quintus' treatment of dreams in Book I begins with a flood of "trivial" dreams (*minuta somnia*), drawn from a treatise of the Stoic Chrysippus, who collected prophetic dreams from esteemed peoples of all kinds (I.39-57). Then follow a dream of Quintus and one of Cicero (I.58-59).

Next, Quintus responds to often-used objection that many dreams are meaningless. He states:

> Yet, someone might object, many dreams are false. On the contrary, perhaps they are [not false but merely] obscure to us. What then should we say about true dreams? These would happen much more often if we should go to sleep in the proper condition. As things are, burdened with food and wine, we discern perturbed and confused dreams[7] (I.60).

He then goes on to relate what Plato says at *Republic* IX[8] about preparing for sleep in the proper manner to secure the least error in the soul and to improve its capacity to divine.[9] To this, he contrasts the accounts of Epicurus[10] and Carneades,[11] both of whom railed against divination by dreams (I.60-63).

At I.64, he gives the Stoic Posidonius' threefold classification of dreams.[12] Quintus states:

> He maintains that people dream under the influence of the gods in three ways: first, because the soul, which is preserved through a kinship with the gods, foresees by its own accord; second, because the air is fraught with immortal souls on whom, as it were, the clear marks of truth are visible; third, because the gods themselves converse with people who are sleeping[13] (I.64).

Strangely enough, Quintus says nothing more about this classification. Sandwiched in a text that deals with the power of moribund people to prophesy, it seems to be thrown in clumsily and hastily, as if it is an afterthought.

I.71 presents the one-clear-instance argument of Cratippus, a peripatetic friend of Cicero: If there exists even one clear instance of divination that rules out chance, then divination is firmly established. And, the argument runs, there are many such instances. At I.82-83, he presents the Stoic proof that the propositions "The gods exist" and "The gods do not make the future clear [through divination]" are inconsistent. Moreover, though the cause of any form of divination cannot be given, this is no proof that it is ineffectual (I.85-87). In summary, Quintus maintains that the weight of evidence greatly favors divination. His overall strategy, Malcolm Schofield correctly argues, is the rhetorical device of persuasion through "swamping". Swamp readers with a large number of examples and if at least one is too extravagant to be due to chance, then they will be persuaded that divination exists.[14]

Skeptical Reply in Book II

Cicero answers each of these arguments in the course of Book II. From II.9 to II.12, drawing from Carneades, he argues that there is not one field of inquiry where divination is helpful. At II.17-18, he states that anything foreseen must have a cause or distinguishing mark (*nota*) that tells of its coming. Moreover, all such cases of successful prediction, like predictions involving the movements of heavenly bodies, are successful because they follow a course of reasoning that divination, by definition, does not follow.[15] Then, at II.27, he challenges the credibility of the testimonies Quintus has given throughout the first book, while at II.41 he calls into question the Stoic proof of divination given at I.82-83 (i.e., "The gods exist" and "The gods do not make the future clear through divination" are inconsistent).

For purposes of this undertaking, at II.127-128, Cicero advances his most interesting argument, which I give below *in toto*. Here, dealing exclusively with dreams, he contends that the dearth of criteria by which god-originated dreams are distinguishable from soul-originated dreams is ultimately evidence that only the latter exist.[16] He argues:

> (1) Still, in reality, who would dare to say that all dreams are true? (2) "Some dreams are true", says Ennius, "but nothing requires that all are". (3) After all, what is your means of distinguishing them? (4) What do the true have? (5) What do the false have?
>
> (6) And if true dreams are sent-by-god, from where do false ones arise? (7) For if these are also divine, what is more capricious than god? (8) In addition, what is more absurd than to stir up the minds of mortals with false and mendacious dreams (*visa*)? (9) If, however, true dreams are divine while the false and inane are human, what makes you think that god made one and nature made the other, rather than supposing that either god made all, which you deny, or nature made all? (10) But since you deny the former, the latter must be admitted....
>
> (11) Now, if some are false and others are true, I truly would like to know by what kind of mark they can be distinguished (*nota internoscantur*). (12) If there is no mark, why should we listen to your interpreters? (13) If there is one, I long to hear what it is; but they (the Stoics) will be at a standstill.

The text is an ambiguous, winding piece of reasoning. Typical of Academic skepticism, it is designed more to bring to light the confusion of the Stoic position regarding divination than to settle on a fixed line of thought regarding it. Lines one through five and 11 through 13 say that, even if both true and false dreams exist, we would never be in a position to demonstrate this, because nothing distinguishes in advance prophetic dreams from nonprophetic ones before the former "turn out true".

Lines six through 10 develop a different argument. Cicero argues that, since it is more likely that all dreams are either due-to-nature *or* sent-by-god (instead of true dreams being sent-by-god and false being due-to-nature) and since even Quintus denies the latter, the former must be admitted as more likely. A reference at II.128 to Aristotle's account of dreams and the text at II.129 that immediately follows provide additional support for the wholly natural explanation. At II.129, for instance, Cicero writes that it is beneath the dignity of the gods to send prophetic dreams, especially those dreams in need of interpretation, to all mortals.

> For now, let us debate about which of the following is more probable. Do the immortal gods, by their superiority of excellence in all things, run around not only to the beds, but even to the low couches of all mortals everywhere and, when they see someone snoring, throw at him certain twisted and obscure dreams (*visa*), which he, terrified while asleep, takes to the interpreter in the morning? Or does it happen by nature that an easily agitated soul seems to see in sleep what it sees when it is awake? Which of these is more worthy of philosophy: to interpret your visions by the superstition of fortune tellers or by means of a natural explanation?

Cicero's explanation of how dreaming occurs at II.139-140 attempts to rule out divine causation altogether.

When everything is said, the argument at II.127-128 leaves the matter of the divine causation of dreams on unsettled grounds. "Prophetic" or "divine" dreams are, he suggests, likely fully explained by chance and, therefore, such dreams must occur only infrequently (II.48-49, 121, and 146).

In all, Cicero shifts the burden of proof to his brother. If you, Quintus, believe that some dreams are false (which, as it were, simple attention to your dreams would likely confirm) but also unremittingly cling to the proposition that some dreams are nonaccidentally true, then you must provide me with compelling evidence for the latter and, in addition, a reason for positing that these must be god-sent. Otherwise, it is best to conclude that no dreams are divine and those that are true are merely accidentally so. At the end of this burden-of-proof argument, there seems to be no room left for prophetic dreams of any kind.

Quintus' Oneiromantical Program

Cicero does, nevertheless, leave himself open to persuasion by scientific principles that would distinguish prophetic dreams from false ones so that we could know in advance when to regard a dream as prophetic or not. Having put the burden of proof foursquare on Quintus' shoulders, does Quintus anywhere and in any manner develop or disclose such principles?

Assuming, as Cicero does, that the Stoics did believe in both true and false dreams, Book I has a response to the argument at II.127-129. Quintus employs it to vindicate all forms of divination from the charge of fraud and show that prophecy is an art or science like any other. I restrict its scope to oneiromancy in an effort to show, first and foremost, whether it can legitimize interpretation by dreams as an art and, second, whether it provides an empirical method for distinguishing prophetic from nonprophetic dreams.

At I.12-13, Quintus states that we must examine the outcomes (*eventa*) rather than the causes of the phenomena at issue through carefully observing signs over time in connection with certain future events. Once carefully observed, these signs indicate to us what will be through divine excitement and inspiration. He adds, "[T]here is nothing that length of time cannot bring about and attain when memory receives connections[17] and written annals transmit them".

Hereafter follows a swarm of examples, from sensible to absurd, of certain signs that have come to be indicative of particular outcomes. Herbs and roots have been found to have medicinal value (I.12-13). The gray heron's raving and the heaving sea warn of an impending storm (I.13-14). Little frogs with their comical croakings also give signs (I.15). Soft-footed oxen lift their nostrils to the illuminated sky to draw moisture before a storm, thereby acting as signs of the storm (I.15). The mastic tree, in exhibiting its berries three times, shows the seasons for plowing are three (I.15-16). The aristolochia plant cures the bite of a snake because of a cause unknown (I.16). "Scarcely ever do we see these signs lying", Quintus says, "yet still we do not grasp why such things happen as they do" (I.15).

Though some of the examples at I.12-16 are strained, the argument from experience (at I.12-13) is compelling. A great deal of scientific investigation today concerns correlation between seemingly unconnected phenomena and the subsequent search for an underlying causal relationship. Though in many cases no such aetiological relationship can be found, this does not render the correlation valueless. For example, in nutrition science it is well documented that the ingestion of caffeine prior to either short-term intense exercise or long-term endurance exercise enhances athletic performance. We still do not know precisely why this happens, yet the many controlled laboratory studies heretofore performed clearly indicate that it does happen.[18] And so, many athletes use caffeine regularly for performance-enhancement. In the same way, if we should carefully observe that those bitten by venomous snakes do not suffer the dangerous effects of the poison when given a certain part of the aristolochia plant, then we would be warranted in concluding that this part of the plant cures snakebite regardless of whether or not we know how it cures snakebite. Cicero's insistence that we need reasons and causes, since without these we cannot be absolutely sure that something is the case (II.17, 27), seems unjustified. If our observations are carefully noted, we can determine that part of the aristolochia plant cures snakebite without knowing why it does. We may not have causal understanding, but this means little to someone who is bitten by a snake. Moreover, it does not necessarily make treating snakebite in such a manner unscientific. What matters is *that* such a treatment cures snakebite, not *why* it cures it. The question now is this: By having carefully observed and recorded links between signs in dreams and certain future events, could the ancients have begun or have developed a craft or science of oneiric prophecy in some rudimentary sense?

By careful observation, it is possible to establish correlations among signs in dreams and future events (if they exist) and it should be possible to know whether a dream is prophetic or not before it turns out or fails to turn out true—a strategy avowedly employed by the oneirocritic Artemidorus in the second century A. D. (see next chapter) and, most likely, other oneirocritics. For instance, if a certain dream of type ο (where ο indicates some element or aspect of oneiric content such as a theme, episode, or symbol) has been always or even usually[19] followed by a particular, seemingly arbitrary event of type τ, we are inductively justified in concluding that future dreams of type ο will result in events of type τ. In short:

> All dreams of type ο portend events of type τ.[20]

In such a manner, through careful observation and attention to detail over time, an oneirocritic can fashion a catalog of oneiric signs and correlated events that may be judged prophetic or not by an appeal to content alone in accordance to the strength of the correlation. The question now becomes "Did the ancients essay to develop such a science to any extent?"[21]

Catalog of Dreams in *de Divinatione*

I mention above that Book I contains a list of fulfilled dreams from I.39 to I.59 and the few others scattered elsewhere—27 dreams in all.

Of these 27 prophetic dreams,[22] Quintus acknowledges, two are probably poetic fiction.[23] Since Quintus himself doubts their validity, I ignore them also. Those at I.4, I.16, I.43, and I.96, as well as the two dreams recorded by Xenophon at I.52 are referred to without sufficient detail, while the dream at I.99 is the same as that of I.4. So none of these deserves attention. The 18 remaining are neatly separable into 10 *straightforwardly prophetic dreams* (hereafter, S-P dreams) and eight *enigmatically prophetic dreams* (hereafter, E-P dreams).[24] Since only the latter require interpretation, I examine these alone in this section.

With the aid of the eight E-P dreams, let me now evaluate the Stoic oneiromantical program as both a defense of oneirocriticism and a response to Cicero's reasonable demand for criteria for differentiating prophetic and nonprophetic dreams. Since the meaning of these dreams is up for grabs, perhaps a closer look at each and its interpretation will enable us to gain some insight into the worth of the program that Quintus has sketched.

At I.39 Quintus mentions the dream of the mother of the tyrant of Syracuse, Dionysius. When pregnant with Dionysius, she dreamed that *she gave birth to an infant satyr*. The Galeotae (interpreters) predicted that *she would have the most eminent son of Greece, one who would live a long and fortunate life*. Quintus says nothing about why *satyr* portends *most eminent son* or how the Galeotae decided his life would be long and fortunate. In contrast, the second-century A. D. oneirocritic Artemidorus, in his *Onirocritica*, writes that to dream of a *satyr*, in general, forebodes *great danger* (II.37).

At I.44-45, Quintus talks of the dream of Tarquin the Proud. Tarquin dreamed of *choosing two rams from a herd. The more handsome of the two he sacrificed, while the other butted him to the ground. While looking up, he saw the sun reverse its course.* The diviners said to Tarquin that this meant that *one bereft of intellect could take your throne* and that, since the sun changed course, *there would be imminent change.* The *sun moving from left to right* indicates that *Rome would reign supreme over all the earth*. The Hippocratic author of *Dreams* states that, when a *heavenly body moves opposite its natural motions*, it is a sign of *good health*, as long as it is *pure and bright* (IV.lxxxix). Artemidorus writes that *the sun rising in the west* indicates that *secrets will be brought to light*, *the return of a foreign traveller*, or that *every endeavor and hope will meet with struggle and go unfinished* (*Oniroc.* II.36).

I.46 relates two dreams worth noting. One is a dream of the mother of Phalaris. Having fallen asleep while looking at the sacred images of the gods in her domicile, she saw *the statue of Mercury holding a bowl in his right hand and pouring blood, which eventually filled the room*. The *inhumane cruelty of her son* subsequently fulfilled the dream. The interpretation seems reasonable enough, but it must be admitted that why this dream portended that specific outcome and no other is a mystery.

The second is the dream of Cyrus of Persia. Once, Cyrus dreamed that he saw *the sun at his feet and thrice he tried to grasp it, while thrice it escaped him*. The Persian magi interpreted *his grasping for the sun thrice* as *his reign lasting for 30 years*. Having begun his reign at 40, he lived until 70 years. The closest thing to this for Artemidorus is a *disappearing sun*, which is inauspicious for all but those in hiding or those wishing to do unmentionable things (*Oniroc.* II.36).

At I.52 he relates the famous dream of Socrates in Plato's *Crito*. Here Socrates tells Crito of his dream that *a fair and comely woman visited him saying: "O Socrates, on the third day hence you will go to fertile Phthia*". And so this dream turned out to forebode Socrates' death.[25]

I.53 tells of a dream of Eudemus the Cyprian, handed down to us presumably through Aristotle in a lost work called *Eudemus*. Aristotle says that Eudemus, while in Pherae and on his way to Macedonia, became desperately ill. In sleep, he dreamed that *a beautiful youth told him that he would get well quickly*, that *the tyrant Alexander would die in a few days*, and that *he (Eudemus) would return home five years later*. The first two prophecies came true immediately, in the manner of an S-P dream. Five years later, Eudemus was killed in battle at Syracuse. This aspect of the dream was interpreted to mean that *his soul left his body upon death and returned home.* Obviously, this last aspect of the interpretation is strained.

The least sensational and most believable dreams are those related by the two brothers themselves, and Cicero himself acknowledges this.[26] At I.58 Quintus relates a dream of his own. When he was proconsul of Asia, he dreamed that *Cicero, on horseback and riding toward some river, suddenly plunged into the river and wholly disappeared, only soon to reappear cheerfully on the horse on the other side of the river, where Marcus and Quintus embraced.*[27] The dream was interpreted by an expert in Asia to foretell those events that actually befell (*Cicero's banishment in 58 B. C. and subsequent recall in 57 B. C.*). Yet we are told nothing about how the practitioner came to this interpretation. Artemidorus tells us that *horse* is like *ship* because of the horse's link with Poseidon (I.56), that *river* is like *judge* because neither is accountable to anyone (IV.66), and that *to be unable to get out of a river* is bad, while *crossing one*, especially on foot, is good (II.27).

Finally, Quintus relates a dream of Marcus himself (I.59). While banished and in a country house at Atina, he dreamed that *he was wandering about sadly when Gaius Marius, with his fasces wreathed in laurel, met with him and asked about his condition. Marcus told him that he had been driven from his home by violence. Marius then took Cicero to the nearest lictor to be taken to a memorial temple for safety.* Sallustius then predicted *a speedy and glorious return for Cicero.* It turned out that Cicero was recalled by the Senate from Marius' temple.

What principally concerns us with this collection of E-P dreams is that there is no evidence whatsoever that any of the interpretations, different sources notwithstanding, were derived through correlating oneiric elements with events subsequent to the dream. In fact, Quintus tells us nothing at all of the methods behind the interpretation of such dreams. These interpretations do not even square with interpretations of similar dreams in other extant Greco-Roman works. Thus, these E-P dreams nowise aid us in our evaluation of the plausibility of constructing and employing a science of oneiric prophecy.

Cicero's Criticism of Oneiromancy

Let us now turn to Cicero's own criticism of the E-P dreams in Book II. Here Cicero counters that none of the E-P dreams have anything divine about them. Instead, all likely have the following explanation. With sleep, the soul is freed of its bodily responsibilities of discerning, thinking, and perceiving. It moves of itself and attends to the many confused and diverse forms and sounds—the remnants of the things which we have seen, thought of, and done—that are turned this way and that. Out of this disorder, dreams emerge[28] (II.139-140). Relating this to the two most promising candidates for genuinely prophetic dreams, Cicero's dream and that of Quintus, Cicero states that Quintus' dream was due to the latter's worry over Cicero's banishment, while his own dream happened at a worrisome time for himself when Marius, being an exemplar of courage and strength, was often in his mind (II.140-141). The argument is a natural extension of the one at II.127-129, dealing with the impossibility of distinguishing true dreams from false ones. Without such criteria, Cicero believes, it is probable that all dreams are naturally caused.

From II.144-145, Cicero adds that the conjectures of the interpreters are more a product of their own cleverness than the power and accord of nature. Here he gives three examples of inconsistent interpretations of E-P dreams. The first is of an aspiring Olympic runner who dreamed *he was riding in a chariot drawn by four horses.* One interpreter, in the morning, told the runner that *he would win because of the swiftness and the might of the horses*. However Antiphon said, "*Do you not know that four ran before you?*" The second deals with another runner who dreamed that *he had been changed into an eagle.* Again, while one interpreter told him that *he would win since no bird flies faster than an eagle*, Antiphon told him that *he would lose since eagles, always pursuing, are ever in the last position.* Finally, a married woman who was pregnant and in doubt of her pregnancy dreamed that *her womb was sealed.* One interpreter told her that *she would bear no child since no child could come from a sealed womb.* Another told her that *she would bear a child, since one only seals that which is not empty.* Now, without question, each of these interpretations seems reasonable. Cicero's point, then, is that these dreams admit of more than one and perhaps even a multitude of reasonable interpretations. Therefore, an interpreter's so-called "art" is more a product of whim and fancy than careful observation.

Consequently, Cicero demonstrates that while Quintus has set out to establish divination through dreams as a valid art—one that is actually practiced successfully in antiquity—he only shows that, with careful observation and correlation, such a science *can* exist.

Cicero, in a rhetorical and decisive objection at II.146, even has something to say against the *possibility* of a science of oneiric interpretation:

> Dreams can be observed? In what way? We cannot think of anything too preposterous, too confused, too monstrous about which we cannot dream. How, then, can we grasp through memory or record through observation these countless and ever new visions?

Astronomers, he relates, can carefully observe and record astral observations, but, next to the interpretation of dreams, their art is simple. Dreams, he adds, are of an infinite variety and there is nothing inconceivable that cannot be dreamed.

There follows another brief reference to the difficulties involved in differentiating true from false dreams. "In what way, then", he asks, "can true dreams be distinguished from false ones, since the same dreams turn out otherwise for different people and not always in the same way for the same people?" In other words, no appeal to content alone can tell us inviolably how to regard a dream.[29]

The examples Quintus catalogs are sometimes lengthy and he offers no explanation as to how interpreters arrived at an interpretation. First, unlike Artemidorus in his *Onirocritica*, Quintus does not give us even one instance where the same dream or oneiric element has been connected with the same event more than once. In addition, the argument from experience needs some nonarbitrary criteria for culling significant elements or themes of each dream in order to secure correct interpretation.[30] Quintus gives us none. Last, as Cicero himself says, there must be some assurance of the credibility of each testimony.[31] Because of the tendency to forget dreams and the influence of secondary revision, even first-hand reports are seldom true to the dream as it was actually dreamed. The problems with secondhand reports are considerable as well. Against the Stoics, Cicero has shown that Quintus cannot ensure that the interpretations he has given are not ineliminably arbitrary and that the interpretations of professional oneiromantics will not often or even customarily be flatly inconsistent. Quintus' argument, next to these objections, lacks cogency; Marcus, it seems, has won the day.

Analysis of Cicero's Criticism

Nevertheless, there are problems with Cicero's objections. First, the problem of differentiating prophetic and nonprophetic dreams through an appeal to oneiric content alone is based on the assumption that the Stoics believed in both true and false dreams. Now it is clear that the Stoics believed in prophetic dreams, but whether they actually believed in nonprophetic dreams is uncertain. Although, at II.127, Cicero clearly states that Quintus (as spokesperson for the Stoics) does not believe that all dreams come from god (*omnia deus [fecerit], quod negatis*), we have also seen that I.60 suggests that nonprophetic dreams exist for the Stoics only in the sense that many people, overwrought by food or drink, do not go to sleep "in the proper condition" and, thus, have "false" dreams. Here the falsity of such dreams is due to the vicious character of the dreamer and not god. This intimates that all dreams are god-sent and that the falsity of any dream is a contamination of that message by a less-than-virtuous sleeper.[32]

Even if the Stoics did believe in both prophetic and nonprophetic dreams, it need not be the case that they believed that these were distinguishable by an appeal to content alone. Put simply, perhaps they merely thought that the same dream could both function prophetically at one time and, at another time, be wholly void of meaning. What if the prophetic nature of a certain dream, for example, is decidable in advance by comparing oneiric content to the circumstances attending the dreamer's life at the time of a dream—his occupation, name, habits, nature, and so forth? In short, certain dreams in specific circumstances have meaning; otherwise they are insignificant. As will become evident later, such dreams played a large part in Artemidorean oneirocriticism in the second century A. D. (*Oniroc.* I.3 & IV.2) and even the Hippocratic author of *Dreams*, almost 600 years earlier, makes reference to them in his work (xc.40-47 & 64-69, see chapter eight).[33]

Now if there is any plausibility to either of the two alternatives just mentioned, and I suggest that neither can be surely ruled out, then we have some reason to be suspicious of Cicero's right to demand *internal* criteria[34] for differentiating between true and false dreams. Therefore, Cicero has not shown the impossibility or even the unlikelihood of prophetic dreams and the demand for oneiric criteria to vindicate oneiromancy (at least, with respect to the content of dreams exclusively) is unwarranted.

In addition, Cicero has not demonstrated the *impossibility* of a science of prophetic dreams. At best, he has shown that there are many forbidding obstacles to surmount before attempting to put such a science into practice. In fact, most of the problems mentioned by Cicero in Book I (such as ensuring the reliability of the report of a dream and the need of criteria for culling significant elements in dreams) are problems that haunt us today in our nonprophetic science of oneiric interpretation. Put simply, we have no right to expect from these ancients greater scientific understanding of dreams than we have today. Still it is reasonable to assume that these weighty difficulties would likely have made oneiromancy *impracticable* in Ciceronean antiquity, even were we to presuppose the validity of prophetic dreams.

When the arguments on both sides have been heard, the debate concerning the existence of prophetic dreams and the possibility of a science of them in antiquity is perhaps best construed as a true stalemate. Yet consistent with the aims of Academic skepticism, a stalemate gives Cicero the edge. Marcus has indeed won the day. What Cicero has truly shown, however, is that, even if there were prophetic dreams in antiquity, the many complications concerning dreams and their circumstances would have made an art or science of their interpretation impossible in practice.

Dreams as a Form of Knowledge?

I wish to take up a final question in this chapter. Just what sort of divine assistance did the Stoics believe sleepers would acquire through dreams? The Posidonian classification of I.64 is unhelpfully vague, but the many recorded dreams of Book I suggest that dreamers would gain a practical insight into their own affairs.

Stoic cosmology, as expressed by Quintus, seems to demand much more than this. Quintus tells us that, for the Stoics, *fato omnia fiant* (I.125, 127). Fate in turn implies a causal connection between all events.[35] Yet we are not gods and cannot aspire to be divinely wise and thereby know the relation of each thing to all others, so the gods have foreordained events so that certain things are significant of certain other, seemingly unrelated things. Consequently, to aid us in gleaning these signs, we must employ divination (I.127).

For the Stoics, Quintus relates that divination through dreams enables dreamers to gain insight into the divine mind through contact with divine souls[36] (I.110 and 126). Sleep allows for this, since it is a special condition of human existence where the sensitive, motive, and appetitive parts of the soul cease from activity, while the rational and intellective parts are drawn outside of the body to mingle with these divine souls[37] (I.34, 70, and 110). In a word, through communion with immortal souls, dreamers clearly seem to gain a share of what these souls *know*, and this gives reason to believe that sleepers acquire knowledge through dreams.

Nevertheless, a look at Stoic epistemology outside of *de Divinatione* creates problems for this picture of dreams. For the Stoics, all knowledge (ἐπιστήμη) begins with sensation. The soul, a blank slate at birth, receives impressions (φαντασίαι) and, in time, memories accrue, then experiences form, and universal conceptions[38] develop—all of which conduce to knowledge for the properly disposed soul.[39] Certain types of impressions, cognitive impressions (φαντασίαι καταληπτικαί),[40] perceived to be qualitatively different by the Stoics, reveal themselves and their cause or impresser (φανταστόν) with such distinctness and clarity that one having such an impression can do no other than assent.[41] For the Stoics, all knowledge is built upon such impressions. In contrast, dreams are images (φαντάσματα) seen in sleep that arise not from any impresser, but from imagination. From imagination there arises the impressions of the mad and melancholic as well as those of dreamers.[42] In short, only the cognitive impressions, being unshakeable and fixed, conduce toward knowledge first by exacting our assent, then by securing cognition (κατάληψις[43]). Certainly, this suggests a low regard for the images of dreams and seems quite inconsistent with the Stoic insistence that some (perhaps even all) dreams are divinely prophetic.[44]

Still it is not by virtue of their being *phantasmata* that oneiric images cannot be linked with knowledge, since concepts (ἐννοήματα[45]), the building blocks of knowledge in a rational mind, are themselves images.[46] Rather it must be because they are further removed from or are bastardizations of particulars, the true realities of the Stoic cosmos, that they cannot conduce to knowledge.

Patricia Cox Miller argues, though without much elaboration, that frequent employment of the words *praesensio* and *praesentio* in connection with divination indicates that dreamers gain merely a "sense or feeling for the shape of things", not any sort of knowledge through dreams.[47] If this is true, then it neatly explains the perceived disharmony between what one acquires through Stoic divination by dreams and what one acquires through receiving cognitive impressions. The gods do not grant *knowledge* through the inspection of signs or the straightforward messages of certain dreams, but give humans a *presentiment* of what will be. As with Plato and Aristotle, knowledge is reserved for sober people of moderate ways.

Yet Miller's account ignores key, conflicting passages. First, at the very beginning of Book I, Cicero defines *divinatio* as a "a presentiment and *scientia* of future events". In addition, at I.109, Quintus states that the repeated observation over a long time—whether of one thing coming about from another (causal) or one thing signifying another (semiotic)—brings about *incredibilem scientiam*. Quintus' oneiromantical program is certainly of this kind. Also, at I.126, Quintus says that we somehow discern the *causae* of future events through frenzy or dreams, as well as the artificial types of divination. These passages strongly suggest that sleepers gain causal understanding, knowledge of some sort, through dreams. Thus they present sincere difficulties for Miller's interpretation.

In spite of these troublesome passages, Stoic cosmology (and the general tenor of Book I) are in agreement with Miller (that we gain a *sense* of things to come and not any kind of knowledge through prophetic dreams). Let us look at I.118, where Quintus relates how the Stoics believed the gods set up the cosmos. In the beginning, the world was created so that certain signs would precede certain events and, thereby, would be semiotic designators of them. The perspicacious reader of these signs will note simply that they precede other events, without assigning a causal significant to them. In this way, those who read signs aright will not, properly speaking, gain knowledge, but get a certain and, in general, an accurate feeling for what will come to be. The ability to read these signs properly, then, need not require any apprehension of universal principles or causal understanding, but may merely be guided by divine dispensation.

Concluding Remarks

That Cicero wrote an Academically styled treatise on divination tells us that the variously practiced forms of prophecy were under fire during his time. Following empirical medicine, Book I of *de Divinatione* challenges Academic skeptics with an argument designed to show that genuine science is possible without knowledge of causes. It is sufficient for science merely to know that something is the case, instead of knowing why it is so.

Related to oneiromancy, in Book II, Cicero shows that this argument from experience, which looks to correlate oneiric signs with particular subsequent events, is difficult to apply to dreams because of the elusiveness of dreams. Many of his objections to oneiric prophecy are still pertinent for oneiric theorists today.

Overall, for so rich a source of reported dreams, the treatise is disappointing for the aims of this project. Apart from the appeal to the argument from experience (which is not so much an argument on behalf of the various branches of prophecy as it is an argument for a nonrationalist approach to science) and various other tidbits of information on oneiromancy scattered throughout the two books, there is little in *de Divinatione* that indicates just how ancient oneiromancists practiced their craft. This, however, was not Cicero's intent. Our best source for the actual practice of oneiromancy or oneirocriticism is Artemidorus' *Onirocritica*, the subject of the following chapter.

---

[1] Quintus states that the Romans have done better than the Greeks in calling "the prescience and knowledge of future events" *divinatio* instead of μαντική. The latter is derived from *furor* (i.e., μανία; see Plato's *Phdr.* 244c); the former, from *divi* (*Div.* I.1). Because of this and because of constant references to prophetic dreams as "divine", in this chapter, I shall follow the generally accepted tradition of translating *divinatio* as "divination".

[2] *Att.* XII.52.

[3] The Academy shortly after the death of Plato.

[4] *Acad.* II.24-30.

[5] The influence of Book I is mostly Posidonius from the work περὶ μαντικῆς and possibly, περὶ θεόν. That Quintus himself was a Stoic seems unlikely, since at *Fin.* (V.96) he is presented in sympathy with the Peripatetics.

[6] The source is likely Carneades through the pen of Clitomachus, with the exception of the astrological section, II.87-97, which is drawn from Panaetius, probably from the work περὶ πρόνοιας (Pease 1920, 25-26).

[7] Cf. Plato's *R.* 571d-572b. Advice about what to eat and what not to eat to ready for sleep alludes to the Pythagorean/Platonic position of how to prepare oneself for sleep to induce true dreams (*Div.* I.62, 115, II.119). For instance, the Pythagorean prohibition of beans is believed to have come about because the flatulence they cause generates an internal, physical condition at odds with the soul. That food had a noticeable affect on sleep and dreams was commonly accepted not only by the Neoplatonists, but almost every oneiric thinker in antiquity. Tertullian gives an especially interesting account in chapter 48 of his *de An.* For a fine list of references on this topic in antiquity, see Behr 1968, 180 (fn. 17). In modern times, the "Heavy-Supper Theory" of dreams came into prominence in the nineteenth century. Hatfield says of this school of thinking, "A heavy supper, by drawing blood for the digestion, may affect the circulation of the brain and so give rise to the dream" (1954, 5).

[8] *R.* 571c . See also *Ti.* 71e-72b.

[9] Cf. *Div.* I.121.

[10] *Sent. Vat.* #24.

[11] Cicero notes that Carneades rejected all forms of divination and gives some of Carneades' arguments at *Div.* II.9-12.

[12] This is perhaps the same classification used by Philo of Alexandria (c. 20 B. C.-50 A. D.), in reverse order.

[13] Drawing from Cratippus, Quintus states that during sleep or frenzy, the human soul is drawn and pulled outside of the body, where the divine soul can influence it. Thus, while the appetitive, motive, and sensitive part of the soul is no longer active in the body, the rational and intellective part thrives when it is most distant from the body. The explanations for frenzy and sleep come at I.114 and I.115, respectively. During sleep, the soul, freed from the encumbrances of the body, sees everything and is engaged with innumerable souls. This is most unlike Plato's account in *Ti.*, where

the basest part of the soul was judged most suitable for prophecy (71c-d), or Aristotle's depiction of the lucky man (*EE* VIII.2), who receives divine succor with reasoning disengaged, yet it has much in common with the Neoplatonism of Synesius in his *Insomn*.

[14] Schofield 1986, 52.

[15] The reasoning is designed to show that Quintus' definition of *divinatio*, given at I.9 as a prediction and presentiment of those things that are fortuitous, is flawed. See also II.27 & 60.

[16] In a letter to Evodius, Augustine expresses similar thoughts: "[W]ords fail me to explain how those seemingly material bodies (dreams), without a real body, are produced; yet, as I know that they are not produced by the body, so I wish I could know how we perceive those things which are seen sometimes by the spirit and are thought to be seen by the body, or *how we are to distinguish the visions of those who are deluded by error or impiety, when they are generally described in the same terms as the visions of the good and holy*" (my italics) (*Ep.* #159). Gregory the Great also recognized problems with differentiating kinds of dreams. He acknowledged six kinds of dreams: two caused by the body, two by demons, and two by God or divine messengers. With such a variety of causes and, presumably, because of similarities of oneiric content, he advocated mistrust in them (*Dial.* IV.50).

[17] That is, he notes a semiotic and correlated relationship between dream and future event.

[18] Spriet 1995, 84-85.

[19] We can effectively argue for the universality of this relationship even in such cases where certain signs usually give rise to a particular outcome. For instance, the failure of a certain sign to forecast a highly correlated outcome could be explained by another sign in the dream, some forgotten segment of the dream, the state of the dreamer prior to sleep (I.60), or even inexpert interpreters (I.118).

[20] Here the relationship between oneiric element and future event is not causal, strictly speaking, but semiotic. In the Stoic universe, the god preestablishes the harmony of all the constituents in the cosmos. The relationship between certain signs and events that follow, preestablished at the beginning, testifies to this harmony (I.118).

[21] There is one major impediment to this approach as it applies to oneirocriticism. Book I mentions two types of divination: artificial (divination involving art) and natural (divination employing no art) (I.11-12, 34, 70, 109-110). Those diviners employing art, he says, learn what is old through observed and recorded signs, and then proceed toward new matters through conjecture and reason. These include the readers of entrails, interpreters of portents and lightening, augurs, astrologers, and interpreters of oracles. This link with the divine is indirect and, requiring a diviner, artificial. Those not using art divine through a certain disturbance of the soul by means of either the frenzy of madness or unrestrained and free motion brought on during sleep (I.11-12, 34). Their link to the divine, involving no human skill, is more direct. Since divination by dreams belongs to the category of natural divination, which is an unmediated type

of divine communication, the argument from experience, it seems, only applies to artificial divination, thereby excluding dreams. However, at I.116, Quintus mentions Antiphon, who had an incomparable knack for interpreting dreams and who staunchly believed that the interpretation of dreams (as well as oracles and frenzied utterances) did not occur naturally, but demanded art. Quintus admits, here, that some dreams, especially enigmatic ones, require art. And so, the argument from experience is applicable to dreams as well.

Blum takes I.116 as evidence that Quintus has adopted a later Stoic (Posidonian) approach to prophecy by dreams in which dreams are both naturally (where the soul moves "through sympathy with The All") and artificially (where the soul moves "through its own power") interpreted. The first is a case of θεῖα πρόγνωσις, the second is a case of τεχνικὴ πρόγνωσις. To these two ways of divining, Blum says, correspond two ways of knowing, direct communion with the universal mind and the usual empirical way. The Latin equivalents to θεῖα πρόγνωσις and τεχνικὴ πρόγνωσις are at *Div.* 1.109 (*divinae praesensionis* and *artificiosae praesensionis*) (1936, 64-65 & 82-83).

[22] Twenty-two occur from I.39-59, while five others are scattered throughout Book I.

[23] I.40-41 and 42.

[24] Called by Cicero *aperta et clara* and *obscura*, respectively (II.135).

[25] Phthia was Achilles' home (*Il.* IX.363), so Socrates' dream of going to Phthia is a return home for him.

[26] In Book II, Cicero discusses these only after having dismissed the testimonies of the other E-P dreams on account of their incredibility (II.136).

[27] From a Babylonian-Assyrian book on dreams dating perhaps prior to the first millennium, we find that *sinking into a river and emerging again* indicates *riches and worries. Crossing a river* signifies *confusion* (Lewis 1976, 18).

[28] Roughly the account elaborated in Aristotle's *Insomn.* Cf. II.128, where Cicero gives a sketch of this account and a reference to Aristotle and also to the Hippocratic account of the soul in sleep in *Insomn.* lxxxvi.

[29] Cicero does not address the further complication of the impossibility of verifying reports of dreams. Dreams, being *only* personal experiences, cannot be witnessed by others. Moreover, nothing about a dream can be related until after the sleeper has waked. Here the lapse of time, forgetfulness, and obtrusion of other dreams make this problematic.

[30] Though, of course, most of the dreams that Quintus lists are so concise that many inessential elements must have been removed prior to this account.

[31] Cicero himself mentions that the S-P dreams of Chrysippus (catalogd by Quintus from I.39-59), however straightforward they may be, are so far removed from their sources that no one can guarantee their reliability (II.136). For our purposes, in dealing with such dreams, we must bear in mind that we are dealing with ancient reports of dreams, and not the actual dreams. Moreover, knowing the substantial effects of secondary revision,

as we do today, it is almost certain that it occurred amply in these more remarkable dreams catalogd by Chrysippus. Like a story that is passed from person to person (with each passing, the story takes on some attribute of the new teller or some detail that it did not have before), the ancient reports of dreams may have changed each time they were told until all perceived incoherence and absurdity—due to forgetfulness, vagueness, ambiguity, or anything else—were smoothed out. And so, it is easy to see how any short, verbal dream could have been worked up, with the passing of even a little time, to an S-P dream like the kinds catalogd by Quintus.

[32] At *ND* III.93, the Academic Sceptic Cotta tells the Stoic Balbus, *vestra est de somniorum veritate sententia.* See also *ND* III.95.

[33] It is strange that the work as a whole makes no reference to the influence of attendant circumstances on the interpretation of a dream, since taking such circumstances into consideration was doubtless part of established oneirocritical practice in Cicero's day.

[34] That is, dictated by oneiric content alone.

[35] By "fate", Quintus means "an order and series of causes, where cause, linked to cause, brings about an effect of itself" (I.125) and also "the eternal cause of things, why also these things, which have passed, were brought about and those things, which are impending, come about and those things, which follow, will come about" (I.126). In short, everything that happens has a cause (I.126, 127). Consequently, should we see through to the causal links between all events, we would never be deceived about the order of things past, present, and future.

[36] In his paper, "The Original Notion of Cause", Frede (1980, esp. 217-226) argues correctly that the interest in causes, for the Stoics, does not arise from an interest in "actual explanation", but instead from an interest in responsibility. Along this line, dreams can be construed as instruments of moral betterment. In stark contrast, Tertullian argues the soul is restive or ecstatic in sleep, but acts to no effect. Like a gladiator without arms, "there is the fight, there is the struggle; but the effort is a vain one". Good deeds are in vain, bad actions are useless. "We shall no more be condemned for visionary acts of sin, than we shall be crowned for imaginary martyrdom" (*de An.* §45).

[37] Quintus is drawing from Cratippus here.

[38] These, like dreams, are called φαντάσματα because, unlike φαντασίαι, they arise from no impressor.

[39] Aetius, *Dox.Gr.* IV.xi.1-4; Cicero, *Acad.* I.41-42; and Sextus Empiricus, *M.* VII.151-153.

[40] All such impressions have propositional content (λέκτα) in that they present themselves to the mind for assent or denial. Only such impressions warrant *firm* assent in that they are derived from and in accordance with a real object—that is, nothing unreal could have produced them. See Diogenes Laertius' *Vit.* VII.46 & 54; Cicero *Acad.* I.40-41, II.30-31, 77-78, 83-84, & 141; and Sextus Empiricus *M.* VII.247-260 & 402-408. Sextus relates that Carneades objects to the assertion that φαντασίαι could not have been produced by what is not real. For even in dreams the thirsty person takes pleasure in a drink and one terrified feels fear (*M.* VII.402-

404).

[41] Cicero uses the analogy of a scale sinking when weights are placed in the balance (*Acad.* II.38). Sextus states that these impressions seize us by the hair and pull us to assent (*M.* VII.253-256). These analogies notwithstanding, assent is an entirely voluntary process (*Acad.* I.40-41).

[42] Diogenes Laertius' *Vit.* VII.49-51 and Aetius, *Dox.Gr.* IV.xii.4-5. For a link between melancholy and prophecy, see Aristotle's *Somn.Div.* 464a32-b2 & *EE* 1248a28-b3.

[43] Κατάληψις, as a *secure* type of grasping, is perhaps midway between both either ignorance (Cicero, *Acad.* I.41-42) or opinion (Sextus, *M.* VII.151-155) and knowledge.

[44] Against the Stoics, Carneades believed that dreams, ecstasy, deliria, insanity, and hallucinations afford evidence that other impressions, either without an impressor or that deviate from the immediate impressor, are equally as striking and evident as φαντασίαι καταληπτικαί so that we assent to them and even act upon them (Sextus, *M.* VII.403-408, VIII.67-68; Cicero, *Acad.* II.88-90).

[45] I.e., universals.

[46] Diogenes Laertius' *Vit.* VII.60-61. For instance, the concept of "warrior", for the Stoics, is not something in itself, but in some sense a construction of the mind through its experiences of actual warriors.

[47] Miller 1994, 53.

Chapter Six
Artemidorus' *Onirocritica*

Introduction

The deficiencies of Quintus' empirical program are addressed in roundabout fashion in the *Onirocritica* of Artemidorus of Daldis, the second-century A. D. diviner. His *Onirocritica* is the only complete oneirocritical guidebook that survives from antiquity. Thus, it is an invaluable source for the methods ancient oneirocritics used in interpretation, and it also gives us some indication of the state of oneirocriticism (and prophecy) during his time.

Of Artemidorus, little is known with any certainty. Aside from his own comments in the *Onirocritica*, there are few references to him in antiquity. Pseudo-Lucian in *Philopatris* (XXI-XXII) records that Artemidorus was an interpreter of dreams. The second-century physician Galen refers to him briefly in *de Victu Acutorum*. We also know from a tenth-century Byzantine lexicon *Suidas* that he wrote works on methods of divination other than oneirocriticism.

The *Onirocritica* itself tells us that Artemidorus was born in Ephasus and that he chose to associate himself with Daldis, the place of his mother's birth, with the hope of making famous the small, Lydian town (III.66). Inspired by Apollo himself (perhaps through a dream) (II.70 and IV proem), the proem to Book I states that his work is no mere copy of preexisting books on dreams, but rather it is the culmination of many years of listening to fulfilled dreams while travelling in Greece, Asia, Italy, as well as the largest islands in the Mediterranean. His oneirocritical insights are derived from experience (ἀπὸ πείρας), not conjecturing or putting together words according to verisimilitude (II.32[1]).

The work as a whole consists of five books. The first three, Artemidorus dedicates to a certain Cassius Maximus.[2] These are written for general readership (I.proem) and feature a loose categorization of dreams, selected methods and guidelines for interpretation (scattered throughout), and a catalog of oneiric signs and outcomes. The arrangement of the material as a whole is casual and tendentious. The third book, for instance, Artemidorus adds sometime after the first two because certain critics have objected to deficiencies in those books and because Artemidorus himself wants to satisfy his own intuition that no small and insignificant things were left out (IV.proem).[3] Books IV and V, written for his son of the same name who was learning oneirocriticism, are even later additions to the first three books. Of these, the fourth book is a hodgepodge of dreams, given mostly to illustrate certain rules of interpretation, while the fifth book is a catalog of "actually fulfilled" dreams, collected to show how to interpret prophetic dreams properly (IV.84 & V.proem).[4]

The proem to Book I indicates unambiguously that oneirocriticism around the second century A. D. was generally considered disreputable.[5] Consequently, Artemidorus makes two pledges. First, he pledges to do battle with those trying to do away with divination in its various forms by employing both his experience and the testimony of actually fulfilled dreams (τὴν τῶν ἀποτελεσμάτων μαρτυρίαν). Second, he pledges to give those who have never found an accurate treatment of oneirocriticism just such a treatment (I. proem). In doing so, he strives for completeness (II.70, III.proem, 28, 66, IV.proem), sufficient detail (II.70), order and good arrangement (III.66), and freedom from error (I.proem, IV.proem). At the end of Book IV, he vaunts: "And so, O son, these things are sufficient and faultless, since all the difficulties of oneirocriticism have been resolved. Being laid open in such a manner, they too will be easily understood by you".

In this chapter, I look at Artemidorus' account both of the nature and function of dreams, then turn to his own empirical program for a science of oneiric prophecy. The question I ask is this: Given his goal of vindicating oneirocriticism from the reproofs of skeptics and critics and given the inchoate nature of science in antiquity, does Artemidorus deliver at all on his promise to establish the interpretation of dreams as a prophetic science?

Classification and Principles of Interpretation

At I.1, Artemidorus begins his fivefold classification,[6] distinguishing between two main types of dreams: *enupnion* (empty dream) and *oneiros* (prophetic dream). He says: "For *oneiros* differs from *enupnion* in that it is proper for the former to point out things that will be, for the latter, things that are". Concerning *enupnia*, he elaborates:

> Certain of the affections naturally approach and draw themselves up besides the soul and bring about the manifestations of sleep (τοὺς ὀνειρωγμούς). For example, the lover necessarily sees that he is together with his beloved in a dream and the frightened man sees what he fears,[7] and again the hungry man eats and the thirsty man drinks[8] and, in addition, the person who has stuffed himself with food vomits or chokes...[9] (I.1).

He adds that *enupnion*, as the word itself suggests, occurs in sleep and, because it conveys to mind only what currently is, is limited to the duration of sleep (I.proem & IV.proem).

Oneiros, though also an *enupnion* in a way (since it too is something seen "in sleep"), is a prophetic dream that calls to the dreamer's attention a prediction of future events. Yet after sleep, it awakens and excites the soul to activity—possibly, he relates, receiving its name in such a way[10] (I.1, I.2, & IV.proem).

Oneiroi he divides into two classes: theorematic and allegorical dreams. Theorematic dreams are those that turn out in exactly the manner they were dreamed and happen immediately after the dream. Allegorical dreams, in contrast, "are those signifying certain things by means of other things". Here the soul of the dreamer portrays an obscure message or riddle to the dreamer. Its meaning comes true after a lapse of time that is rarely long (I.1, IV.1). Understandably, the whole work is devoted to a deeper apprehension of this particular kind of predictive dream.[11] Given a curt reference to three other types of dreams—*phantasma* (which corresponds to the nonsignificant *enupnion*) and *horama* and *chrematismos* (which correspond to *oneiros*)—we may ascribe a fivefold classification to Artemidorus: three types of significant, prophetic dream and two kinds of nonsignificant dream.[12]

At I.3 (and IV.2), Artemidorus elaborates on six elements or principles (στοιχεῖα) by which all dreams should be interpreted: nature (φύσις), law (νόμος), and custom (ἔθος) at the generic level; occupation (τέχνη), names (ὀνόματα), time (χρόνος), and custom[13] (again) at the particular level.[14] Each of these are interpretable through one of two qualifiers: "in agreement with" (κατά) and "against" (παρά). Dreams in agreement with any of the principles bode good outcomes; dreams against these bode ill.

These principles, Artemidorus warns, are not universal in application. He illustrates in Book IV by mentioning a certain potter's dream of *beating his mother*. Though this activity is against the law (παράνομος), the dream means *profit for him* because his craft is one of beating his mother (i.e., τὴν μητέρα τύπτειν = τὴν γῆν τύπτειν) (IV.2). In other words, one of the personal circumstances of the dreamer at the time of the dream (his craft) predominated over a general circumstance concerning the dream (the law).[15]

Methods of Interpretation

The general rule for interpreting dreams requires that we have knowledge both of the overall customs and habits of men and of the working of nature (I.8-9).[16] The oneirocritical methods of interpretation are many and dispersed throughout the work. These include interpretation through literalness;[17] letter-, word-, and number-play; analogy; metonymy; homonymy; antinomy; converse signification; and intuition.

Artemidorus also makes considerable use of word-, letter-, and number-play. At IV.24 he mentions the dream (made famous by Freud in his *Interpretation of Dreams*)[18] where Alexander, while besieging Tyre, dreamed of a *satyr dancing on his shield.*[19] At Alexander's service, Aristander divided the word σάτυρος into σά and Τύρος and interpreted the dream to mean *Tyre is yours*. Here also and again at III.34, Artemidorus talks about the numerical value of letters in dreams that enable one word with an equivalent number value to another to end up being interpreted as the other—isopsephism (ἰσόψηφος).[20]

Artemidorus also uses analogy abundantly. One of his most interesting examples occurs at IV.67. A woman dreamed that *she gave birth to a serpent*. It turned out that *her child became an excellent orator*, since both serpents and orators have forked tongues. A second woman, with the same dream, had *her child become a hierophant* (a priest who initiates others in the sacred mysteries). She was a priest's wife,and serpents, like priests, play a part in sacred rites. There follow four other cases with four different interpretations , each using analogical reasoning and each being explicable by differences in the attendant circumstances of the dreamer at the time of the dream.[21]

Metonymy, where one word takes on the meaning of another through association, is another method Artemidorus employs. At II.3, Artemidorus says that *dressing like a foreigner* or *wearing foreign clothes* signifies good for those who wish to go there. He says that when Temenus the Arcadian sailed through the Ionian gulf, he was favorably received by the inhabitants. Consequently, the garment worn by him in his style, called τήβεννος by the Romans (through a later corruption), is indicative of good when worn by one in a dream.

Artemidorus also refers to homonyms and near homonyms throughout. He says that *defecating a large amount of fecal matter while seated on a stool* is good for all, especially travelers, since ἄφοδος means "a going away" and "a departure" as well as "excrement"[22] (II.26).

Similar to, if not reducible to homonymy is the appeal to colloquial usage. Here Artemidorus argues for a type of homonymy based on the common-usage equivalence of one term with another. Such instances are characterized usually by verbs of speaking, such as καλῶμεν, λέγομεν, or φαμεν (or something equivalent). For example, "goats" (αἶγες) are inauspicious for seafarers because *we call* (λέγομεν) great waves (μεγάλα κύματα) "goats" *in common parlance* (ἐν τῇ συνεθείᾳ) (II.12).[23] In contrast to colloquial usage, we have the appeal to usage by authorities—references to ancient poets (especially Homer) and other literary figures. Artemidorus states at I.67 that "watermelons" (πέπονες) indicate good things for friendships (φιλίαι) and unions (συμβιβάσεις) because *poets call* (οἱ ποιηταὶ καλοῦσι) what is loved most "my watermelon" (πέπον)—that is, "my friend". II.12 contains five such instances.[24]

Antinomy occurs in Artemidorus at II.59, where he tells of a dream in which a man sent his son off to earn some money. His son, still abroad, appeared to the man in a dream and said, "*I have 3800 coins*". It was interpreted that *his son would return home without money* because, in part, "opposite things always turn out [in dreams] (τὰ ἐναντία ἀεὶ ἀποβαίνουσι)".

Artemidorus gives another method at IV.24, which I call "converse signification". He writes, "what is indicated (τὸ δηλούμενον) by something is in turn significant (σημαντικόν) of that thing". For example, a woman dreamed that *her eyes were sore* and, soon, *her children became sick*. Another woman, dreaming that *her children took sick, got sore eyes*.

Last, though strictly not a method, creative experimentation with words is worth noting because Artemidorus himself advocates its use for troublesome dreams. He writes:

> But we must employ further art to mutilated dreams (τοῖς καταπήροις) or, as it were, dreams that have nothing to hold on to and especially to difficult ones (ἀπόροις[25]) where certain letters or a word are seen not to contain a complete thought. Sometimes you must place [oneiric] items differently (μετατιθέντα), sometimes change them around (ἀλλάσσοντα), sometimes add (προστιθέντα) letters or syllables, but at other times you must think up numerically equivalent words through which the meaning (λόγος) might become clearer (I.11).

Artemidorus' Oneirocritical Program

Concerning the employment of his oneirocritical methods of interpretation, let us recall the oneiromantical program of Quintus

Cicero in the previous chapter. Quintus argues that it is possible to establish correlations among signs of dreams and future events. Thereby, one can also know whether a certain dream is prophetic or not before it turns out or fails to turn out true. In short, in such a manner, through careful observation and attention to detail over time, an oneirocritic can fashion a catalog of oneiric signs and future events that may be judged prophetic or not by an appeal to the strength of the correlation between signs and events.

Artemidorus clearly recognizes that an oneirocritical program like that of Quintus is oversimplified. He constantly reminds us that it is not only a bald look at oneiric content that determines an interpretation. The circumstances of the dreamer at the time of the dream, both at the general and specific levels, influence interpretation as well. In other words, the same prophetic dream can mean different things for different people under different circumstances. Adding these attendant circumstances to the picture, Artemidorus' account might be generalized in the following manner:

> All dreams of type o, given the generic circumstances attending the dream, $(\gamma_1,\ldots,\gamma_n)$ as well as the idiosyncratic circumstances $(\iota_1,\ldots,\iota_n)$, portend events of type τ.

To illustrate, at III.62 Artemidorus says that "marketplace" (ἀγορά) in general is a sign of confusion (θορύβος) and tumult (ταραχή) because of the large crowds that gather there. But for those who live there (particular modifying circumstance), it is auspicious. An empty marketplace in general indicates much safety (πολλὴ ἀσφάλεια), while it is inauspicious for those who live there, since it indicates unemployment (ἀπραξία).

Evaluation of Oneirocritical Program

I now turn to the serviceability of Artemidorus' methods of interpretation. Here problems abound, the most important of which is how Artemidorus knew when to use one method of interpretation in preference to another.

Perhaps addressing this problem, Artemidorus gives many guidelines for interpretation scattered throughout the five books. Since these are too numerous for an exhaustive study, I take a selective, though representative, look at those dealing with dreams at a more general level.

At IV.68, Artemidorus relates that all things seen in sleep that "move in the same way" have the same interpretation. "Serpent" (δράκων) means the same thing as "wheel" (τροχός), since both move "with their entire body". According to such reasoning, many aquatic animals should be interpretable as "serpent" or "wheel". Yet, for instance, his interpretations of dreams about "fishes" at II.14 deal almost exclusively with their outward appearances. Furthermore, as the comparison of wheel and snake shows, "moving in the same way" can mean very many things. The analogical reasoning here is anything but tight and compelling.

Additionally, he tells his son to divide compound dreams into their main components and interpret each of these separately. He then gives an example of someone dreaming of *sailing and then getting out of the boat and walking upon the sea* and calls "sailing" and "walking upon the sea" components (IV.35). Why *getting out of the boat* is not a third main component, he does not say. What is lacking is a rule for what makes something a "main component" of a dream.

IV.20 says that whatever always follows in waking life follows necessarily in dreaming life also.[26] Consequently, a man who dreamed that *he had sexual intercourse with his mother* woke and *antogonized his father*, since, if he had taken pleasure with his mother when awake, he would have antagonized his father afterward.[27] Likewise, a dream of *eating the flesh of another's child* should bring about guilt, disgust, a desire for retribution by the child's father, or some such thing. Instead, at I.70, he only mentions that it signifies good luck.

Throughout Artemidorus shows disregard for consistency. One can almost arbitrarily pick out a particular guideline and search for and find another that explicitly contradicts it. This makes interpretation relatively arbitrary. A few instances suffice for illustration.

Artemidorus remarks that interpretations of dreams not fully remembered must remain doubtful because everything in a dream is important (I.12, III.66, IV.3, 28, 72) and the slightest omission can change the entire meaning (I.9, IV.4). Yet at IV.42 he says that certain things seen by one entering a house—like vestibules, doorposts, and lintel—are in dreams only for embellishment. At IV.63, he even cautions against seeing too much hidden meaning in dreams, for the gods do not involve men in so much twaddle. At IV.4 he says that the more universal custom always prevails over the less universal custom in interpretation. Yet as he often remarks, the particular circumstances of the dreamer at the time of the dream almost always change the entire meaning of the dream.[28] IV.proem states that *enupnia* do not occur to those who practice a good and morally upright way of living; instead, only the masses, being led on by their desires and fears, have such dreams. Yet among the list of dreams given in Book V, he mentions prophetic dreams of a household servant (οἰκέτης) (V.23), a gladiator (μονομάχος) (V.58), and a slave (δοῦλος) (V.85).

In short, the guidelines, having been woven into the fabric of the work in a tendentious and unstructured manner, afford little assistance in enabling an interpreter to get at the meaning of any "prophetic" dream. They exist in abundance within the *Onirocritica* and merely add to rather than clear up the overall confusion. Instead, they steer oneirocritics in innumerable directions.

For illustration, let us look at one of Artemidorus' own examples of how readily his work facilitates correct interpretation. At the end of Book III, he acknowledges the difficulties involved in oneirocriticism and offers "some small and easy-to-follow suggestions" (μικράς τινας καὶ εὐπαρακολουθήτους ὑποθήκας) to add to what has already been said. Here he considers hypothetically a dream of a poor man (with a rich father) who sees in sleep that *he dies because a lion removes his head.* The interpretation is that *the father will die and declare him, the son, heir* because "head" (κεφαλή) is a symbol for "father" (πατήρ), "lion" (λέων) is a symbol for "king" (βασιλεύς) or "illness" (νόσος), and "the death of poor men" (τοῖς πενομένοις τὸ ἀποθανεῖν) is a symbol of something "advantageous" (λυσιτελές) or "useful" (χρηστόν). Each of the significant elements fits into the whole, which in turn confirms the interpretation of the elements (III.66). Schematically:

> *Lion* (~~king~~/illness) removes *his head* (his father) and *he [a poor man] dies* (advantage/utility).

Given this simple depiction, it seems that the only other possible interpretation is that *his father dies, because of a king, and the son comes to some advantage*. Yet the particular circumstances surrounding the dreamer at the time of the dream are an indefinitely large set for any individual. Why was "poor man" picked by Artemidorus and not, say, "husbandman" or "young man"? In the case of any real dream, his choice would be fairly arbitrary: Having chosen one, there would be many possible interpretations he did not consider.[29] At the very least, he would owe some explanation of why he preferred the particular circumstance that he chose from the indefinitely large set that surrounded the dreamer at the time of the dream. Consequently, perhaps the most significant feature of Artemidorus' oneirocritical program—his insistence that the attendant circumstances play a crucial role in the interpretation—winds up also as one of the greatest practicable defects of the whole program.

In addition, if we consider what Artemidorus states elsewhere about these symbols, the number of possible combinations increases dramatically. At II.12, he says that "lion" also represents "fear", "threats from leonine men", or "fire". IV.56 adds that it signifies "noble men", "free-spirited men", "energetic men", or "formidable men". In all, there are nine possible significations. At I.21 we learn that "head" in general is a sign for "one's relations". At I.35, we learn that it signifies "children", "wife", "an overseer", and, if a person has more than one of these three, "head" signifies the most important of them. It also is a sign of "what is most excellent" (IV.25). In all, there are minimally six things to which it refers. Last, allowing the unlikely circumstance that the dreamer's being a poor man is the most prominent or most relevant circumstance at the time of the dream, II.69 tells us that "poor man" also portends "false hopes". Thus, "death of false hopes" indicates perhaps "realistic perspective" in addition to "advantage". In all, this parsimonious analysis demonstrates that there are at least 108 possible interpretations! And this is supposed to be a paradigmatic example to show how easily, when done properly, one can arrive at the "right" interpretation?

In sum, the guidelines for application do more to confound matters than to alleviate uncertainty. Artemidorus' insistence that what is most important or relevant of the dreamer's attendant circumstances is part of the interpretation is the very thing that makes his program unserviceable, since it is posited without any guidelines for how to cull from the indefinitely large set of attendant circumstances at the time of the dream. When he does show how an "unexpected" outcome is just what is expected, given a particular circumstance of the dreamer, it is generally done after-the-fact.[30]

On all levels, the number of circumstances surrounding any dreamer at the time of a dream is indefinitely large. With no means to cull relevant from irrelevant circumstances, oneiric interpretation becomes a vagarious "science". There can always be more than one reasonable interpretation within such a system.[31] An oneirocritic can find an interpretation for every prophetic dream by digging deeply into the personal circumstances of a dreamer. What is worse, *enupnia* on such a program can easily be interpreted prophetically.[32] It is fair to say that given the rules of Artemidorus' art, there is no *conceivable* dream that cannot be "shown" prophetic. Judging from Artemidorus' own objectives—to provide dissenters with such a sober account of oneiric prophecy that they can do no other than believe in it and to give nondissenters an accurate treatment of oneirocriticism—the *Onirocritica* fall short of its aims.

Artemidorean Oneirocriticism as Science

I have shown that Artemidorus' methods of oneirocriticism and their guidelines for application were impossible to employ systematically and not always consistent. These defects would unquestionably make his oneirocriticism unscientific for our time, but do they make it unscientific for Artemidorus' time?

In answer to this question, I return to what I have emphasized earlier in this book: Ancient Greeks and Romans had nothing comparable to our notion of science today. Consequently, an evaluation by contemporary standards is fruitless. Nonetheless, how well does Artemidorus' oneirocritical science stand up to ancient canons of science?

Following Aristotle's threefold division of scientific investigation (see chapter one), Artemidorus' oneirocriticism is an admixture of both technical and empirical science. At the technical level, it critically involves knowledge of universal principles and is not governed by chance. In addition, it concerns knowledge for the sake of some end—successful interpretation of each allegorical dream's meaning. At the empirical level, Artemidorus asserts that it is experience that separates his work from those of others. Though he postulates universal principles of interpretation, he recognizes that experience of particulars may alter or modify interpretation that is guided by these principles. Experience, he constantly boasts, is the final arbiter.

As a whole, Artemidorus' program is eclectic, though it is predominantly empirical. While he frequently refers to or falls back upon rules and principles of interpretation in his *Onirocritica*, these are not inviolable canons that uniquely determine the interpretation of a dream. Instead they function merely as heuristics to guide interpretation where there is a dearth of experience. Their worth too, as the language Artemidorus employs when referring to them suggests, is no greater than the experience upon which they are founded. Thus, it is difficult to fault him for inconsistencies in his work, since consistency was no prerequisite of ancient empirical science as described by Aristotle or as practiced in antiquity (e.g., empirical medical science). Empirical science was judged by its utility or success, not by adherence to established, inviolable principles. So, if Artemidorus' *Onirocritica* has proven itself not to be a fully serviceable text for interpreting dreams, it is because, being mostly an empirically driven text, it could not have been one. For empiricists, experience guides but can never determine practice, since no amount of experience can be welded into an unbreakable rule.

Concluding Remarks

In closing, Artemidorean oneirocriticism, judged by its aims of striving to battle those who would do away with oneirocriticism and of providing believers with an accurate treatment of the subject, was ambitious but ultimately unsuccessful. Yet given the notion of science in antiquity, the failure is not one of lack of science; it is not even the result of bad science. The shortcomings of his overall program are more the effect of the slipperiness of the phenomena that he was trying to explain.

Overall, Artemidorus should be lauded for his realization that many factors—external, attendant circumstances as well as psychological and physiological elements—go into the making and interpretation of dreams. Recognizing this, Artemidorus was faced with difficulties that were insuperable for his time—difficulties that plague theoreticians today. One might even say that our nonprophetic science of the interpretation of dreams today has not gone much further in its understanding of the meaning of dreams.

---

[1] See also I.proem, 32, II.37, 66, 70, III.28, 66, IV.4, 20, and V.proem.

[2] Believed to be Maximus of Tyre. See Blum (1936, 23) and Pack's introductory comments to his edition of the *Oniroc.* (1963, xxv-xxvi).

[3] See also III.proem and 66.

[4] The language throughout is Attic and often in the popular vernacular, sometimes crudely and even vulgarly expressed. Claes Blum believes that this is not the direct result of popular speech or later textual corruption, but of drawing from the mantic literature of his time, namely astrological literature (1936, 23-51). See also Behr 1968, 181 fn. 21.

[5] Artemidorus tells us that, rather than acquiring and mulling through every book on dreams he could find, his procedure was to consort with "the much maligned diviners of the marketplace" (I.proem).

[6] Concerning how Artemidorus arrived at his classification, Blum says that external and internal evidence point to Posidonius as his ultimate source (externally, the parallels in Macrobius and Chalcidius; internally, the themes of morality and divination, the link of prophetic dreams with a κίνησις of the soul, and the notion of the image producing activity of the soul). He adds that Hermippus of Berytus (believed by Waszink [1947, 474-475] to be the source of Tertullian's classification) could be the immediate source (1936, 71, 80-91).

[7] The same examples given by Aristotle at *Insomn.* 460b5-8.

[8] Cf. Lucretius' *Nat.* IV.1024-1025.

[9] Cf. Macrobius' *Somn.Scip.* I.iii.3.

[10] If not, *oneiros* may have come from of "telling" (τὸ εἴρειν) "what is real" (τὸ ὄν) (I.1).

[11] Allegorical dreams are divided into five subclasses or forms (εἴδη): personal (ἴδίοι) (about and having consequences for the dreamer alone), alien (ἀλλοτρίοι) (about and having consequences for another seen in the dream, if familiar), common (κοινά) (about and having consequences for the dreamer and the acquaintances seen in the dream), public (δημόσια) (about market places, gymnasia, harbors, and the public monuments of the city), and, last, cosmic (κοσμικά) (about cosmic conditions) (I.2). Furthermore, each of these can be understood generically and specifically, and there are four types of each (I.3). In all, given that dreams can occur in agreement with or contrary to reality, there are 80 different possible combinations of allegorical dreams.

[12] Macrobius gives us a fuller version of this classification in his fourth century work *Somn.Scip. Enupnion* he defines in much the same way as

Artemidorus does. For the mental variety, caused by mental distress, the lover dreams of his beloved, while the fearful man sees his enemy in sleep. For the physical kind, one overindulgent in eating or tippling sees himself choking or eliminating the burden, while one hungry or thirsty dreams of searching and finding food or drink. Such irrational fancies flee once the sleeper awakens (I.iii.4-5). *Phantasma*, which Artemidorus mentions but fails to discuss (*Oniroc.* I.2), comes about for Macrobius in the first clouds of sleep. The sleeper, believing himself still awake, sees all kinds and sizes of specters and creatures flitting about (I.iii.7). Like *enupia*, these have no prophetic value (I.iii.8). In contrast, *chrematismos*, *horoma*, and *oneiros* are predictive. *Chrematismos* occurs when a parent, pious man, priest, or god reveals what will come about or what the dreamer should do or avoid doing (I.iii.8). *Horoma* corresponds to Artemidorus' theorematic dream, being a dream that turns out true precisely in the manner in which it was dreamed (I.iii.9). Last, *oneiros* corresponds to Artemidorus' allegorical dream in that it veils through signs what it portends. Here Macrobius gives us the same five subkinds: personal (*proprium*), alien (*alienum*), common (*commune*), public (*publicum*), and cosmic (*generale*) (I.iii.10-11).

[13] I.8-9 and IV.2 explain that there are both general and idiosyncratic customs. The former include sacred mysteries, festivals, national games, and marriage; the latter involve clothing, food, and hairstyle.

[14] This conforms neatly to diagnosis in Hippocratic and, later, Empirical medical practice. E.g., the Hippocratic author of *Epid.* states that, in forming a judgment about disease, both general and personal circumstances must be taken into account, even dreams (I.iii.1).

[15] Immediately after, Artemidorus says that *the greater custom prevails over the lesser in interpretation* and supports this with an example contrary to the potter's dream. Aristides, who customarily wore white as a barrister, dreamed that *he wore white*. He soon died, not mindful that *dead wearing white* is a more universal custom than *barrister wearing white*. Artemidorus makes little use of this principle throughout. His *modus operandi* in oneirocriticism is overwhelmingly to regard the particular circumstances as superior to the general circumstances (e.g., I.9, 13, II.36, 45, IV.2, 59, & 67.) The example at IV.2 is the only contrary example of which I am aware.

[16] See also I.13, II.36, 45, IV.2, 4, & 67.

[17] Literalness, obviously, is the method employed for theorematic dreams, which unambiguously and clearly portend their outcomes.

[18] This example was a footnote added to the great work in 1911, Freud states, "this is the nicest instance of dream interpretation which has reached us from ancient times...based on a play in words" (1993, 99).

[19] Due to the similarities of some of the methods (i.e., metonymy and homynomy) and inherent textual difficulties, my subsumption of certain of Artemidorus' examples is sometimes fairly arbitrary.

[20] Since the words πεζῇ (on foot), πέδαι (fetters), ἀνγελία (message), μένε (remain), and νέμε (pasture) each have letters whose value, when added together, equals "100", anyone of these words is interpretable as any of the others. For instance, πεζῇ = νέμε, since (π + ε + ζ + η = 80 + 5 + 7 + 8 = 100) and (ν + ε + μ + ε = 50 + 5 + 40 + 5 = 100). For more, see White's

commentary on the *Oniroc.* (1975, 290-291). Concerning the nonnumerical significance of letters in dreams, he mentions that when the Jewish war was being waged in Cyrene, a military commander dreamed of *the letters ι, κ, and θ being on his sword.* Since the ι signified 'Ιουδαίοις (for the Jews), the κ signified Κυρηναίοις (at Cyrene), and the θ signified θάνατος (death), the dream foretold of *great fame for the commander* (IV.24). See also II.70 & IV.23).

[21] Other instances of analogy occur at I.80, II.6, 10, 12, 36, 37, 61, 68, III.16, 26, 28, 41, IV.30, 65, 66, and V.87.

[22] Other instances occur at I.26, 45, 78, 79, II.12, 14, 24, 26, 32, 35, III.58, IV.80, V.59, and 89. Near homonyms occur at I.70, II.12, 24, and III.35.

[23] See also I.17, 22, 44, 45, 78, 79, II.12, 32, 36, 37, 45, 68, III.28, IV.4, and 18.

[24] See also I.4, 77, II.4, 5, 10, IV.43, and 47.

[25] 'Απείροις in manuscript **V**.

[26] See also III.66.

[27] At I.79 Artemidorus states that dreams of intercourse with one's mother admit of multiple interpretations, depending upon the manner of embraces and the various bodily positions during the event.

[28] E.g., I.13, 35, IV.59, and 67. At most, the more universal custom provides an interpretive base for the oneirocritic.

[29] See also Blum (1936, 73) and Meseguer (1961, 17).

[30] See, for example, IV.8, 27, 59, V.3, or 39.

[31] Cf. Cicero, *Div.* II.144-145.

[32] Artemidorus states of the difficulties in distinguishing between *oneiroi* and *enupnia* at I.1: "Therefore, it is possible to see these things not as aiming at a prediction of what will be, but as attempting to call to mind what is, since the affections already underlie [in *enupnia*]". The logical modality of the sentence here clearly indicates that even Artemidorus recognized that *enupnia* were often indistinguishable by content from *oneiroi*. More importantly, given his characterization of nonprophetic dreams, there is a host of prophetic dreams in the five books that could easily be categorized as nonprophetic (e.g., II.26, dream of sitting on a firm night stool and discharging much fecal matter).

Chapter Seven
Synesius' Mantic Science in *On Dreams*

Introduction

By the second century A. D., the belief that mediating powers between gods and men (i.e., angels, demons, or spirits) filled the upper regions was nearly universal in Greco-Roman culture. This *Weltanschauung* was the culmination of a type of soul/body dualism, beginning roughly in the fifth-century B. C., in which the soul was seen as an unwilling captive of the body. During sleep, however, the body's tight reigns on the soul were loosened and the soul became free through dreams to pursue its own, nobler interests. In some dreams, the soul was said to leave the body and to commingle with mediate spirits. In others, the soul, unimpeded by the baser physical interests of the body, was thought to remain in the body and to receive divine communications. This notion of mediate spirits and divine communication through dreams was characteristic of Stoic philosophy. It was also fundamental to Neoplatonism, an important philosophic genre in the Late Roman Republic, evident in such writers as Philo Judaeus,[1] Iamblichus,[2] and, the focus of this chapter, Synesius of Cyrene (c. 365-c. 414 A.D.). In what follows, I look at a treatise of Synesius known as *On Dreams*.

Caught in the latter fourth-century A. D. battleground of Hellenic paganism and Christianity, Synesius was inquisitive in nature and of complex character. Though he was a pagan, he was appointed bishop of Ptolemais by Theodorus in 410 A. D., a few years after *On Dreams*.[3]

On Dreams itself was written between 404-406 A. D., while Synesius was in Alexandria.[4] This work is not a systematic treatment of dreams, but a loose collection of engaging oneiric insights in stream-of-consciousness style as well as a paean to the excellence of divine prophecy through dreams. It is the best example of a study of dreams in Neoplatonism.

Avowedly written while he was inspired, the work has been much lauded by psychologists for its depth of insight. Morton Kelsey calls it "the most thoughtful and sophisticated consideration of dreams to be found until we come to the modern studies of Freud and Jung".[5] Erich Fromm, quoting the beginning of Synesius' work, says that the author "makes one of the most precise and beautiful statements of the theory that dreams stem from the heightened capacity of insight during sleep".[6] Though thoughtful and beautiful in places, there is little that is sophisticated or precise in *On Dreams*. The work is sometimes contradictory and often obscure, and there is scant regard for grammatical soundness in its composition. Consequently, a clear, exact, and consistent articulation of Synesius' views on dreams is an impossible task and this, of course, makes philosophical (and philological) analysis even more tedious.[7] Yet this is the approach that I undertake here—essaying to disclose for Synesius a consistent account of the kinds of dreams, the nature of dreaming, and the art of oneiromancy, insofar as the work allows. (I follow the enumerated columns in the text of Migne throughout.)

Phantasia, *Pneuma* and the Neoplatonic Cosmos

Synesius prefaces *On Dreams* by saying that he follows the tradition of Plato in veiling profound philosophic thoughts by a light treatment of dreams. In concealing the profundity, he says, he is making the account inaccessible to the profane[8] (1281b). Synesius begins:

> If dreams (ὕπνοι[9]) are prophets and the things seen in them offer for people who reach out to them (τοῖς ἀνθρώποις ὀρέγουσι[10]) puzzles of what will come about in waking reality, then they would be wise but not clear prophets. Indeed, their wisdom is just their lack of clarity. For the gods keep life concealed[11] (1281c).

In the second section, Synesius speaks of the cosmic interdependence of all things (Σημαίνει...διὰ πάντων πάντα) (1284d) in Platonic and Stoic fashion.[12] We are "brothers in a single living being (ἐν ἑνὶ ζώῳ), the cosmos", which allows for an understanding of how arbitrary signs in dreams can signify seemingly unrelated outcomes (1284d). "And he who knows the relationship of the parts of the cosmos", he adds, "is wise" (1285a).

Section III begins by informing us that, though prophetic dreams are obscure, they share obscurity with the commonly accepted ritualistic initiations and oracular responses.[13] Yet the prophecies in sleep have an advantage over other divine blessings. Coming from within us, dreams are personal prophecies and thereby readily accessible. It follows that we ought to embrace oneiric prophecy, not shun it. For in wakefulness the one who teaches is man; while a god, through courage, instructs dreamers in sleep (1288a and 1289a).

At 1288b, we discover that *nous* holds possession of the forms of being (τὰ εἴδη τῶν ὄντων); *psyche*, in turn, holds possession of the forms of becoming (τὰ εἴδη τῶν γινομένων).[14] The latter puts forward only what concerns it and mirrors the *phantasia* (here, an image) of these generated things. Yet ultimately, it is *phantasia* (here, the faculty generating images) where impressions are initially received, that indicates to us what will be through dreams.

The end of 1288b on through to the end of Section V is part of a lengthy, yet discursive, description of the faculty of *phantasia* and the *pneuma* that it utilizes.[15] Considered in itself, *phantasia* seems to be a living being, capable of perception and of governing the other senses. It perceives things through its own sensory organs (αἰσθητήρια) with the whole of its *pneuma*, even when the bodily sense organs are at rest.[16] It distributes its powers to each part of the body and each power stretches out separately from the center of the living being, then loops around back to this center. Moreover, *phantasia* is the "perception of perceptions,[17] because this imaginative *pneuma* (τὸ φανταστικὸν πνεῦμα) is the most common sense organ and the first body of the soul",[18] since this *pneuma* governs each living being. Thus, perceiving by means of *phantasia* is a more divine, direct way of perceiving, in contrast to the bestial and common means of sensing through bodily organs[19] (1288c-1289d).

Phantasia is not a part of the soul, but a personal vehicle for the soul (ἴδιον ὄχημα). It exists at the borders of reason and unreason, body and nonbody, and what is divine and what is demonic. Through *pneuma*, *phantasia* borrows from each of these extremes as it transports the soul (1292b-c). *Pneuma* enters into the physical cosmos from the realm of intelligibles and unites with bodies to become the elements of *phantasia* (1297b). It descends even into animals without reason and guides their behavior.[20] "Whole races of demons", he adds, "have existence by such a life (i.e., *phantasia*)" (1292d). Yet *phantasia* also enables the inferior elements in us (the corporeal or irrational elements) to accompany the soul as it ascends upward as far as the "summit of the elements"—the realms of fire and air (1293c).

During sleep, by virtue of its *pneuma*, *phantasia* conveys the soul to all parts of the cosmos, obtains true impressions of things, and either draws one to god or creates a vacuum for evil spirits.[21] Synesius adds that whoever keeps this imaginative *pneuma* pure through living according to nature has in dreams a readily disposed tool for personal gain (1292b). Souls that live moderately become light; those acting otherwise are sullied and become heavy. The former, by virtue of their warmth and dryness, ascend to the gods, while thick and dry souls sink into the hollows of the earth, where other moist spirits lurk[22] (1293a).

The rest of section V on through to section VI discusses at length the voyages of pure and corrupt souls via the imaginative *pneuma* to the extremes of light and darkness, especially during sleep. He tells us that when one's imaginative *pneuma* is pure and well defined, it receives true impressions of things that are (ἀληθῆ τῶν ὄντων ἐκμαγεῖα) (1297d-1300b). Against the things that might injure the *pneuma*, intellectual application (νοερὰ ἐπιβολή) is our most incisive weapon, for it refines the *pneuma* and raises it toward god. In contrast, in those whose intellect is shrunk and condensed through desuetude, a wicked *pneuma* (πονηρὸν πνεῦμα) enters (1300b-c).

Dreams and Self-Understanding

Sections VII and VIII concern the ritualistic initiation into the art of prophecy through dreams. In VII, he illustrates the ease of prophecy by dreams:

> I think it worthy to have at my side this art of prophecy (μαντική) and to leave it behind to my children. By this art, it is not necessary for those who have readied themselves to go on a long journey or a foreign voyage, as if to Pytho or to Hammon. It is enough that they, after having washed their hands and observed a solemn silence, fall asleep (1301b).

Section VIII tells us that no one is privileged by social status. The god appears to one who is worth 500 *medimnoi* as well as to the person worth 300 *medimnoi*, to the yeoman as well as to one who works the boundary lands to eke out a living, to the galley slave as well as to the journeyman, and to the taxpayer exempt from the *metoikion*[23] (ὁ ἰσοτελής[24]) as well as to him who pays the *metoikion* (1301c-d). Concerning the prophetic art's virtues, Synesius says: "Its democratic nature is especially humane, and its plain and artless quality is especially philosophic, even its lack of force is pious" (1304a). In addition, oneiric prophecy employs no tools and happens at no inconvenient time for the sleeper (1304a-b). Each person is his own instrument (1304c).

Synesius says that everything from what is worst to what is most profitable is found in dreams, and because of this, even the most misfortunate are moved by hope through dreams (1304d-1305a). Because of hope, a man in fetters dreams he enters the army, immediately becomes a lieutenant, then a captain, and last a general, who gets crowned by garlands on account of military victories (1305b). He summarizes this cryptically, "And yet, all this is the waking reality of the dreamer (ὕπαρ...ὀνειρώττοντος) and the dream of one who has awakened (ἐγρηγορότος ἐνύπνιον),[25] for both are engaged in the same underlying state, the imaginative nature (τὴν φανταστικὴν φύσιν)". When awake, *phantasia* enables us to make mental images (εἰδωλοποιεῖν) whenever we wish; in sleep, such images are formed spontaneously as a pledge from the god (1305b-c).

Synesius then states that if Homer's Penelope did truly tell us that two different gates allow the passage of dreams—one for deceitful dreams and another for true ones—then she must have lacked a correct knowledge of the nature of dreams. "If she had understood the art (τέχνη) concerning these things, she would have let all dreams pass through the gate of horn". Synesius means that the apparent deceitfulness of "false" dreams is just an inability to grasp the divine riddle through the proper use of the prophetic art (μαντικὴ τέχνη)[26] (1305d-1307a). Along these lines, Synesius tries to show that the baneful dream that Zeus had sent to Agamemnon (*Il.* II.5-84) was no deceitful dream, but merely a prophecy misinterpreted (1307a-b).

Section IX is a testimony of the efficacy of dreams in people's lives, especially his own. He says here that dreams help to make clear or explain some of the problems people encounter while awake. At one moment in a dream, one seems to be inquiring into some matter, while at the very next moment one is pondering a solution (1308c). He adds that dreams have helped him in his own writings to bring forward the right words, to add something here, or to excise something there. They also have admonished and assisted him regarding his speaking: They have told him to avoid novel uses of archaic Attic and have helped to smooth out roughness, to cut out excrescences, and to give and explain neologisms. In sum, they have restored sobriety to his diction (1308c). Moreover, dreams have enabled Synesius to devise clever hunting strategies (1308c-d) and had also greatly assisted him when he was an ambassador (1308d-1309a).

Clear and Enigmatic Dreams

At section X, Synesius talks about the kinds of dreams:

> Indeed, these kinds of dreams (i.e., his own and those of other upstanding people)[27] are more divine, and are either wholly or almost wholly clear and obvious, and require art least of all. But

> they can assist only those who live in accordance with virtue that has come about through intellect or habit. And if at any time [such] dreams should come to any other [nonvirtuous] person, they would certainly come with difficulty. For there is no good reason that a dream of the best kind will be present to anyone whatsoever (τῷ τυχόντι). The remaining and by far the most common sort (τὸ λοιπὸν...γένος) [of dream], then, would be the enigmatic dream (τὸ ᾐνιγμένον), for which it is necessary that art be provided. For it has had an origin (γένεσιν...ἔσχεν), so to speak, unusual (ἄτοπον) and different ἀλλόκοτον). And, as it has sprung from such origins, what is most unclear advances[28] (ὡς ἐκ τῶν τοιούτων βλαστῆσαν ἀσαφέστατον πρόεισιν[29]) (1309b).

Is Synesius positing here that two types of divinely prophetic dreams exist—one clear and one enigmatic—or are the differences more nominal than actual?[30] It seems plausible that Synesius' intention is not a strict demarcation into types. If so, then there is only one type of dream for Synesius, the divinely prophetic dream, and he is merely following a common oneiric tradition that virtuous people have better, less puzzling dreams, while those who are base have enigmatic dreams.[31] As with the Stoics (see chapter five), the fault here lies not with the dream, but with the purity of a dreamer's soul.

Behr, who takes this approach, argues that the varieties of prophetic dreams for Synesius are explicable merely by the moral nature of the dreamers—the condition of their soul. He writes, "Among prophetic dreams, Synesius distinguishes gradations, which range, depending on the purity of the soul, from the highly sanctified and restricted 'presentation of being,' through dreams whose unreal images are distorted in various degrees…".[32]

Fitzgerald, too, takes this line. He states that an illuminated and dry soul has a higher destiny than a heavy, moist soul. As the soul is, so is the imagination; only a virtuous soul can receive clear images. It is, therefore, up to all people to keep their imagination pure to enable it to have unclouded dreams.[33]

Nonetheless, 1309b introduces a difficulty for this view. Here Synesius says that this most common sort of dream has *an origin* (γένεσις) that is unusual (ἄτοπον) and different (ἀλλόκοτον[34]). "And, as it has sprung from such origins (ἐκ τῶν τοιούτων), what is most unclear advances". It seems obvious that it is the difference and strangeness of the origin of enigmatic dreams that accounts for their obscurity. Having an origin that is different from that of clear, divine dreams suggests that there are two types of divinely prophetic dreams. Yet just what is this different origin?

The Platonic characterization of enigmatic dreams[35] that immediately follows 1309b tells us what this different origin is.

Nature, he says, possesses all the things that have come into being, all the things that are, and all the things that will come into being. From these, as combinations of form and matter, images flow off (ἀπο'ρῥεόντα εἰδώλων). The images of *things that have come into being* are distinct initially and dull with time. The images of *things that are* are truest to life and most distinct. Finally and most importantly, the images of *things that will be* are the most indefinite and indistinct. Falling in with the psychic or imaginative *pneuma*, these images find a suitable home and the imaginative *pneuma* within each of us is a most clear mirror of all these.

> In this manner, art too is necessary for the things that will be, for shadowy images proceed from them, and the likenesses [from future things] are not manifest as they are from the things that are. In truth, they are by nature extraordinary, even as they are, because they have come about from things that have not yet happened (1309b-1312a).

In short, the origin of enigmatic dreams is found though the images that emanate from future things, whose nature is obscure. The description, however, suggests that they are enigmatic due to the tenuity of their images; if the images responsible for such dreams are shadowy, the dreams themselves should appear shadowy and difficult to perceive. The passage at 1309b strongly suggests, since these images are somewhat muddled, that these are the prophetic dreams of baser sorts of people.

Against Fitzgerald and Behr, I argue that there are two distinct types of prophetic dreams distinguishable by genesis: the clear dreams of virtuous people and the enigmatic ones of the nonvirtuous. Yet this seems to generate more questions. First, what is the different origin of clear, prophetic dreams? At this point, the only plausible candidate is that they are caused by the images of the things that are, but this, of course, would be to say that clear, prophetic dreams have their origin in things that presently exist, which seems absurd. Next, since the account of enigmatic dreams is wholly naturalistic, why is it that those who live virtuously will tend not to have such dreams? Last, given that obscurity is one of the hallmarks of their divinity (1281c-1284a), just what is so divine about enigmatic dreams? I return to these questions later.

Oneiromancy as Idiosyncratic Science

Section XI states that we should prepare ourselves to receive clear dreams by calming the divine *pneuma* through the study of philosophy and living a moderate and sensible life. He then tells us just how (enigmatic) dreams and the art of their interpretation can assist us (1312a-b).

How there can be an art of interpretation through dreams can be understood by analogy. Mariners at sea, when first they see a rock and then a city of men, will take the former as a sign of the latter. If a ship's skipper fails to take the rock as a sign of the city, then he is at fault for not utiliing a helpful sign. In a similar manner, anyone who has often seen something without noticing that it portends another thing is equally a fool. The conclusion is obvious: Certain dreams clearly portend specific outcomes and those who fail to notice this or put it to good use have only themselves to reproach (1312b-c). Yet this analogy is of limited use. The portents for the skipper are clear enough if only he chooses to observe them, while shadowy likenesses of future things responsible for the enigmatic images in dreams are not clear even for those who choose to regard them (1312a).

Next, he tackles the query of general rules or nonidiosyncratic elements of oneiromancy. Aristotle and reason assert that from sensation comes memory, from memory comes experience, and from experience comes art.[36] Now, he adds, this may be adequate for developing a science from waking perceptions and experiences, but it will not work for dreams. Along these lines, Synesius says, many useless books on dreams have been written. The imaginative *pneuma* for each of us is unique, because the *pneuma*, which enables us to have prophetic images in dreams, streams off from different astral spheres for each person and, thus, affects each person differently (1313a-b).[37] And so, he asks, "In things unlike in nature (φύσις), law (νόμος), and affection (πάθος),[38] how do the same things appear through the same [dreams]?" They cannot (1312d-1313c). So, how is an art of oneiromancy possible?

The answer comes in section XII and this is where Synesius deviates most noticeably from Artemidorus and other oneirocritics. No man, he says, is under the same laws; each person is his own best interpreter (1313d-1316a). Having a peculiar astral influence, the personal experiences of each dreamer are unique and this uniqueness prohibits any secure generalizations concerning oneiric elements and future outcomes.[39] As a consequence, Synesius encourages everyone to keep a log of both waking and sleeping visions (ὕπαρ καί ὄναρ ὁράματα), for this will enable each person to develop technical principles of interpretation for himself (1316a-b).

Schematically, Synesius' program looks something like this:

> All dreams of type o, given the idiosyncratic circumstances at the time of the dream ($\iota_1,\ldots,\iota_n$) for any one dreamer, portend events of type τ for that person.

Synesius, as we have seen, is not looking for laws of interpretation—rules categorically applicable to and useful for all dreamers everywhere. He is not even looking for customary or cultural similarities in dreams. The circumstances surrounding each dreamer at the time of each dream, the $\iota_1,\ldots,\iota_\nu$ depicted above, are not generalizable to other dreamers. For Synesius, they are peculiar to each sleeper.

It follows that we would never be in a position to state, as does Artemidorus in his *Onirocritica*, that dreaming of *combing one's hair* is a good sign for all since "comb" signifies "time" and time *untangles and smoothes out what is rough* (*Oniroc.* II.6). What comb means for one dreamer, according to Synesius, would almost certainly differ from its meaning for another. Instead, he thinks, the rules we would find in interpreting our own dreams come from a careful inspection of our own personal circumstances and life history as well as the peculiar astral influence we receive in sleep. In consequence, there are and can be no laws of interpretation: Nothing seen in a dream is and can be a universal or even a cultural or conventional symbol of some future event.

Nevertheless, that there can be no laws of interpretation need not imply that some type of nomological consistency does not exist for all people who examine their dreams. It is probable that for Synesius I may come to know that my dreaming of *combing my hair* is, say, a good sign for me whenever there is a certain set of circumstances unique to me that attend such a dream. Yet this too may change over time.

Formation of Dreams

What these circumstances are depends critically upon one additional query: Precisely how do enigmatic dreams come about? Do the images of these dreams visit dreamers as they sleep or do the souls of sleepers leave their body and mingle with the images? The account at 1309b-1312a tells us merely that enigmatic dreams have an origin different from clear dreams. The former emanate from things that have yet to come into being and fall and rest within the psychical *pneuma*, our vehicle for both what is most and what is least divine. Additionally, he has not told us what the origin of clear, prophetic dreams is.

Solutions to these difficulties, if they exist, lie buried within the tangle of Synesius' inspired prose. Though he tells us that there are two types of divinely prophetic dreams distinguishable by origin, he seems to give us only one account of how we come to have dreams.

Still I think that it is possible to tease out the genetic differences between clear and enigmatic dreams, and I attempt to do so next.

Though *nous* contains the forms of generated things (most importantly, the forms of what will be), *phantasia* is ultimately responsible for gleaning the images of such things (1288b). *Phantasia* is a living being, a governor of the senses, and the most common sense organ. Through it, we perceive more divinely and directly (1288c-1289d). *Phantasia*, in dreams, makes use of the psychical *pneuma*, which is in sympathy with our psychical disposition (ψυχικὴ διαθέσις) (1292b). As souls ascend to the regions of air and fire or descend to the subterranean parts, they carry with them *pneuma* and gain either the divine and lucent influence of good or the dark and material persuasion of evil (1296b-1297d). Purified souls, being warm and dry, tend to ascend; cold, wet, and corrupt souls generally descend (1292a-1293c).

Being warm and dry by nature, purified souls readily ascend as far as the regions of air and fire, though, not being *noi*, they do not reach the realm of intelligibles and can never truly acquire or apprehend the forms of being (1288b). Therefore, we must assume that, among the things souls acquire from these higher regions, they receive images of things yet-to-be, since they have a capacity to do so. Conversely, sullied souls will tend downward to the murky and colder regions where impressions of what will be are themselves murky, indefinite, and deceitful[40] (1297d-1300a). Such souls will be improperly disposed to receive the images from the higher regions, since such images are unsuited to a corrupt nature (1313a-d).

In this manner, two of the three questions posed earlier are solved. First, concerning the different origins of the two types of dreams, purer souls, tending upward by nature, will glean the brighter, more divine images of future things. They will have clear or relatively clear dreams of what will come to be. Contaminated souls tend downward and receive the indistinct and corrupt images of material things yet-to-be, thereby having enigmatic dreams. As such, the origins of clear and enigmatic dreams are different, though the account given both is roughly the same. Second, better people have fewer enigmatic dreams because their souls, while dreaming, spend most of their time in the astral regions, where the images that emanate from objects are clear and distinct as opposed to the obscure and shadowy images of the subterranean regions. Regarding the third query—"What is divine about enigmatic dreams?"—we may respond in Aristotelian fashion that there is more that is demonic than divine about such dreams.[41]

At 1317a, Synesius points out one of the greatest difficulties in coming to terms with dreams—a problem just as prominent today as it was then. How does one relate the incredible, mostly visual experiences in dreams through the plainness of language? He asks: "Furthermore, one conquers and walks and flies *at the same time*[42] (my emphasis) and *phantasia* has room for everything. But how will speech find room?"[43] One soars to the loftiest spheres and looks upon the earth and talks with stars and meets the unobserved gods of the universe[44] (1317a-b). As Freud and others after him have emphasized, our dreams are every bit as grand and absurd at times, and the problem of relating through language what we have dreamed—due to forgetfulness, the length of dreams, and their obscurity or complexity—is every bit as real for us today.

Finally, Synesius tells us in Section XIII that even myths take their authority from dreams (1317c).

Assessment of Synesius' Oneiromancy

By dismissing the possibility of laws or any generalizations for interpreting dreams, Synesius directly challenges the worth of professional oneirocriticism. Professional interpreters of dreams, like Artemidorus, begin with the assumption that elements in dreams have different meanings—from universal or near-universal meanings to those built upon the dreamer's own experiences. Synesius' elements, in contrast, are exclusively idiosyncratic and interpretable only in terms of each dreamer's personal experiences. Moreover, dreams themselves are part of one's experiences. Consequently, by denying what Artemidorus and other oneirocritics assume—that certain elements in dreams have generic meaning—he poses an alluring nomological query for other ancients (and for us today): Can there be an art or science of oneirocriticism if there are no generic elements in dreams?

Synesius certainly believes that there can be such an art even though we are all unlike in nature, law, and affection (1313c). He even tells us in section XII how this can be so. We must simply commit to memory an accurate catalogue of oneiric images along with the events that follow. Thus we should keep logs of our daily and nocturnal experiences and compare the character of these two lives (1316a-b). In short, though the circumstances surrounding our dreams are decidedly unique, this does not mean that each of us cannot match repeated elements in dreams (like themes, symbols, or episodes) with future events in our own lives for some profit. All cultural or conventional influences put aside, I may notice that every time that I dream of *combing my hair*, given certain circumstances, I *receive a windfall* on the very next day. In such a way, Synesius says, I can develop an art of interpretation for my own dreams over time. Yet the question arises: "Is this art a science?"

In our own time, Freud realized the value of symbols in dreams, yet recognized the difficulties in establishing a science of symbolic interpretation. He said of symbolic interpretation that it is "perhaps the most remarkable chapter of the theory of dreams", since symbols are stable translations that "realize to some extent the ideal of the ancient as well as of the popular interpretation of dreams".[45] They are an unconscious knowledge—a legacy from a more primitive time when what is today symbolically connected was likely once a sign of "conceptual and linguistic identity". Nonetheless, he considered symbolic interpretation to be subordinate and complementary to his method of free association, the former to be used to fill in the gaps left behind by free association. Considered by itself, he thought that symbolic interpretation merely follows intuition and is thus exempt from criticism. Therefore, without free association, symbolic interpretation is scientifically unreliable.[46]

There are two important points that Freud makes here. First, concerning scientific methodology, he is saying that an integral and indispensable part of scientific practice is scientific criticism. Science that is immune to scientific criticism—objective standards for testing the reliability of scientific claims—is held in check by the caprice of an individual and so is not science at all, but rather a frivolous form of intellectual self-indulgence. Consequently, independent of scientific criticism, the prophetic science that Synesius takes himself to be promulgating is itself a "baneful dream".[47]

Still, it is reasonable to object that we certainly cannot hold any of these ancient oneirocritics to our standards of observation and collecting and evaluating data. Nevertheless, as we have seen with Cicero and Artemidorus, ancient scientific practice was not immune to the criticisms of the ancient scientific community. Even though satisfied customers were all that was necessary for an oneirocritic to establish himself securely, to gain credibility as a scientist in antiquity, oneirocritics had to respond to the objections of their critics, at least at some level. In dismissing scientific criticism of the interpretation of dreams, Synesius is simply doing shoddy science even by the standards of his own time.

Freud also makes a second point: one related exclusively to dreams. He says that certain oneiric symbols are meaningful because they are universal, unconscious remnants of a common ancestry we all share. Other early twentieth-century pioneers of the scientific study of oneiric content agree with Freud.[48]

Many, if not most, current experts of oneiric content regard nonidiosyncratic symbols, especially cultural or conventional symbols, as important elements in the interpretation of dreams.[49] Synesius' claim that there are no nonidiosyncratic elements in dreams, given his own oneirocritical tradition (as well as what we know of dreams today), seems less motivated by observing oneiric content and more influenced by the tenets of the Neoplatonic epistemology—especially the theory of psychic ecstasy during sleep.

Concluding Remarks

With respect to Synesius' empirical attitude, Fitzgerald writes:

> There was nothing "unscientific" to the mind of Synesius in the idea that dreams portend coming events. It would only be the fulfilment of a natural law, and the whole drift of *Dreams* is rather in the direction of a rationalization of all manners of divining the future, but pointing to the inferiority of these to the law, as he conceived it to be, that operates in dreams.... We must not therefore suppose that Synesius was superstitious because he speaks of magic, incantations, and spells, as the commonplaces of experience. On the contrary he has rather the scientific mind, seeking a rational explanation.[50]

Synesius' mind may not have been unduly superstitious, but by the standards of ancient times, it was not especially scientific either. In the final analysis, Synesius' contribution to oneiromancy—when compared to the Stoic empirical program for a science of oneiromancy or Artemidorus' *Onirocritica*—takes us away from the possibility of an oneiromantical science, prophetic or otherwise. His insistence that there are no generic elements in dreams and that each person is his own best judge of his own dreams exempts Synesius' prophetic art from scientific criticism, a standard acknowledged even during ancient times. Moreover, in ridding dreams of nonidiosyncratic elements, we do away with social, cultural, and possibly even remotely past influences on dreams that undeniably affect many aspects of our waking and subconscious personality. Shunning scientific criticism, we fall into the Heraclitean fog of private understanding: We hold fast merely to what seems to be real, instead of striving for common understanding.[51] In such a fog, no science of oneiromancy could have been possible.

In spite of this defect of Synesius' oneiromantical "art", Synesius must be applauded for proposing that dreams are meaningful and democratic. Each person, from the highest to lowest, can and should use analysis of dreams as an important instrument for self-understanding. Few oneirologists today would disagree.

---

[1] *Insomn.* I.i.2 & II.i.2.
[2] *Myst.* III. 2-3.

[3] Traditionally, scholars have taken this as evidence of a conversion to Christianity. However, internal evidence shows that no conversion ever really took place. For Synesius, the Neoplatonic ideals that he embraced before his bishopric were the same that he upheld thereafter. Historical circumstances led him to the Church, not a change in philosophic vision. For him, the true conflict was not between Christianity and paganism, but between barbarism and Greco-Roman culture, with Christianity being construed a part of the latter. Thus, we need not assume that *On Dreams* represents the ideas of an uninitiated thinker before breaking free from the manacles of Neoplatonism. See Bregman 1982, esp. 13 & 177-184.

[4] Ibid, 61.

[5] Kelsey 1968, 142.

[6] Fromm 1951, 130.

[7] Fitzgerald argues that the difficulties with Synesius' writings, especially the "fascinating and quite untranslatable" *Insomn.* may be dealt with by assuming corruption of the text, obscurity as an artistic device, *and* obscurity as failed clarity (1930, 67-71).

[8] Nicephorus Gregoras (14th century) had this to say about Synesius' treatise on dreams in a letter to a friend. "[T]his work is the best of all that he has written, and he has made every effort that it should appear so.... God inspired him, and he had no recourse to his forces as a man...in this work. He simply lent his pen to it. God did all. Thus the work is the production, so he writes, of a man possessed by a prophetic inspiration, and full of the Divinity. For this reason the greater part of the book has been composed in an obscure style, as were the oracles that the Delphic Tripod gave forth, and that were, as you know, full of prophetic phrases sedulously concealed and unintelligible to the ignorant, phrases which screened them as if behind a curtain of heavy obscurity" (Ibid, 437).

[9] Following Fitzgerald here (Ibid, 326).

[10] In contrast to Fitzgerald's "...to anxious men" (Ibid, 326). "Anxious" has a primary connotation of "troubled" or "worried" and is thus unsuitable for ὀρέγουσι here.

[11] We must not take this too literally, for we learn at 1309b that better people have clearer dreams. He is likely just cautioning against shunning dreams that are unclear. Artemidorus at *Oniroc.* IV.71 tells us that gods send puzzling dreams because, in their wisdom, they do not wish us to accept anything before thoroughly examining it. The Neoplatonist Iamblichus states, "[N]ot only is the presence of the gods manifest in a degree by no means inferior to those who understand such things, but if we must tell the truth, it is necessarily more exact and distinct, and effects a more perfect consciousness in the former case than in the latter" (*Mys.* III.ii.105). Philo in *Insomn.* says that divine matters are clearer at night because mind is then unobscured by the objects of sensation (I.xiv.80-84), adding that a symbolic understanding surmounts literal apprehension (I.xxi.127). See also Plutarch's *Pyth.Or.* XXVI.407e, Plotinus' *Enn.* VI.8.xiii, and Porphyry's *Antr.Nym.* IV-V.

[12] Cf. Plato's *Ti.* and Cicero's *Div.* I.118. See also Plotinus' *Enn.* IV.iv.35.

[13] Synesius' approach to interpreting dreams has more in common with

allegorical approaches to interpretation—characteristic of Philo, Augustine, Macrobius, and Origen—than Quintus Cicero's (*Div.* I) or Artemidorus' (*Oniroc.*) more scientific approach. See Miller 1994, 95.

[14] Precisely the same with Iamblichus (*Myst.* III.iii.106). Plato also believed that dreams give knowledge of the past, present, and future (*R.* IX.571d-572a & *Ti.* 72a).

[15] The theory of *phantasia-pneuma* is difficult to understand due to the rambling nature of the work. For more on *phantasia-pneuma* for Synesius, see Bregman 1982, 145-154, Lang 1926, 45-48, and Kissling 1922, 318-330. For a good account of the crucial role of *pneuma* in Neoplatonism, see Smith's *Porphyry's Place in the Neoplatonic Tradition*—especially Appendix II where the accounts of Porphyry and Plotinus are compared with each other and with other Neoplatonists like Synesius and Iamblichus (1974, 152-158).

[16] This *pneuma*, so indispensible to Neoplatonists and the Stoics, Synesius also calls ἴδιον ὄχημα (1292b), τὸ ψυχικὸν πνεῦμα (1300b and 1309c), πνευματικὴ ψυχή (1293b), σῶμα ἀκήρατον (1297b), τὸ πνεῦμα τὸ θεῖον (1312a) and φανταστικὸν πνεῦμα (1289c, 1292a, 1300a, 1309c, and 1313a). With Synesius—as with Porphyry, Plotinus, and other later Neoplationists—it acts not only as an organ of higher perception, but also as a substrate to the lower soul, as the body of deemons, and as the subject of magical and theurgic rites (A. Smith 1974, 153).

[17] Cf. Aristotle's discussion of αἴσθησις αἰσθήσεων, beginning at *de An.* 417a, and Lucretius, where he calls the unknown fourth element of the anima, "*anima animae*" (*Nat.* III.273-275).

[18] Fitzgerald (1930, 333)—translating "For this [imagination] is the perception of perceptions, inasmuch as the imaginative *pneuma* is the most widely shared organ of sensation, and the first body of the soul"—takes the phrase "and the first body of the soul" as descriptive of imagination and *not* the imaginative *pneuma*, as do I. The Greek, αἴσθησις γὰρ αἰσθήσεων αὕτη ὅτι τὸ φανταστικὸν πνεῦμα κοινότατόν ἐστιν αἰσθητήριον καὶ σῶμα πρῶτον χυχῆς, is ambiguous. Terzaghi, in placing a comma after αὕτη, obviously agrees with me (1944, 152-153).

[19] Cf. Iamblichus, *Myst.* III.iii.107.

[20] Aristotle says *phantasia* exists even in insects (*de An.* II.ii 413b23-25). For his account of *phantasia*, see *de An.* III.iii 427a17-429a9.

[21] Cf. Philo (*Insomn.* I.viii.43-44 & 174) and Iamblichus (*Myst.* III.iii.105 & 107), where each speak of sleep too as a freeing of the soul from bodily encumbrances.

[22] Concerning Synesius' psychology, Fitzgerald writes: "It is interesting to observe how the Platonism of Synesius interprets a tentative psychology founded on observation and reasoned hypothesis. He begins, as always in the language of poetic similes, to define the imagination, that 'perception of perceptions', as the 'first body of the soul', and speaks of it as 'lurking there in its fastness and directing the government of the living being as from a citadel....' From all this it follows that the life in dreams, as being one raised from a participation in the lower category of perception to the imaginative faculty alone, by just this step stands so much nearer to the

life of mind, pure and unadulterated, and (for he pushed his conclusions to this logical sequence also) approaches more closely to the life of the soul after death. As our waking life is to our dreaming life, so is our dreaming life, if I understand him aright, to our future and, for he is always a Platonist, to our past existence" (1930, 80-81).

[23] A tax assessed to metics (resident foreigners in Athens) of 12 *drachmae* per year.

[24] The *isoteleis* were a favored class of *metoikoi*, alien settlers in Athens who paid taxes and alien duty but enjoyed no privileges of citizenship. *Isoteleis* paid taxes but no alien duty.

[25] Cf. Heraclitus, *Vorsokr.*, vol. i, fr. 88: "And, as <one and> the same thing, there is present <in us?> living and dead and the waking and the sleeping and young and old. For the latter, having changed around, are the former, and the former, having changed around, are <back> again <to being> the latter" (Robinson trans.).

[26] Cf. Cicero's *Div.* I.64 and Macrobius' *Somn.Scip.* I.vii.4-6. Patricia Cox Miller notices that Synesius' μαντικὴ τέχνη provides a nice contrast to the oneiromancy of Artemidorus. "In marked contrast to this Synesian view of the revelatory potential of all oneiric images was the position of the master-classifier of dreams in late antiquity, Artemidorus. More circumspect with regard to the image-world, he put greater trust in the interpreter than in the dreams, thus reversing Synesius' formula" (1994, 76).

[27] The sorts of dreams referred to in section IX.

[28] I.e., an enigmatic dream.

[29] Because βλαστάνειν chiefly means "to sprout" or "to burst forth" (LSJ), like Fitzgerald, I take ἐκ τῶν τοιούτων to be referring to γένεσις. However, Fitzgerald translates this latter part as "...its development is most obscure" (1930, 350). It seems better to take ἀσαφέστατον as the subject of πρόεισιν.

[30] Cf. Macrobius' *Somn.Scip.* I.iii.8-11. For Macrobius two types of prophetic dreams were clear, *horama* or *visio* (which turns out exactly as dreamed) and *chrematismos* or *oraculum* (which is a future revelation by some divine or divine-like figure), and one type is enigmatic, *oneiros* (or *somnium*).

[31] Cf. Plato (*R.* 571d-572b), Aristotle (*Pr.* xxx.957a26-32), Cicero *Div.* I.60), Artemidorus (*Oniroc.* IV.proem), Macrobius (*Somn.Scip.* I.iii.14-16), Philo (*Insomn.* II.iii.20 & III.xv.105), Iamblichus (*Myst.* III.iii.107), and Epictetus (*Diatr.* III.ii.1-5).

[32] Behr 1968, 174, fn. 10.

[33] Fitzgerald 1930, 83.

[34] Fitzgerald (Ibid, 350) translates this as "portentous". This is a possible reading, but untoward given that Synesius has spent much time in attempting to justify the divine and prophetic nature of *all* dreams prior to this. Here he is more concerned with showing that the origins of such dreams are unusual and different, not portentous.

[35] Cf. *Ti.* 70d-72d.

[36] *Metaph.* A (980a28-981a30).

[37] See Kissling 1922, 327.

[38] Cf. Artemidorus' six *stoicheia*: nature, law, custom, occupation, names, and time (*Oniroc.* I.3). It is interesting to note how neatly Synesius' three influences of dreams correspond to Erich Fromm's three types of oneiric symbols: accidental symbols, conventional symbols, and universal symbols. For Fromm, an accidental symbol (cf. πάθος, also meaning "accident") is a semiotic relationship that occurs by a chance pairing of symbol and that which it symbolizes that is personal. A conventional symbol (cf. νόμος), involving a particular group, is established by convention of a group, such as stringing the letters T-A-B-L-E together to represent table. Last, a universal symbol (cf. φύσις) indicates an intrinsic relationship between symbol and that which it represents and is shared by all men. All of these symbols are involved in the formation of dreams for Fromm (1951, 13).

[39] As Kissling states, it is probably the uniqueness of the astral influence for each dreamer that prohibits there being a science of oneiromancy (1922, 327)

[40] Synesius tells us here that the luminosity of the astral regions is conducive to truth in the soul, while the darkness of the subterranean parts disposes it to obscurity and falseness. Truth is divine, while error belongs to those who wallow in matter (1309b-1312a). It seems a safe conclusion that the images of future things here are themselves *even more* indefinite and indistinct. Therein lies their deceitfulness.

[41] *Div.Somn.* 463b12-15. Early in this chapter, Synesius says that demons, as intermediaries between gods and men, inhabited these regions (1292a).

[42] The Greek reads: ἤδη δὲ τις ἅμα καὶ νικᾷ καὶ βαδίζει καὶ ἵπταται, which Fitzgerald (1930, 356) translates "Now <in dreams> one conquers, walks, *or* flies simultaneously...". He is emphasizing that any possible combination of two or more of these would show the incredible nature of certain dreams, but there is no warrant for this. Instead, I see Synesius giving an example of a dream in which even the impossible occurs. In addition, Fitzgerald bids us to compare these three activities in dreams to the three ways in which men dream according to Posidonius at *Div.* I.64 (472). I fail to see any resemblance.

[43] I.e., to explain such things. Iamblichus speaks of the energy of the dream as being "superior to language" (*Myst.* III.iii.108). He is certainly correct.

[44] Philo mentions dreams where (1) god sends *phantasiai* to the sleeper, (2) our intellect (διάνοια) moves in sympathy with the soul of the whole, and (3) our soul sets itself in motion and, becoming frenzied, foretells what will be. The first are clearest, the last are most obscure (*Insomn.* I.i.1-2 & II.I.iv). It is conceivable, but unlikely, that Synesius here is referring to another way in which dreams are prophetic, perhaps something like Philo's second type of dream. For Synesius, all dreams essentially involve *psyche*, and *psyche*, unlike *nous* or other higher faculties, is limited in its sleeping sojourns by its capacities. Containing the forms of things having a beginning and end (1288b), its most important role during sleep seems to be gleaning the images of future things (1309b-c). For more on the distinction between cosmic and hypercosmic gods in Neoplatonism, see

Fitzgerald 1930, 441-442.
[45] Freud 1966, 151.
[46] Freud 1993, 350-352.
[47] Cf. the baneful dream that Zeus sent to Agamemnon at the start of *Iliad* II.
[48] Like Freud, Jung too founded his belief in universal symbols in dreams on an unconscious knowledge of our past. He writes, "Hence one could say—*cum grano salis*—that history could be constructed just as easily from one's own unconscious as from the actual texts". For Jung, universal symbols in dreams are archetypes or structural components of the "collective unconscious", inherited tendencies of our minds to form representations of mythological motifs such as the "wise old man" or the "unknown mother". However, he warns that they must not be construed in practice as fixed and archetypal, but rather as "relatively fixed" expressions of unconscious content, because in no case can we have "*a priori* certainty" that a particular symbol must be interpreted in a particular manner (Jung, 1990, 76-77, 104-105, & 160). Havelock Ellis—who, like Plato (*Ti.*), Aristotle, and Lucretius, is more concerned with how dreams come about than what they are about (and giving them a psychophysiological underpinning)—states that symbols are a "synaesthesia" where one sensory impression is involuntarily and automatically linked with another so that the one comes to be regarded as a symbol for the other. Still, he admits that some of our symbols in dreams are progeny from "an antiquity so primitive that we usually fail to interpret it" (Ellis 1976, 150-151 & 156).
[49] One of the foremost experts in the study of oneiric content in modern times, Calvin Hall, has argued against symbolic codification and emphasizes the role of personal experience in dreams. Yet even he grudgingly acknowledges the validity of near-universal oneiric symbols: "Dream symbols are private, personal emblems of thought and cannot be codified in the form of a dictionary. There may be a few symbols that are shared by a number of people but even these are probably not timeless or universal in meaning" (Hall 1966, 108).
[50] Fitzgerald 1930, 82.
[51] See Heraclitus, *Vorsokr.*, Fr. 2.

Part III
Oneirology and Ancient Medicine

Introduction

I have given a full account of ancient Greco-Roman medical practice, both secular medicine and religious incubation, in the first chapter. In this part, I focus on the role of dreams in both medical traditions.

On the magical side, healing deities at religious sanctuaries were believed to offer a type of medical assistance that centered on dreams. The ill traveled to a religious sanctuary, gave a votive offering, and then retreated to a sleeping parlor where a healing god was believed to visit them in a dream and administer or suggest a cure for what ailed them.

On the secular side, medical practice was sometimes guided by the conviction that certain dreams were indicative of bodily health—either somatic normalcy or current or incipient illness. Unlike medical dreams in incubation, it was the physical constitution of sleepers themselves that was thought to generate diagnostic dreams.[1] A person's soul, ancient physicians argued, surveyed one's bodily functions during sleep and brought about dreams that indicated, by a scrutiny of their content, bodily health. Many experts on dreams today consider this to be an authentic kind of dream.[2]

In chapters eight and nine, I look at diagnostic dreams in secular medical practice. Chapter eight is a critical analysis of Book IV of the Hippocratic treatise *Regimen* (often simply referred to as *Dreams*[3]), while chapter nine examines short works on dreams by the second-century A. D. physicians Galen and Rufus. In these chapters, I ask the following questions. First, how, if at all, did diagnostic dreams differ from other recognized kinds of dreams—for instance, meaningless or prophetic dreams? Second, did physicians have empirically reliable methods to interpret diagnostic dreams?

Chapter ten, in contrast, focuses on dreams in incubation. Here, by perusing the extant testimonies found at ancient healing sanctuaries and scattered references to cures at them, I draw up a picture of the perceived function of dreams in this type of medicine by a thorough analysis of the extant reports of dreams. Content of such reports gives a fairly reliable picture of how these sanctuaries operated over time.

---

[1] Today called "prodromal dreams." This term was coined in the nineteenth century by M. Macario (Van de Castle 1980, 365). For mention or discussion of medically diagnostic dreams by nonphysicians in antiquity, see Aristotle, *Div.Somn.* 463a8-22; Cicero, *Div.* II.142; and Artemidorus *Oniroc.* IV.22.

[2] See, for example, Harry Hunt's *The Multiplicity of Dreams*, 1989, 111-112.

[3] I follow the convention in footnotes of referring to the four books of *Regimen* themselves as *de Victu* I-IV and the fourth book as *de Insomniis.*

Chapter Eight
Diagnostic Dreams in Hippocratic Medicine

Introduction

Our earliest evidence for the use of dreams in Greco-Roman secular medical practice is the fourth book of a work called *Regimen* that is part of the Hippocratic Corpus.

The Hippocratic Corpus, a group of some sixty medical writings probably collected by Alexandrian scholars in the third century A. D., has received its name from the historical Hippocrates, of whom we know little. Plato, Aristotle, and Meno (a pupil of Aristotle) tell us that Hippocrates was roughly a contemporary of Socrates and that he came from Cos. We are also told that he was a famous doctor who taught medicine for money. Apart from these things, there is nothing that reliably links him to any of the writings in the corpus that bear his name. In fact, disagreement within the corpus concerning correct methodology, treatment, etiology, and overall aims shows that the works were written by many different authors.[1]

Most of the Hippocratic works were written within a relatively short span of time, from the late fifth century B. C. to the middle of the fourth century B. C. They covered a vast array of important topics—medical initiation, etiology of disease, justification of medical practice as art, explication of the humoral approach to medicine, effects on climate and place on health, proper practice of medicine, and even philosophy of medicine. Because of their wide-ranging subject matter, they are an indispensable source for our knowledge of Hippocratic medicine and early Greco-Roman science.[2]

Despite these differences, Hippocratic medical practice was by today's standards a holistic approach to medicine that centered on regimen: the effects of diet and exercise on overall physical health. Regimen was introduced as a relatively new approach to health that complemented older pharmacological and surgical approaches. For Hippocratic physicians, physical health was deemed a matter of internal bodily harmony. For the Hippocratic physician, Galen tells us,[3] excess or defect of any one of the internal humors ("juices" or "flavors" and their properties or powers)—phlegm (cold and wet), bile (hot and dry), black bile (cold and dry), or blood (hot and wet)[4]—was generally believed responsible for ill health. Corrective remedy was designed to return one's body back to a state of physical equilibrium through a variety of regimens: inducing sweat, blood letting, drinking wine, enemas, ingesting much dry food, vomiting, rapid walking, and so on. In short, the elements of nature and their powers—fire (warmth), air (wetness), water (coldness), and earth (dryness)[5]—as elements or constituents of humors, were believed causally responsible for our physical well-being. A physician's task was to maintain or restore internal equilibrium of these natural powers.

Composition of *Regimen*

Regimen is plainly a Hippocratic work in style and substance, and, like most of the other works, it is one of unknown authorship. In addition, there is no consensus as to when it was written. Arguments have been put forth for its composition anywhere from the late fifth century B. C. to 320 B. C.[6] These arguments are mostly based on comparisons between *Regimen,* and scholars admit that there is little that is decisive on this issue.

Of the four books in *Regimen*, Book I deals with preliminary, theoretical matters. The author states that to prescribe regimen rightly for cure, a physician must know the nature of man, the nutritive and curative capacities of food and drink, the effects of exercise, the constitution of the patient, the season of the year, the patient's age, the change of winds, the region in which the patient lives, the constitution of the year, and the rising and setting of celestial bodies—each in proportion to its contribution to illness or health[7] (I.ii). All of these factors are reducible to the activity of fire (hot and dry), which moves things, and water (cold and wet), which nourishes things (I.iii-iv). Fire and water together are the elements of all existing things, of their parts, and of their attributes. Through elemental interaction, all change occurs (I.iv-xxxvi). I.x tells us that the human body has within it three groupings of fire-made circuits (ἐξποιήσατο τὸ πῦρ περιόδους[8] τρισσάς), with the apposite bodily materials in them: those around the periphery, the middle ones, and those around the hollows of the moist (αἱ...πρὸς τὰ κοῖλα τῶν ὑγρῶν). Book II talks about the effects of climate, foods, drinks, baths, ointments, exercise, and sleep.

In the third book, perhaps the most important one to the author, he discusses first a seasonal approach to regimen for the majority of people (III.lxvii & lxix) and then a special regimen he has discovered (μοι δίαιτα ἐξευρημένη). This regimen, he relates, helps those who employ it and has brought him great honor. It involves an early diagnosis of the illness and a diagnosis of those things that are overpowering in the body—whether food overpowers exercise or exercise overpowers food (in either case, illness is incipient or present)[9] (III.lxvii, lxix). Afterward, he examines the symptoms of food overpowering exercise and the apposite corrective regimen (III.lxx-lxxxiii) and then, briefly, the overpowering of exercise on food and how to use regimen here to restore balance (III.lxxxiv-lxxxv).

Regimen IV

The fourth book of *Regimen*,[10] often simply referred to as *On Dreams*, is the earliest existing Greco-Roman treatise on the subject. At *Regimen* IV.lxxxvi, the author begins: "Whoever has learned correctly about the signs (τεκμηρίων) occurring in sleep will find that they have a great influence (μεγάλην δύναμιν) on all things" (1-3). The reason is that the soul—while a servant to the body when awake and attending to such duties as sensation, walking, feeling, pain, and thinking—is stirred and moved to do similar things while the body rests in sleep.[11] He sums, "And so, whoever knows how to judge these things correctly knows a great part of wisdom" (18-19).

The author of Book IV suggests that interpretation of dreams is often difficult, because there are at least two basic kinds: divinely prophetic dreams that forecast bad or good to cities or individuals, and diagnostic dreams in which the soul signifies what ails the body. The interpreters of prophetic dreams, he says, also interpret diagnostic dreams, though with mixed results. Sometimes they hit the mark, at other times they miss it. Because they do not know the causes of their successes or failures, these interpreters urge people simply to beware so that nothing bad will befall them. Yet unlike physicians, he points out, they do not teach people how to be on guard. They merely urge them to pray to the gods.[12] In short, many interpreters of prophetic dreams have no understanding of the physical etiology of dreams for medical diagnosis. Consequently their results are hit and miss. In contrast to this approach, the author encourages his readers to pray to the gods, but also suggests prayers would be more effective were people more actively involved in their own affairs (IV.lxxxvii).[13]

The author goes on to give in some detail a psychogenic account of diagnostic dreams. At IV.lxxxviii, he tells us that dreams that repeat our diurnal thoughts and activities "as if they were done or planned during the day in the normal occurrence (ὥσπερ τῆς ἡμέρας ἐπρήχθη ἢ ἐβουλεύθη ἐπὶ δικαίῳ πρήγματι[14])" signify health, showing a proper balance within (2-10). Dreams contrary to daily events (πρὸς τὰς ἡμερινὰς πρήξιας ὑπεναντιῶται τὰ ἐνύπνια) forebode bad, indicating disturbances of the body (10-14). Here and throughout, the reasoning is analogical and the prevailing rule for interpretation is this: Dreams in accordance with (παρά) the way things generally turn out in waking life indicate somatic health; those contrary to (κατά) the way things usually happen indicate incipient or existing illness, caused either by surfeit or depletion.[15] In the contrary cases, the greater the discord, the greater the illness.[16]

Throughout the lengthy section IV.lxxxix, the reasoning is exclusively based on an assumed resemblance, first mentioned at I.x, between celestial movements and the movements of matter in the human body. Each person's body is likened to the cosmos, which has an outer sphere (ἡ ἔξω περίοδος) (where stars orbit), a middle sphere (ἡ μέση) (where the sun orbits), and a sphere around the hollows (ἡ πρὸς τὰ κοῖλα) or inner sphere (where the moon orbits) (9-11). In a similar manner, the human body is presumed to have three such circuits (περιφοραί), with the apposite bodily materials in them. Disturbances in the normal bodily flow of things may bring about anomalous cosmic dreams, symptomatic of a corresponding underlying condition (6-9). Consequently, given a grasp of the capacities of fire (hot and dry) and water (cold and wet), a physician directs regimen toward returning bodily constitution to normal. For example, he says that to dream that *any one of the stellar bodies (ἄστρα) is harmed or vanishes or is hindered from its circuit by mist, cloud, rain, or hail*—all conditions of wetness—signifies that *a moist, phlegm-like secretion has moved to the outer circuit of the body.* The condition is *less severe* if the cause in the dream is *mist or cloud* (since these merely obscure in the waking world); *more severe*, if *rain or hail* are obscuring causes (since these actually cause damage) (14-17). Here, since excess coldness and wetness exist in the outer circuit, purgation should be directed through the skin. In the less severe instance, a dreamer should take long runs with a cloak to induce sweat, take long walks afterward, skip lunch, reduce food by one-third and then gradually increase it to normal within five days (14-23). In the more severe case, he should employ the vapor bath to induce sweat and eat dry, acrid, astringent, and unmixed foods in addition to what he prescribes for less severe cases[17](23-29). If anyone dreams of these phenomena *in the innermost circuit*, a revulsion of phlegm should take place from within (29-38). Last, if excess phlegm is indicated by a dream *in the middle, "solar" circuit*, then revulsions must be directed in both directions[18] (38-45).

Section IV.xc[19] discusses dreams depicting things occurring on earth: Things occurring as they should signify underlying normalcy and things happening anomalously indicate underlying physical pathology. Seeing and hearing clearly *what happens on land*; *walking or running surely, quickly, and fearlessly*; seeing *flat and well tilled earth or luxuriant trees with copious fruit*; observing *rivers and springs flowing freely, and wells with the right amount of water*; these are all indicative of health (2-12). Whatever is dreamed to be the opposite of these is a sign of something insidious that underlies (12-13). For example, to dream of *trees shedding their leaves* indicates *a moist and cold (phlegm-like) disturbance* (23-25). If *leaves abound, though without fruit, a hot and dry (bilious) disturbance* is indicated (25-26). *High water* signifies *excess blood*; *low water, depletion of blood* (29-31).

Importantly, he maintains, the physical circumstances surrounding the dreamer at the time of the dream can also affect its interpretation.[20] For instance, dreaming of *diving into a lake, sea, or river* indicates *excess moisture* and was generally bad. Yet for *someone with a fever* it was good, since it showed that *moisture was suppressing the heat within.*[21] In a similar vein, Section IV.xci of *Regimen* talks about clothes, footwear, their colors, and other such things as they relate to the dreamer.[22] Section IV.xcii discusses dreams of the dead, and the final section takes up dreams of monsters as well as dreams concerning nourishment, anxiety, and frustration. At the close of Book IV the author sums up his contribution to medical oneirology: "By employing the things I have described, one will become healthy, and I have discovered regimen with the help of the gods as far as it is possible for one, being but a man, to discover."[23]

In short, what these passages from *Regimen* IV reveal is that, while physicians were looking for a medical interpretation of dreams based on analogical reasoning and an understanding of natural phenomena, oneirocritics were at least sometimes looking for a prophetic meaning in the same kinds of dreams.

Regimen IV and Artemidorus' *Onirocritica*

If dreams were interpreted both prophetically and diagnostically, the question is to what extent the content of diagnostic dreams may have differed (if at all) from that of divine dreams to offer clues for the proper method of interpretation . We can gain some insight on this issue by comparing *Regimen* IV with the *Onirocritica* of Artemidorus.

There are at three notable comparisons to be made between the two manuals. First, scrutiny of the dreams in *Regimen* IV reveals that most are about natural phenomena unrelated to human involvement (stars, planets, storms, trees, seas, rivers, earth, etc.). Dreams of human affairs (receiving something from a god, injured legs, diving into water, seeing the dead, eating and drinking, running, and fighting) make up a noticeably smaller portion of the work. Artemidorus reverses the emphasis: Dreams of natural phenomena without human involvement are a very small part of the *Onirocritica*. Nevertheless, scrutiny of Artemidorus' five books shows plainly that none of the Hippocratic dreams would be out of place in the oneirocritic's collection—for instance, dreams about celestial bodies.

This brings me to a second distinction between the two works. In dreams about such natural objects as the sun, moon, and stars, Artemidorus shows a sociological rather than diagnostic slant to his interpretive strategy: The heavenly bodies are treated entirely and properly (given the cosmology of the times) within a section on the gods.[24] In other words, it is not the content of dreams that these two authors consider that is so radically different, it is the conceptual framework and interpretive strategy that each one emphasizes.

Third, there is a remarkable difference between the two oneirological manuals in the way each handles elements of dreams. All of the dreams mentioned in Book IV of *Regimen* appear to be elements or episodes of larger dreams. Nowhere does the author attempt to deal with dreams as a whole. This is in stark contrast to the approach of Artemidorus, who explicitly provides a system of interpreting oneiric elements in order to get at the meaning of an entire dream.[25] If physicians were looking chiefly at discrete naturalistic elements of dreams as diagnostic clues, this would explain the tendency of the author of *Regimen* IV to privilege analogy as a method of interpretation. In contrast, to get at the meaning of a whole dream, diviners like Artemidorus found that they needed to employ a variety of interpretive principles or techniques (not all of which worked harmoniously, see chapter six) from letter-, word-, and number-play to simple intuition. This difference highlights yet again the distinct interpretive strategies of the two authors regarding content of dreams.[26]

Based on my comparison of these two texts, it is likely that physicians who used dreams as diagnostic tools looked at all dreams of patients as potential diagnostic tools, though they only focused attention on particularly striking elements or on certain key episodes. Most of these concerned natural phenomena that were taken as indications of underlying bodily conditions. Oneirocritics, on the other hand, at least sometimes looked for prophetic significance in the same dreams. Nonetheless, they found each dream as a whole more significant than the elements of it taken as discrete units of meaning, and they used a broader range of interpretive methods to help them unravel that meaning.

As for the question posed earlier—"How did Hippocratic physicians who used dreams diagnostically know when to regard a dream as a medical tool?"—I can now offer a simple answer: They did not. Since there were no manifest features to distinguish diagnostic from prophetic dreams, physicians who examined their patients' dreams probably considered all of them as possible diagnostic indicators. Physicians, following analogical reasoning (or perhaps using mere intuition) only needed to search for certain signs or episodes in dreams that could offer clues for diagnosis. Such clues could be added to and compared with other symptoms of a patient and diagnosis would follow. More ambitious physicians could have embarked upon an empirical program of establishing links between certain episodes of dreams and future health-related events. The question is: "Did they?"

Regimen IV's Empirical Program

Since the primary aim of *Regimen* is to prescribe regimen (IV.ciii.39-41), one could argue that the work implicitly assumes that the empirical groundwork has been done already—a justification of how dreams could be diagnostic tools had been previously given elsewhere. In support of this is the fact that the treatise nowhere attempts to justify the use of dreams as diagnostic tools by physicians. If this is plausible, then the empirical program upon which *Regimen* IV is based looks something like this. Having observed that certain oneiric elements in dreams (here episodes) generally signify a particular somatic malady, while others signify somatic well being, we are justified inductively in concluding that all such similar dreams are likewise somatically indicative. In summary:

> P_1: All dreams of type o_υ, given the idiosyncratic circumstances attending the dream $(\iota_1 \ldots \iota_n)$, signify outcomes of type τ_υ

and

> P_2: All dreams of type $o\pi$, given the idiosyncratic circumstances attending the dream $(\iota_1 \ldots \iota_n)$, signify outcomes of type τ_ν

(where "o_κ" indicates a diagnostic dream whose content is in accordance with waking reality, "o_π" indicates a diagnostic dream contrary to waking reality, and "τ_υ" and "τ_ν" symbolize existing or incipient health and illness respectively for the dreamer).

Though the Hippocratic program involving interpretation for diagnosis in *Regimen* seems to be driven by empirical factors (collecting dreams, looking for links with events that follow, and establishing right principles of interpretation), there is no mention that the interpretations at any time were derived in such a manner and no reason to believe that they actually were. Whether dreams indicate bodily illness or wellbeing is based exclusively on the assumed analogy between the human body and the visible world outside of it. The most prominent use of this analogy is the comparison between the celestial spheres and the circuits of the body mentioned at I.x and elaborated upon in the lengthy section IV.lxxxix. It is plausible to conclude that prescriptive regimen dictated by dreams in *Regimen* IV had little to do with an empirical study of oneiric content and future events and more to do with the assumed analogical principles underlying the burgeoning science of the Hippocratic accounts of good health and disease.

Concluding Remarks

Overall, *Regimen* IV provides us with a wealth of information on the use of dreams in ancient medicine and gives a clear and comprehensive vision of the practice of diagnostic interpretation of dreams in contrast to oneirocriticism. I enumerate my findings:

- *Regimen* IV posits that diagnostic and divine dreams, though presumably differentiable by origin, were scarcely, if at all, distinguishable by content. Thus, by appeal to content alone, physicians and diviners were interpreting the same dreams.
- While physicians were looking for diagnostic significance in the episodes of dreams, diviners were principally concerned with the dream as a whole for prophetic purposes.
- The methods many physicians employed in oneiric interpretation probably had little to do with experience (i.e., relating symbols in dreams to symptoms or illness) and everything to do with the perceived similarity between cosmic and bodily circuits (i.e., the normal occurrence of natural circuits and the harmonious intercourse of bodily circuits).

In summary, the underlying assumptions behind diagnostic dreams for the author of *Regimen* IV are that physical symptoms often influence the imagery in dreams and that a proper understanding of how images are affected leads to a correct diagnosis of illness. These are exactly the principles assumed by many oneirological experts today who maintain that dreams often function diagnostically.

For two later accounts of diagnostic dreams in secular medicine, I turn to Galen and Rufus in the next chapter.

---

[1] Temkin 1991, ix-xii, 5-6, & 39-75.

[2] Ibid, xi & Lloyd 1983, 9-59.

[3] Galen believed that the majority of the treatises we now have were indeed written by Hippocrates and ascribes the theory of the four humors to

Hippocrates. He writes in *Nat.Fac.* (I.2): "Of all the doctors and philosophers we know, he [Hippocrates] was the first who undertook to demonstrate that there are, in all, four mutually interacting qualities, through the agency of which everything comes to be and passes away" (Lloyd translation).

[4] The most important of these for disease were bile and phlegm (*Aff.* I & *Morb.* II). *VM* XVI states that the hot and the cold are the weakest of the four powers.

[5] The author of *Vict.* mentions only fire (hot & dry) and water (cold & wet).

[6] Fredrich and, more recently, Joly argue that it was written sometime between the end of the fifth century B.C. and the beginning of the fourth (Fredrich 1899, 217-230; Joly 1960, 206-209, and 1984, 49). Van Lieshout, seeing the influence of Xenophon, narrows the date to the first quarter of the fourth century B.C (1980, 187-188). Jones gives 400 B.C. as a good approximation (1992, xlvi.). Rehm, arguing that the work was influenced by Eudoxus, believes that it was written around 370 B.C. (1941, 38-40), while Kirk thinks the work could not have been written before 350 B.C. (1954, 27-29). Diller gives an approximate date of the mid-fourth century (1952, 408). Jaeger dates the work around 320 B.C (1944, 33-40).

[7] Similar to Rationalist medical practice as Galen describes in *Sect.Intr.* III. See also *Vict.* III.lxvii and *Ep.* I.23 & VI.viii.9.

[8] The same word that Plato uses to describe the circuits of the soul (*Ti.* 42e-44d) as well as the circuits of intelligence in the heavens (*Ti.* 47a-b).

[9] When food and exercise are in proportion, there is good health.

[10] There is concern about the originality of Book IV. In all, there seems sufficient agreement on certain details (e.g., mention of bodily circuits at I.x and IV.lxxxix, talk of surfeit and depletion throughout, and similarities in the manner of regimen in Books I-III and Book IV, etc.) to indicate that whoever wrote the earlier books also wrote the final one. However, Fredrich (1899, 206), Joly (1960, 168-171), and van Lieshout (1980, 185-187) have convincingly argued that there must have been a book of dreams from which this author drew the material for Book IV. From their arguments, the following points are worth noting. First, the author's assessment of "good" and "bad" to dreams indicates a preexisting compilation. Second and most importantly, the infusion of religious ritual is unique to *Insomn.* (lxxxvii, lxxxviii, lxxxix, and xc) and cannot be the brainchild of the author of the other three books. Third, the change from great to scant detail of presentation that begins at IV.xc suggests that this author is copying from another work and hurriedly trying to finish his presentation, leaving out his own comments, present in the chapters of the book prior to IV.xc.

[11] Cf. Galen who writes, "For the soul—having slipped into the depths of the body and having withdrawn from external, sensible things—seems to perceive the condition throughout the body. And it receives an image of all the things that it desire as if these things were truly present" (lines 39-43, Kühn). See also Plato (*Ti.* 45b-d), Aristotle (*Insomn.* 458b30-459a6), Cicero (*Div.* I.114-115), and Lucretius (*Nat.* IV.949).

[12] Praying to the gods is also suggested at IV.lxxxviii.30, IV.lxxxix.28-33, and IV.xc.63. Concerning the Hippocratic corpus, the emphasis on prayer as

complementing regimen is unique to Book IV. *Dec.* VI talks of the gods as the real physicians for cures and physicians merely as their instrument. *Prog.* I (line 21) has a passing reference to something divine in diseases (εἴ τι θεῖον ἔνεστιν ἐν τῇσι νούσοισι) in all manuscripts (regarded by most scholars today as an interpolation). *Morb.Sacr.* considers, then rejects, any direct divine cause for seizures. Seizures are explained by natural causes (cold, sun, & wind) and, thus, are only divine insofar as the things that cause them are divine.

[13] The author probably had in mind that, by praying to the gods to rectify a certain illness, one was in a sense attributing a divine and unnatural cause to the disease. Ludwig Edelstein argues that there existed a reticence, even a renunciation, concerning prayers in medical practice that in no way reflected a belief in the ineffectuality of prayer (Temkin et al. 1967, 240-41).

[14] Jones, who translates δικαίῳ πρήγματι as "in the normal act", and Joly (1967, 98) after him ("à propos d'une affaire convenable") are certainly correct in not attributing any moral significance to the terms as Littré (1962, 643) does ("dans une just affaire") and Ermerins (*in re iusta*) as well does before him. See Jones's (1931) commentary of *Insomn.*, 425 fn. 1. Such dreams, as we shall see in chapter eight, constitute a separate category for Galen.

[15] Spelled out as πλησμονή and κένωσις at IV.lxxxix.105. These refer to illness brought on by excess or want of food or excess or want of exercise.

[16] Cf. Artemidorus' *Oniroc.* IV.2.

[17] Following the Hippocratic therapeutic principle in *Flat.* I.33-34: τὰ ἐναντία τῶν ἐναντίων ἐστὶν ἰήματα.

[18] The notion of elemental balance (i.e., the humors) is certainly influenced by Heraclitean ethics, epistemology, and metaphysics and is characteristic of Greek ethics, especially Aristotle's *EN*.

[19] There is a noticeable change in the author's style from here to the end. Concerning this, Joly (1967) writes: "Comme à la fin du livre III, l'auteur semble ici pressé d'en finir: il se fait avare de détails dans la description du régime; il multiplie les rêves, mais abrège son commentaire sur chacun d'eux" (105 fn. 2).

[20] *Oniroc.* I.8-9, IV.2, 4, & 59.

[21] *Insomn.* IV.xc.40-48.

[22] Joly argues that this section refers exclusively to clothing and footwear (n.15, 107 fn. 3). He is probably correct, though the Greek is too imprecise for a definite answer.

[23] *Insomn.* IV.xciii.34-41.

[24] *Oniroc.* II.33-39.

[25] E.g., *Oniroc.* I.12, III.66, IV.3, 28, & 72.

[26] An interesting exception being dreams of incubation and the appearance of a healing god to assist or administer cure.

Chapter Nine
Dreams in Early Roman Secular Medicine

Introduction

In the previous chapter, I looked at the use of dreams for diagnosis in Hippocratic medicine. In this chapter, I examine in turn two treatises on diagnostic dreams in first- and second-century A. D. humoral medicine: one by Galen and another by Rufus of Ephasus.

Galen was born at Pergamum in 129 A. D. His father Nicon wanted his son to enter into politics or philosophy, but Galen tells us that Asclepius himself prescribed a career in medicine for the young man through a dream of his father.[1]

When Galen was around 20, his father died. Galen then traveled to Smyrna, Corinth, and Alexandria to further his medical education. When he returned to Pergamum in 157 A. D., he was appointed physician to the gladiators—a position that he would keep until 161 A. D. Afterwards he moved to Rome and spent the lion's share of the remainder of his life there. In Rome, he lectured extensively, wrote prolifically, and practiced medicine on some of the most important Roman citizens, including Marcus Aurelius himself.

His medical interests, covering almost all elements of second-century medicine, were varied and comprehensive. His copious writings, however, advance beyond medical texts to philosophy of science.[2] He wrote commentaries on the *Hippocratic Corpus* in an effort to disentangle proper medical procedure from what he considered to be sham medical practice. Galen's overall dedication and contribution to medicine make him perhaps the most important figure in the history of medicine.

Galen's *On Diagnosis*

Just as the author of *Regimen* IV, in addition to believing that dreams assist diagnosis, Galen openly acknowledges in treatises the divine influence of dreams on his choice of career, his surgical practice,[3] and his writings.[4] He also admits that the prophetic dreams of others have impacted him.[5]

Galen's most definitive statement for medical diagnosis through dreams is in a work entitled *On Diagnosis from Dreams*. Other than brief references to it, this treatise has not received much serious attention in the secondary literature.[6] Because of its shortness and incompleteness, Steven Oberhelman argues that this treatise is probably a piece from a lost work *On Healthy Regimen* (which Galen refers to in his *Commentary on Epidemics* I). Consequently, he believes the work is prior to the treatise on epidemics, which he dates around 176 to 179 A. D., and gives the period of 169-175 A. D. as most likely for its composition.[7] Other scholars question its authenticity as a Galenic treatise.

On Diagnosis from Dreams begins as follows: "The dream indicates to us the condition of the body". Then follow four examples of dreams (lines 2-6K[8]) to illustrate how oneiric content is indicative of underlying humoral imbalance or disturbance for Galen. If someone sees a *conflagration* in a dream,[9] this indicates *bile* (hot and dry). If one sees *smoke, mist, or deep darkness*,[10] this is a sign of *black bile* (cold and dry). Seeing a *thunderstorm*[11] indicates that *cold moisture increases* (phlegm: cold, wet). Last, seeing *snow*, *ice*, or *hail* in sleep indicates *cold phlegm* (again, cold and wet).[12] Lines 6-16K tell us to pay attention to the time of the dream and what the dreamer has consumed, for these circumstances can have everything to do with a proper medical interpretation of the images in a dream.

From 16-20K, we find mention of three other types of dreams,[13] each of which has a cause other than the body: some dreams originating from what we habitually do each day; some from those things we have thought about;[14] and some coming about because certain things are prophetically foreshadowed by the soul (τινα μαντικῶς ὑπ' αὐτῆς προδηλοῦνται).[15] On distinguishing between the medical type among these, he writes:

> The diagnosis of the body on the basis of dreams that are set in motion from the body becomes difficult (δύσκολος ἡ διάγνωσις τοῦ σώματος γίγνεται ἐκ τῶν ἀπὸ τοῦ σώματος ὁρμωμένων ἐνύπνιων). For were it necessary merely to distinguish (διακρίνειν) [diagnostic dreams] from dreams of deeds and thoughts of the day,[16] then it would not be difficult to suppose that all those dreams that are not from our deeds or thoughts seem to be set in motion from the body. But since, in addition, we acknowledge that

> certain dreams are prophetic (τινα...μαντική), it is not easy to say how these can be distinguished (διακριθείη) from dreams that are set in motion from the body (τῶν ἀπὸ τοῦ σώματος ὁρμωμένων) (20-27K).

For Galen, there are three types of dreams in all: diagnostic dreams, dreams that mirror our diurnal thoughts and activities (hereafter, "mirroring dreams"), and prophetic dreams. Diagnostic and mirroring dreams would be readily distinguishable, Galen thinks, were these the only types of dreams. Presumably, mirroring dreams could be easily picked out by their close correspondence to our daily thoughts and actions and all other dreams would then, by elimination, be categorized as diagnostic. Yet when prophetic dreams are added to the mix, it becomes difficult to decide which dreams are prophetic and which are diagnostic. The implication is that prophetic dreams, indicative of *what will be* for the dreamer, are similar to if not indistinguishable from diagnostic dreams, indicative of *what is* for a dreamer's body. (Precisely what I take to be the case for *Regimen* IV.)

Galen follows with a series of examples of diagnostic dreams (27-39K), the first of which is of singular interest. First, someone dreamed that *one of his legs turned to stone.* Galen states that many professional oneirocritics interpreted this dream as a reference to the man's slaves. The dream turned out, contrary to even Galen's expectations, to be a foreshadowing of *paralysis in that man's leg* (27-31K). Galen's surprise is probably not due to the unreasonableness of the perceived outcome, but to astonishment that the prophets were wrong. Here again we find oneirocritics trying to interpret diagnostic dreams.

Other examples that follow illustrate Galen too was probably picking out episodes of dreams and was not particularly interested in complete dreams. A wrestler dreamed that *he almost drowned, while standing in a cistern of blood.* The dream was medically interpreted to signify *excess blood in the body that needed draining* (32-34K). Galen follows with some generic examples. Some who are discernibly about to sweat dream of *bathing and swimming in hot water.* Thirsty people dream of *drinking without slake of thirst*, while hungry people see themselves *eating without satiation.*[17] Those filled with sperm dream of *sexual union*[18] (34-39K).

Lines 39-43K give us a brief description of the withdrawal of the soul in sleep. Galen states, "For the soul—having slipped into the depths of the body and having withdrawn from external, sensible things—seems to perceive the condition (διαθέσις) throughout the body. And it receives an image (φαντασία) of all the things that it desires as if these things were truly present". Similarities to Plato, Aristotle, the Stoics, Lucretius, Synesius, and the author of *Regimen* IV here are striking.[19]

Finally, from 43-59K Galen tells us that *an abundance of humors* conduces to dreams of *being oppressed or burdened*, while the opposite condition brings about dreams of *flying or fast running* (43-48K). Seeing *feces or filth* in sleep can indicate *excess feces or putridity*, while *smelling sweet things* is good (48-56K). In summary, "Whatever the ill see and seem to do in dreams often will indicate to us lack and excess and quality of humors" (56-59K). Galen's account is certainly in keeping with the pervasive rule that guided all interpretation at its most general level in Greco-Roman antiquity: Dreams in accordance with (κατά) general trends in waking-life reality signify good to come; dreams against (παρά) waking-life reality signify ill.

Composition of *On Diagnosis*

Concerning the composition of *On Diagnosis from Dreams*, Oberhelman argues, "The incomplete state of the work is proved *decisively* (my italics)...by the haphazard arrangement of the material".[20] Giving Kühn's lines in brackets, I quote his subsequent analysis of its composition in full.

> [A]fter an opening sentence that introduces the dream as a diagnostic tool [1K], we have four lines of examples of medical dreams [2-6K]; this is followed by eight lines on the relationship of the dream's contents to critical factors like time and nourishment [6-16K]. It is at this point (lines 13-22 [16-27K]) that we find what would have more logically begun the treatise, namely, Galen's theoretical discussion of the dream. After this, we have ten lines detailing medical dreams [27-39K], all of which would be placed more properly after lines 1-4 [2-6K]. On the heels of this comes another discussion (lines 33-36 [39-43K]) of dream metaphysics and mechanisms: the relationship of these lines with 13-22 [16-27K] is obvious, but the connection has been severed. The remaining lines (37-50 [43-59K]) are also theoretical and are accompanied by examples of pertinent dreams; however, the transitions of both sentence structure and thought are clumsy and lack cohesion.[21]

(To apprehend my criticism of Oberhelman, refer to my translation of Galen's work in Appendix B.)

The four examples of "medical dreams" (2-6K) which follow 1K are given in simple conditional form (as the εἰ from line 3K illustrates) to justify the opening statement at 1K about dreams being somatic signs and to illustrate the relationship that exists between certain instances of diagnostic dreams and specific humoral imbalance.[22] These are relationships between events, presumably through thorough and repeated observation, that have reached near-nomological status and may be understood formally thus:

> Whenever someone has a dream of type o, a bodily condition of type τ is indicated.

The detailed medical dreams (27-39K) that Oberhelman believes would best follow these examples seem better placed where they are. The first two of these (the leg-to-stone dream and the wrestler's dream) at 27-34K are dreams that presumably have actually occurred and serve to illustrate the text that immediately precedes it. So far, contrary to what Oberhelman says, nothing is untoward.

The general examples at 34-39K, however, do seem misplaced. Lines 16-27K, those "theoretical" lines that "would have more logically begun the treatise",[23] seem better placed immediately after 1-6K (and not directly after 1K as Oberhelman would have it), since 2-6K serve to illustrate the point at 1K. In other words, it is not lines 2-16K, but only lines 6-16K that seem poorly placed. These lines seem to be thrown in as an addendum and would be better suited to a later part of the work. The similarities Oberhelman notices between 16-27K and 39-43K are duly noted, though the latter passage seems to be an attempt to justify the dream as *significans* and bodily condition as *significandum* for the examples directly preceding it. The final section summarizes the treatise and does not lack cohesion, though it betrays a somewhat clumsy hand.

A close look at *On Diagnosis from Dreams* shows that the argument that "decisive proof" of its incompleteness is its haphazard arrangement of material lacks cogency. The treatise in general is composed in a logical, not haphazard, fashion. Certainly material could be placed more effectively in some places and the overall presentation could have been smoother, but this does not mean that the arrangement as it stands is "haphazard". At most the treatise gives signs of being written with a certain amount of haste.

Galen's Classification of Dreams

Let me now return to the three different dreams Galen mentions from 20-27K. We may assume that the various dreams form different kinds for Galen, since the implication of lines 20-27K is that there are different origins of the various dreams that he mentions. Given this, Galen is one of the few to acknowledge that distinguishing one kind from another is as a weighty problem.[24] Mirroring dreams are somehow caused by our daily actions or thoughts, which in turn are reflected back by such dreams. These dreams are readily recognizable and easily betray their origin. Diagnostic dreams, in contrast, have a somatic origin that, if we go by the examples Galen uses for illustration, will manifest itself analogically. Such dreams, being analogical indicators of bodily health, differ substantially from dreams of our daily thoughts and deeds, which are fairly straightforward. Last are the prophetic dreams. These, Galen suggests, are similar to if not indistinguishable from diagnostic dreams, yet we must assume that they have an origin that is nonsomatic and not caused by our thoughts and actions. By elimination their origin is likely divine.

Galen does have this to say about diagnostic dreams. He writes in Platonic fashion that when the soul is withdrawn in sleep from outside concerns, it is better equipped to deal with the inner condition of the body, receiving images of the things it desires. When the condition of the body is insalubrious or unbalanced, the soul sometimes forms dreams that correspond to the inner condition. Like Artemidorus, Galen recognizes the indispensability of attendant circumstances when interpreting a dream (i.e., when the dream occurred and what the dreamer ate before sleeping), though the conditions Galen acknowledges relate more precisely to underlying material conditions that generate the dream (6-8K).

Oberhelman also notices, in his 1983 translation of and commentary on *On Diagnosis from Dreams*, that Galen sets down no method for deciphering "the diagnostic dreams of the soul". He says that Galen prefentially uses the micro-macro analogy of the author of *Regimen* IV in interpreting diagnostic dreams. He elaborates:

> This type of analogy—the human body and the external world, or microcosm and macrocosm—explains most frequently the interpretations of dreams *in the Asclepian literature* and in the writings of Hippocrates *and Aristides* (my italics). Apparently Galen followed the Hippocratic tradition, not only in his theory on dreams and dream causation, but even in the interpretation of dreams and their use in medicine. This devotion to the Hippocratic tradition is to be expected from one who considered Hippocrates as his guide and master and as one who was correct in all medical matters.[25]

That Galen followed the author of *Regimen* in preferentially using the macro-micro analogy to guide interpretation seems clear. All of the examples Galen gives in *On Diagnosis from Dreams*, both those that have actually occurred and the conditionalized examples, accord with this model. Lines 2-6K unambiguously state that Galen is working within the parameters of humoral medicine. Yet that medical dreams *in the main* were of the macro-micro sort is a generalization that is unsupported by evidence. Oberhelman conflates the two types of medical dreams here: the medical dreams of the religious practice of incubation and those used by physicians in medical diagnosis. The dreams of medical incubation were believed to be caused by a deity and were most often straightforwardly, not analogically or symbolically interpretable. Unlike the dreams in *Regimen* and those in Galen, the evidence that we have of testimonies from religious healing sanctuaries indicates plainly that most of the dreams were not analogical.[26] The same may be said of the lion's share of the medical dreams recorded by Aelius Aristides in his diary of dreams. The cause of diagnostic dreams, in contrast to those of religious incubation, was thought to be the soul and the preferred if not exclusive method of conveying its message was analogy. I deal fully with the extant testimonies at religious healing sanctuaries and Aristides' diary of dreams in the next chapter.

Moreover, in contrast to the approach of *Regimen* IV, Galen's work is mostly justificatory, not practical. Throughout the short work, his primary aim is to show that dreams *should* be used by other physicians to assist diagnosis; he is not concerned with cataloging dreams or oneiric elements that indicate specific physical conditions. A clear sign of this is the complete absence of any practical advice for physicians regarding cure in cases of dreams that supposedly indicate illness. For instance, in dreams of injured legs, the Hippocratic author recommends induced vomiting through emetics, long walks in the morning and after eating, and much wrestling (*Reg.* IV.xc.17-19). This author offers *practical* advice for the physician who wishes to approach illness from every angle and cites certain dreams only in order to show how they depict a course of corrective regimen by analysis of their content. Galen's intent is otherwise. Referring again to the leg-to-stone dream, Galen notes that the dream's outcome, subsequent paralysis in the dreamer, runs contrary to the interpretation of the practiced oneirocritics. Here (and throughout) the tone is justificatory. He does not wish to give the practicing physician an interpretive manual for assisting interpretation for diagnosis of the patient's well-being, he wants merely to convince physicians that dreams are important diagnostic instruments that should not be neglected. The justificatory tone, I believe, is a simpler explanation for the brevity of the work than Oberhelman's claim that the work is incomplete.

Rufus' *Medical Questions* V.28-33

We get another account of diagnostic dreams from the physician Rufus of Ephesus in a work on medical diagnosis.

Rufus flourished in the second half of the first century A. D. He studied at Alexandria and practiced medicine at Ephesus.

His writings, concerning pathology and dietetics, are numerous. Though often critical of Hippocratic methods and highly eclectic, they show he had a profound respect for Hippocratic medicine. His *Medical*

Questions, containing the account of diagnostic dreams I am about to examine, is remarkably Hippocratic.

Rufus' short account of dreams occurs from V.28 to V.33. He begins by mentioning that physicians must carefully examine a patient's sleeping behavior: whether or not he has slept, what his sleeping and waking habits are, and whether or not he has had any visions or dreams (εἴ τινα φάσματα αὐτῷ ἢ ἐνύπνια γίγνοιτο) (V.28). In section V.29, he reminds readers that it is impossible for him to give a complete account of dreams here, but that he can write just enough to persuade other physicians not to neglect dreams in diagnosis.

Then follow three examples of dreams. First, a wrestler named Myron the Ephesian dreamed of *being all night in a black marsh of fresh water.* While training afterward, he felt shortness of breath, palpitation in his chest, and a loss of control in his limbs. Unable to speak, he soon died. Rufus states that the wrestler was in need of *a large evacuation of blood*, not exercise (V.29-30). Second, a man with fever often dreamed of *an Ethiopian who would wrestle and choke him in sleep.* The person's physician could not interpret the dream until the fever forced bleeding through the patient's nostrils (V.31). Last, a man dreamed of *swimming in the Cayster river.* His illness developed into dropsy (V.32). He concludes:

> I have persuaded myself altogether that visions of dreams (δόχας ἐνυπνιῶν), signifying both good and bad for a person, occur in accordance with the humors (κατὰ τοῦς χυμούς) in the body. There can be no other understanding of these things for one who has listened (ὧν κατάληψις ἄλλη οὐκ ἔστι μὴ ἀκούσαντι[27]).

Rufus' brief account is in keeping with the analogical style of interpreting diagnostic dreams used by the author of *Regimen* and Galen. Like Galen, his account is justificatory also. He says at V.29, "And so, it is not possible to write all things for all people, but I can point out enough by argument (τῷ λόγῳ) to remind the doctor not to neglect such matters". Rufus does not say whether he believes that other types of dreams exist, though being an eclectic like Galen and a contemporary of him, it would not be surprising to find him endorsing the very same categorization that Galen does.

Concluding Remarks

In summary, consistencies in the accounts of Galen and Rufus as well as the Hippocratic author of *Regimen* in the previous chapter allow me to draw certain conclusions about what the early medical account of diagnostic dreams was for ancient physicians, practiced in the humoral approach to medical health.

- The approach to diagnostic dreams was practical. Dreams enabled physicians to probe diagnostically where they would not have been able to probe. In consequence, dreams were not foolproof diagnostic tools, but pieces of a diagnostic puzzle along with other helpful, diagnostic tools. If enough of these data pointed diagnosis in a specific direction, regimen could then be prescribed.
- The preferred or exclusive method of interpretation was analogy. Proper interpretation of such analogies involved a sure understanding of the humoral approach to disease and cure.
- Dreams in accordance with the way things generally turn out in waking reality indicate health; those contrary to waking events indicate incipient or existing illness due to humoral imbalance (excess or want).
- The greater the discord that the dream exhibits with waking reality, the greater the underlying humoral imbalance (e.g., seeing a raging fire in a dream indicates a surfeit of hot and dry matter, bile, in the body).
- The circumstances pertaining to the dreamer's physical condition at the time of the dream can affect the meaning of the dream. Under certain different circumstances, the same dream can signify two distinct underlying physical conditions.
- The kinds of things dreamed of in prophetic or divine dreams were probably thought to be similar to if not indistinguishable from the things in diagnostic dreams. So, it was impossible to differentiate between prophetic and diagnostic dreams by appeal to content alone.

---

[1] *Meth.Med.* IX.4.

[2] One treatise is entitled *That the Best Physician Is Also a Philosopher.*

[3] Here Galen (*Lib.Prop.* II.2) reports that Asclepius appeared to him in a dream and enjoined him to make an incision on his hand to initiate bleeding. Galen states that this dream saved his life.

[4] Upbraided by the demiurge to finish his work on the optic nerve at *UP* X.12.

[5] *San.Tuen.* I.8.19-21, *Empir.Sub.* X, & *Morb.Diff.* IX.

[6] Siegel (1973, 165-172) offers a translation of substantial chunks of the treatise in the section on Galen's view of dreams of his book *Galen on Psychology, Psychopathology, and Function and Diseases of the Nervous System.* However his translation is faulty and his critique is insubstantial. Kessels (1970, 422-424) gives an analysis of Galen's classification of dreams in *Dign.* as it relates to other oneiric, medical classifications. Oberhelman (1983) offers the first complete English translation. Guidorizzi (1973) offers an Italian translation and commentary and Demuth (1972), a German translation with comments in his doctoral dissertation. A recent version, which corrects some of the defects of Oberhelman's translation, is

available on the web by Lee Pearcy (2000).
[7] Oberhelman 1983, 40 & 1993, 140-141.
[8] For ease of reference, I have numbered the lines of Kühn's edition (1965) of the Greek text in his edition of Galen's *Opera Omnia.*
[9] Cf. *Insomn.* lxxxix.52.
[10] Ibid, IV.lxxxix.89 and 103.
[11] Ibid, IV.lxxxix.122.
[12] Galen gives another example of phlegm where one expects, for completeness of illustration, one of sanguinous matter (hot, wet) here.
[13] Aetius (*Max.* V.ii.3), Plutarch (*Plac.Phil.* V.ii.1), and Ps.-Galen (*Hist.Phil.* CVI) tell us that the Greek physician and anatomist Herophilus (fl. 300 BC) gives a threefold classification: dreams inspired or sent by god (θεοπνεύστοι in Aetius and Plutarch, θεοπέμπτοι in Ps.-Galen) and occurring of necessity, natural dreams (φυσικοί) fashioned by the soul for its own best interest telling what will come about, and compound dreams (συγκραματικοί) arising from the impact of images in accordance with our wishes. The first two give identical accounts, while Ps.-Galen gives one that differs slightly. Von Staden argues that, since Ps.-Galen relies heavily on Aetius or his source, we cannot consider this author an independent source. For a fuller account of this classification, see Von Staden's *Herophilus: The Art of Medicine in Early Alexandria.*
[14] Cf. Aristotle's *Div.Somn.* 463a24-26, Artemidorus' *Oniroc.* I.1, Macrobius' *Somn.Scip.* I.iii.3, and Iamblichus' *Myst.* III.2.
[15] He does not call these dreams θεῖα as does the author of *Insomn.*
[16] Oberhelman translates: "For if it were necessary *to base our interpretations of dreams* only on what we do and think each day..". (1983, 44). The Greek reads: εἰ μὲν γὰρ ἀπὸ τῶν ἐφ' ἡμέρας πραττομένων ἢ φροντιζομένων ἔδει διακρίνειν αὐτὸ μόνον.... Διακρίνω *principally* means "divide", "separate", or "make a distinction", as I translate here, not "interpret a dream" as Oberhelman has it (LSJ). The sense throughout this passage is differentiating between types or functions of dreams, not interpreting. Moreover, since it is in the singular, I take αὐτὸ μόνον adverbially ("merely"), as does Oberhelman, and not as the direct object of διακρίνειν, which precedes it. Thus, the object for the verb must be understood implicitly as "diagnostic dreams".
[17] Cf. Lucretius' *Nat.* IV.1024-1025 & Artemidorus' *Oniroc.* I.1.
[18] *Nat.*, IV.1030-1036.
[19] On the withdrawal of sensation in sleep, see Plato (*Ti.* 45b-d), Aristotle (*Insomn.* 458b30-459a6), Cicero (*Div.* I.114-115), Lucretius (*Nat.* IV.949), and Philo (*Insomn.* lxxxvi). Synesius (*Insomn.* 1288c-1289d), in Platonic fashion, believes that sleep allows for a more direct perception of things. Concerning the drawing up of desirable images in sleep, see Aristotle (*Insomn.* 460b3-16) and Lucretius (*Nat.* IV.816-817).
[20] Oberhelman 1993, 140. In footnote 89 on the very next page, he adds that the work is "a compilation of passages taken out of sequential order, without attention to logical and grammatical thought".
[21] Ibid, 140-141.
[22] This conditionalized form is characteristic of books on interpretation of dreams in Babylonian and Egyptian times even before the first millenium

B. C. (Lewis 1976, 7-19).
[23] I.e., "But since in sleep the soul does not dream only of the conditions of the body...".
[24] See also Cicero's *Div.* II.28 and Iamblichus' *Myst.* III.2.
[25] Oberhelman 1983, 42-43.
[26] From Edelstein's collection of Epidaurean testimonies, *at most* only dreams 39, 42, and 43 of the 43 testimonies listed may be taken as analogical, though I believe these too are better understood nonanalogically and in a fairly straightforward sense. Some typical examples of their straightforwardness: *Stela* 18: "Alcetas of Halicis. This blind man saw a dream. It seemed to him that the god came up to him and with his fingers opened his eyes, and that he first saw the trees in the sanctuary. At daybreak he walked out sound". *Stela* 28: "Cleinatas of Thebes with the lice. He came with a great number of lice on his body, slept in the Temple, and sees <sic> a vision. It seems to him that the god stripped him and made him stand upright, naked, and with a broom brushed the lice from off his body. When day came he left the Temple well". *Stela* 34: "...of Troezen for offspring. She slept in the Temple and saw a dream. The god seemed to say to her she would have offspring and to ask whether she wanted a male or a female, and that she answered she wanted a male. Whereupon within a year a son was born to her". Edelstein et al. (their translation) 1945, 220-237.
[27] The sense of the final sentence is unclear as it stands. Oberhelman's translation, "...no comprehension of these matters is possible unless [the physician] has listened [to the patient]" (1983, 42), assumes that it is the physician who is listening to the patient, but why is it not the patient listening to the doctor or any reader of this text listening to Rufus himself? Moreover, Oberhelman takes no notice of ἄλλη and perhaps with good reason. The sentence makes sense without it ("There can be no understanding of these things unless one has listened"), not with it ("There can be no *other* understanding of these things unless one has listened"). A more economical approach, I believe, is to see μή as a mistaken addition to the manuscripts, reading: "There can be no other understanding of these things for one who *has* listened". Support for this reading comes from manuscript **V** from the two manuscripts, **M** and **V**. See Daremberg and Ruelle's edition of *Quaes. Med.*, xxvi & 206.

Chapter Ten
Healing Dreams in Medical Incubation

Introduction

The previous two chapters show that dreams figured prominently as diagnostic tools in ancient Greco-Roman medical practice. Yet many ancients often relied on medical practice of a somewhat different sort—medical practice at religious healing sanctuaries called "incubation".

Our knowledge of medical incubation comes primarily from stone tablets or *stelae* that display various testimonies of cure (recovered first in 1883) and various other extant Greek and Roman inscriptions as early as the fifth century B. C.,[1] scattered references in ancient Greco-Roman literature after Homer, votive offerings left by supplicants' offerings (replicas of body parts that were cured or required cure), and Aelius Aristides' orations and his diary of dreams in the second century A. D.[2]

In this chapter, my main concern is trying to understand just how dreams figured into therapy or cure at these healing sanctuaries. Still the type of medicine practiced at religious sanctuaries and the Greco-Roman attitude toward it are themselves intriguing issues, and I cannot hope to achieve my primary aim by ignoring the broader picture. To apprehend the function of dreams in incubation, I must say something about the nature of these sanctuaries and about how they were perceived by secular physicians and by Greco-Roman culture at large.

In what follows, I tease out a picture of the function of dreams in religious incubation beginning with the early testimonies, especially the early Epidaurean testimonies, and then turn to the second-century A. D. oneiric diary of Aristides called *Sacred Tales*.

Early Religious Incubation

The Sanctuary at Epidaurus

Religious healing sanctuaries were commonplace throughout Greco-Roman antiquity, even in early Christian times. Prominent temples for Asclepius existed at Athens, Delos, Tricca, Pergamum, Carthage, Lebena, Aegae, Orchomenos, Rome, Peiraeus, Titane, Corinth, and even Cos[3] (one of the significant centers of Hippocratic medical practice).

The sanctuary at Epidaurus, the most important sanctuary for incubation in antiquity, became fully developed relatively late (in the fourth century B. C.). Epidaurus, a coastal city in the southern Saronic gulf, lies to the east of Corinth and Argos and due south of Megara (across the gulf). The sanctuary is situated away from the coast in an idyllic, hilly, and woody area, where water is plentiful.[4] Pausanias, in his *Guide to Greece*, describes the sanctuary thus:

> Boundary markers surround the sacred grove of Asclepius from all sides. Men do not die and women do not give birth within the enclosure,[5].... The suppliant, whether he is one of the Epidaureans themselves or a foreigner, gives up the offerings within the boundary markers.... The statue of Asclepius [at the temple of Asclepius[6]] is half the size of Olympian Zeus at Athens, and is made of ivory and gold. An inscription reveals that the artist was the Parian Thrasymedes, son of Arignotus. Seizing a staff, Zeus sits on a throne, while he has his other hand over the head of a serpent. A dog, lying besides him, has also been wrought. Sculpted upon the throne, are the deeds of the Argive heroes, that of Bellerophon against the Chimaera and that of Perseus cutting off the head of Medusa. Beyond the temple is where the supplicants of the god sleep [a building called[7]]. It is [also] worth seeing a round building of white stone, called *tholos*, which has been built nearby. In it is a picture by Pausias, where *Eros* has cast off his arrows and bow and, instead of these, has chosen to carry a lyre. Drunkenness, drinking from a crystalline vessel, has been painted there as well. This is also a work of Pausias. You can even see in the picture a crystalline vessel and the face of a women through it. Within the enclosure, there stood stone tablets (στῆλαι). In my time, six remained, but there were more in antiquity.[8] Inscribed on them are the names of men and women healed by Asclepius, and in addition the illness from which each has suffered and how each was cured. These are written in Dorian dialect (II.xxvii.1-3).

From the extant archeological and literary evidence, it is possible piece together a relatively reliable account of the steps involved in invoking the help of a healing deity such as Asclepius. First, supplicants had to bathe to purify themselves[9] and then offer up honey cakes and certain meats to the god as a sacrifice (T. 421[10]; see also T. 423.v & 511). Nothing other than a holy frame of mind (T. 318), seemed to be required to invoke the blessings of Asclepius. Thereupon, without ceremony or ritual of any sort, supplicants were led by candlelight (T.421, 423.v, & 544) through the temple district to the *abaton*, where they would lay upon a pallet to await the presence of the god in sleep. Asclepius would then seem to appear to sleepers in a dream and, in most cases, either suggest a cure or by himself administer a cure through various means.[11] Sometimes he would demand some sort of payment in return for cure (T. 413 & 423.xxix). Afterward, a supplicant might erected a statue in his honor (T. 442), compose an ode or song (T. 413), bring back to the sanctuary a large stone (T. 423.xv), or even dedicate to the god a silver pig (T. 423.iv). Such votive offerings filled all parts of the sanctuary, perhaps obscuring the buildings themselves.[12]

The Dreams of Medical Incubation

The extant testimonies at Epidaurus and elsewhere show that when the Asclepius appeared, he was seldom perceived as threatening.[13] In one case, when he appears to a boy afflicted with stone and is told that he would receive "ten dice" from the body upon cure, the god laughs (T. 423.viii). In another, an unnamed person mentions that he saw a beautiful youth (νεανίσκον εὐπρεπῆ) administer a drug upon his toe (423.xvii). Testimony 423.xxv mentions a "man of beauty" (εὐπρεπὴς ἀνήρ), while 423.xxxi talks of a "a certain beautiful boy" (παῖς τις ὡραῖς[14]). His voice is even sometimes harmonious (T. 427).

What is *prima facie* surprising, however, is that in almost every extant testimony at sanctuaries where Asclepius is said to have appeared through a dream, there is nothing said concerning what Asclepius looks like. Some typical testimonies are as follows:

> Hermodicus of Lampsacus had paralysis of the body (ἀκρατὴς τοῦ σώματος). This man, while sleeping [in the *abaton*], was healed and was ordered upon leaving to carry into the sanctuary as large a stone as was possible. And he brought the stone that lies before the abaton (T.423.xv).

Or:

> Alcetas of Halicis. This man, who was blind (τυφλός), saw a dream (ἐνύπνιον εἶδε). The god approached and, with his fingers, seemed to him to draw apart his eyes. For the first time [upon waking], he saw the trees in the sanctuary. At daybreak, he came out healthy (T. 423.xviii).

Or again:

> Hagestratus had pain in his head (κεφαλᾶς [ἄ]λγος). This man could not sleep, because of the pain in his head. As he came into the *abaton*, he fell asleep and saw a dream (ἐνύπνιον εἶδε). The god seemed to heal the pain in the head. Erect and naked, he was stood upright by the god, who taught him the lunge of pancratium. When daybreak arrived, he came out healthy and, shortly thereafter, won the pancratium at the Nemean Games (T.423.xxix).

That there should be no mention of Asclepius' manner of appearance in most of the extant testimonies is surprising, even if we know that supplicants were expecting to see the god in their sleep.[15] After all, he was believed to be a god, and as such was supposedly endowed with certain *visibly* superhuman features. In contrast, talk of divine epiphanies in ancient Greco-Roman literature, especially literature concerning dreams, is seldom without some mention of the striking nature of the deities themselves.[16]

Analysis of the Dreams of Incubation

What are the reasons for the neglect of how Asclepius himself looked in the dreams? At Epidaurus, there certainly was need for terseness, since the testimonies are etched into stone tablets and these would not allow for extraordinarily elaborate descriptions. Yet the tablets were displayed, in a word, to promote religious incubation to supplicants and some mention of the extraordinary features of the god himself in a dream would have certainly facilitated this end better. If this is true, then no argument from economy is cogent; there simply would not have been any need to economize words greatly when trying to advertise the actions of the god.

On the one hand, the lack of detailed description of any sort on the appearance of the god in a dream suggests that Asclepius seemed to sleepers to be neither terrifying, nor awe-inspiring, and that he must have appeared to supplicants to be much like he did in artifacts bearing his "likeness". In short, there must have been very little in his "appearance" that was contrary to expectation. On the other hand, "seeing" Asclepius in a dream *was* genuinely remarkable to some sleepers, but not the most remarkable aspect of the dream. Supplicants came to a sanctuary to be healed or to remedy some physical defect. In consequence, their focus was on health and not on the god *per se*. In preparing for sleep, they were not so much expecting to see the god, they were expecting to see the god *doing or saying something to facilitate their own cure*. If this is plausible, then those who inscribed the tablets themselves were promoting incubation by means of the superordinary deeds of Asclepius, not the god himself.[17]

What does strikes one's attention, when reading the testimonies, is the variety of problems and especially the many, often miraculous, methods that the god suggests or employs in cure. Asclepius uses pharmacological or dietetical (T.405, 410, 411, 423.iv, ix, xvii, xix, xl, xli, 427, 432, 434, 436, 438-441, 447, & 504), surgical (T. 422, 423.v, xiii, xxi, xxv, & xxvii, 426, & 450), cheiric (deeds of the hand) (T. 423.iii, vi, vii, xi, xviii, xxviii, xxx-xxxii, xxxv, xxxvii, xxxviii, xl, & xli, 426, 432, & 449), verbal (T. 407. 408, 409, 413, 423.ii, v, viii, xv, xxix, & xxxiv), and even psychological (T. 413) and miraculous (T. 423x & xvi) means to effect cure. Often he brings about cure through animals, such as snakes (T. 423.xvii, xxxiii, xxxix, & xlii) and dogs (T. 423.xx & xxvi), the very symbols of the god, and even a goose (T. 423.xliii). Many of these cures are said to happen within a supplicant's dream. I give some examples for illustration.

> A certain other wealthy man, this one not a native but from the interior of Thrace, set forth for Pergamum, because a dream had compelled him. Then a dream appeared to him, and the god commanded him to drink, each day, of the drug that came from the vipers and to anoint his body from the outside. After a few days, the disease (τὸ πάθος) changed to leprosy. In turn, this illness was cured by the drugs that the god had prescribed (T. 436).

Or, a testimony at Lebena:[18]

> He (the god) ordered Demandrus of Gortyn, son of Calabis, who had sciatica (ἰσ[χια]λικόν) to go away to Lebena to be healed. As soon as he arrived, he (the god?) operated on him in sleep and he became healthy (T.426).

Sometimes the cure through a dream is miraculous or extraordinary. T.423.ix tells of a blind man who came to Epidaurus with one eyeball missing, yet with hopes of regaining his sight. Many in the temple laughed at his foolishness. Asclepius is said to have visited the man in sleep and poured some drug into the vacancy left by his missing eyeball. At daybreak, the man's sight was fully restored. Again, Euhippus had the point of a spear in his jaw for six years before he came to Epidaurus. While he slept, the god was seen to extract the spear. Euhippus held the spearhead in his hands at daybreak (T. 423.xii). Clearly, what astonishes dreamers is not so much the perceived appearance of Asclepius himself,[19] but instead the incredible nature of his words and deeds.

In spite of the incredible nature of many of these cures, medical incubation was not a last resort for desperately ill people, who were shunned by secular physicians. Indeed, there were some avowedly serious cases that secular practitioners may have declined: cases of spear wounds (T.423.xii, xxx, & xl), paralysis (T. 423.iii, xv, xxxvii, xxxviii, & 446), consumption (T. 423.xxxiii, 427, 438, & 456), and perhaps even arthritis (T. 446). Nonetheless, the testimonies clearly show that many of the supplicants were not in desperate or life-threatening straits and chose incubation because of preference, availability, or proximity. For instance:

> Heraieus of Mytilene. This man did not have hair on his head (οὐκ εἶχε ἐν τᾶι κεγαλᾶι τρίχας), but he had much on his chin. Being shamed and mocked by others, he fell asleep [in the abaton]. The god rubbed his head with a drug and gave him hair (T.423.xix).

Another testimony tells of a porter who, chancing to be near Epidaurus, fell and broke a vase. He put the pieces into a bag and took the bag into the temple, where he discovered upon opening the bag that the vessel was again whole (T. 423.x). Last, an inscription from Crete tells of a woman with a sore finger (T. 441).

Though dreams were important elements in the prescriptions and cures in incubation, they were not essential to the whole process. If he so chose, Asclepius could easily have acted without the assistance of a dream, and he sometimes did (T.423.x & xvi).

The Oneiric Diary of Aelius Aristides

Aristides' Early Illness

Next, I turn to a diary of dreams, *Sacred Tales*, from Aelius Aristides of Smyrna (fl. c. 150 A.D.). *Sacred Tales* tells of Aristides' frequent visits to religious healing sanctuaries throughout his life. Though this testimony on behalf of the efficacy of the gods through dreams is self-serving, it is of incomparable value, since it gives us a fairly trustworthy account of what went on in second-century A. D. medical incubation. More importantly, the dreams that Aristides recounts are in key respects different from those in the testimonies of the various healing sanctuaries much earlier and, thus, they might shed light on some of the problems I discuss above.

Aristides, a rhetorician who was schooled by Sophists in Smyrna, Pergamum, and Athens and won fame in Rome with his art,[20] suffered throughout much of his adult life from various illnesses. After his first serious illness, he came to the Asclepian temple at Pergamum for relief. I sketch out Aristides' account of this incident below.

Aristides tells us that he first became ill in January of 144 A. D. at Smyrna. While sick, he nevertheless set out for a scheduled trip to Rome. The journey was arduous, almost unbearable. At the Hellespont, his ears began to trouble him. As he traveled farther, he developed shortness of breath and fever. He even began to worry that his teeth might fall out. In all, it took him 100 days to reach Rome (II.60-62).

While at Rome, he developed shivers and, he says, his intestines swelled. Physicians attempted to purge him with cucumber juice until there was a bloody discharge. His condition worsened such that everyone lost hope for his survival. In a desperate attempt at purgation, physicians made an incision from his chest to his bladder and applied cupping instruments. His purge was such that he felt an unendurable and numbing pain, and, he relates, his breathing completely stopped for a while. All treatments at this point seemed in vain (II.62-64).

By the fall of the same year, he convalesced sufficiently to enable himself to undertake the long and difficult journey homeward. Arriving in Smyrna in October of 144 A. D., neither physicians nor gymnastic trainers could ascertain the nature of his illness. "From such great origins, to speak briefly and obscurely, my disease formed and grew—ever progressing as time went on".[21] In the summer of 145 A. D., he went to convalesce at the Asclepian temple at Pergamum, where he then stayed for two years (II.64-70).

It was at the sanctuary at Pergamum that Aristides was first visited by his "Savior" (Σωτήρ) Asclepius in dreams.[22] The god's first oneiric command to Aristides was for him to record his dreams in a diary. "Straight from the beginning", Aristides relates, "the God ordered me to write down my dreams". He did so and added many missing details to them many years later, when composing his *Sacred Tales*[23] (II.2.4).

The frequent visitations of the god in all of his guises gave Aristides the courage to carry on despite the many debilitating illnesses from which he would suffer in the course of his life. He became passionately and irretrievably involved with his dreams, and his diary, making some allowance for ambiguous references, contains some 155 of his personal dreams through Aristides' visits to sanctuaries at Pergamum, Smyrna, Lebedus, Olympia, Poemanenon, and Epidaurus.

Analysis of Aristides' Dreams

Concerning the characteristics of these dreams, first, quite unlike the archaeological reports of dreams at the various sanctuaries, the people or deities in Aristides' dreams are not always healing deities. In fact, there are over 60 references to persons or gods seen in dreams other than Asclepius and the Egyptian healing gods Serapis (III.46 & 47) and Isis (III.45, 46, &, possibly, V.25): for example, other gods (I.18, II.41, III.47, IV.39, 40, & V.25), temple priests or attendants (I.11, 12, 15, 22, 25, 40, 41, 43, 49, 58, 76, III.21, 25, IV.48, 64, & V.49), and other notables, such as orators (I.34), philosophers (IV.57 & 61), seers or interpreters (V.20 & 65), and emperors (I.17, 23, 34, 36, IV.57, 60, 61, 106, & V.66). What is even more striking, even though there are numerous implicit references to Asclepius, I have found only three references where the god is *explicitly* identified in a dream (II.18, III.46, & IV.50). At II.18, Asclepius appears both as himself and Apollo, while Aristides is at Smyrna. At the temple of Isis in Smyrna, Aristides mentions that Isis, Serapis, and Asclepius appear to him in a dream (III.46). At IV.50, Asclepius appears to Aristides much the same as he looks in statues.

Second, in keeping with Asclepius' bidding, all of the dreams that Aristides relates in *Sacred Tales* are relevant to the supplicant's health or somehow related to the wondrous medical capacities of the healing gods. In some, the appropriate god straightforwardly points out a prescription for convalescence. He prescribes *bathing* (I.3, 7, 8, 21, 34, 35, 50, II.18, 48, 50, 51, 54, 55, 71, 74, 78, III.6, IV.11, V.24, & 42), even in the snow (IV.11), or *not bathing* (I.22, 29, 41, 52, 59-60, & IV.6); *taking in nutriment* (I.26, 45, 65, III.7, 15, 24, 31, 32, V.24, & 26) or *fasting* (I.27, 40, 54, 56, & III.35); *purging through blood-letting* (I.28, II.47, & 48), *through vomiting* (I.32, 54, 65, & II.13), or *through enema* (II.43 & 63); *rigorous exercise* (often of strange sorts)—like horse riding (I.65), running naked in wintertime (I.65 & II.75), or sailing in a stormy harbor (I.65)—or *rest* (I.15); *the application or oral ingestion of some medicine, ointment, or drug* (I.9, 66, 68, III.6, 21, 27, 28, & 36); and *a bath with sand* (IV.11) or *with mud* (II.74, 75, & 77). Once, Serapis himself operates on Aristides in a dream[24] (III.47). Disregarding the stranger ones, these remedies are not at all inconsistent with the second-century practice of secular medicine. Therefore, healing gods differ from physicians not so much in their proposed remedies, but in their application of these remedies. These gods' remedies are the same as physicians', but the gods often prescribe a remedy under circumstances in which physicians would regard the prescription as inadvisable, even foolhardy (I.62-64, II.20-22, & III.8-9).

There are other, nonmedical ways in which healing gods assist Aristides.[25] Often they provide him with *instruction to benefit his oratory career* (IV.26, 29, 30, 38, 39-41, 44, 83, V.1, 8, 10, 17, 19, 38, 47, & 57-66). Sometimes, a god sends *apotropaic dreams* (II.17, 26-27, III.20, 39, 41-43, 45-46, 48, & IV.15). At other times, a god sends a dream as a mere *sign for what will inevitable come to pass* (III.2, 3, IV.93-94, V.18, 44-45, & VI.3).

Additionally, there are other elements of dreams that are of interest for different reasons. For instance, many of the dreams cataloged by Aristides are *self-laudatory* (I.41, 46, 49, III.4, IV.19, 25, 50, 53, 64-66, 106, & V.44-45), which is unsurprising for those who, like Freud, hold that dreams are always or often a wish-fulfillment. Others serve merely as *praise to the munificence of Asclepius and other gods* (I.23, 30, 33, II.7, 26-27, 31, 42, 59, III.4, IV.30, 45, & 56).

Another aspect of certain dreams of Aristides relates to oneiric absurdity. Aristides' dreams sometimes contain elements of gross absurdity that are missing (probably expunged) from archaeological testimonies at the sanctuaries. We need only recall the dream at II.18 where Asclepius stands before Aristides, in a dream *both as himself and as Apollo* at the same time. Furthermore, IV.57 relates the following dream:

> I dreamed that I saw Plato himself standing in my room, directly across from my bed. He happened to be working on his letter to Dionysius, and was very angry. He glanced at me and said, "How suited do I appear to you for letter writing? No worse than Celer?" (meaning the Imperial Secretary). And I said, "Hush! Remember who you are!" And not much later, he disappeared, and I was held in meditation. But someone present said, "This man who spoke with you just now as Plato is your Hermes", (meaning my guardian deity). "But", he said, "he likened himself to Plato".

Such absurdities, which appear in many of Aristides' oneiric reports and seemingly for no particular reason, are entirely absent from the inscriptions at sanctuaries. This is surprising, for as we know today from careful study of dreams in sleep laboratories, elements of absurdity are more the rule than the exception in dreams. This suggests that Aristides' oneiric reports have probably not been substantially revised. These reports, allowing for some forgetfulness and revision, are likely to be fairly true to the dreams as they actually had occurred.

Next, let me consider the length of Aristides' dreams. Aristides' dreams as reported vary in length: Some are extraordinarily short (e.g.,

IV.6); others are extremely lengthy and considerably detailed (V.57-66). The testimonies, certainly abridged, are all very short reports. Again, given what we know of oneiric length today from studies in sleep laboratories, dreams can exceed 45 minutes in length.[26] Here we have more evidence that Aristides' reports are faithful to the dreams that Aristides actually had.

Overall, Aristides' oneiric reports—in contrast to those in the testimonies (or even those recorded by Quintus Cicero and those by Artemidorus)—are very much like dreams as we would expect them to have occurred at sanctuaries in second-century A. D. antiquity. In Aristides' dreams, he sees gods, priests and attendants of temples, notable contemporaries, friends, and even strangers. The content of these dreams ranges from strange to straightforward, and often dreams comprise thematically divergent episodes. Allowing for some faulty recall and secondary elaboration, Aristides reports his dreams in a manner that very likely corresponds to the dreams as they were actually dreamed. Unlike the archaeological testimonies at the various healing sanctuaries, inscribed primarily to promote these sanctuaries, Aristides' diary of dreams is our best evidence for the kinds of dreams people actually had at healing sanctuaries.

Aristides' Diary vs. Oneiric Testimonies

My examination of the dreams in Aristides' *Sacred Tales* as compared to the testimonies on the extant stelae has yielded the following results:

- A healing god, such as Asclepius, was perceived to act in various ways through dreams. Sometimes he himself would appear, while at other times he would act through a dignitary of the sanctuary, another god, a friend of the dreamer, or even an anonymous person. Sometimes a god would send an allegorical dream.
- By the second century A. D., the healing gods were predominantly consulting physicians, not cheiric practitioners. There is little if anything in *Sacred Tales* of gods effecting cure through their own hands in sleep as there is in the earlier testimonies.
- The gods' prescriptions (in terms of specifying a course of treatment) were much the same as those of secular practitioners. What differed was that sometimes a god was perceived to prescribe a remedy when no physician would dare do so.
- Many of the characteristics of Aristides' oneiric reports, such as the length of and elements of absurdity in them, are evidence that his reports have not been substantially revised—unlike the tendentious reports of the earlier testimonies (and those of Quintus Cicero and Artemidorus).

- Unlike the early testimonies where healing gods seem exclusively occupied with physical malady, numerous references to instruction for Aristides' career indicate that second-century healing gods were perceived to concern themselves sometimes with the overall health of a supplicant (matters of soul as well as body).

Explaining Oneiric Reports

The archaeological testimonies have been taken traditionally as evidence of the essential magical nature of medical incubation. Until the work of pioneers such as Herzog[27] and Edelstein somewhat later, the prevalent view in the secondary literature had been that medicine, as practiced in the religious sanctuaries, was wholly irrational or magical, in contrast to the mostly rational procedures of practicing physicians like Herophilus or Galen.[28]

Concerning the dreams and the miraculous cures seen in them, Edelstein argues that it is best to explain these historically. He says:

> [O]ne has to presuppose that cures were actually achieved in the way in which they are described [in a dream], that many of the healings were successful. This assumption can safely be made, for had all cures been failures, the Asclepieia would certainly not have existed for so many centuries.

As they traveled to a sanctuary, Edelstein says, supplicants were preoccupied with their own illness and the excitement of possible cure. When supplicants arrived at a sanctuary, they were immediately impressed by the tablets with cures and hanging votive offerings as well as other distinct features of their surroundings. In such a milieu, how could they not have had such dreams as they were supposed to have had? Specific elements in dreams, he adds, are explicable by the "individual achievements of good dreamers". That a sleeper often reported medical activity on the part of the god, like surgery or the application of some drug, can be explained by the average person's familiarity with somewhat technical medical procedures.[29]

Overall Edelstein is committed to the view that *some* of the dreams and cures must be taken at face value, and this is unhelpfully vague. And these, as his comments about specific elements in dreams intimate, are probably not the more incredible ones, which on the Epidaurean *stelae* are in the majority. But if this is all that Edelstein wants to show, then it amounts to no explanation at all, for it fails to explain the overwhelming majority of "cures" through dreams—at least those on the Epidaurean tablets.

Edelstein, then, really fails to offer any explanation for the general pattern of such dreams, but he does at least give a fairly good explanation of specific elements of them. The perceived, particular activities of the gods, he believes, are explicable by individuals' understanding of the secular medical art, while miraculous deeds must be accounted for by idiosyncrasies of dreamers themselves.

Dodds acknowledges that it is difficult to attain certainty about the inscriptions. Unsatisfied with Edelstein's general account, he argues that the notion of a "culture-pattern dream"—where oneiric structure is dependent upon a "socially transmitted pattern of belief" that ceases "when that pattern of belief ceases to be entertained"—is a preferable explanation, at least in terms of the perceived general pattern of such dreams.[30] Here, presumably, oneiric content is determined by the social customs and norms of a people.

If we accept Dodds' explication of the general pattern of the dreams of religious incubation, what then is the precise influence of Greco-Roman culture on the content of these dreams? In what specific sense does culture shape such dreams? More precisely, does culture act on the dream itself, or merely on how one "sees" and reports the dream?

Dodds answers "yes" to both aspects of the last question. He says of such dreams, "their form is determined by the belief [in such dreams], and in turn confirms it; hence they become increasingly stylized". He adds, quoting E. B. Tylor, "what the dreamer believes he therefore sees, and what he sees he therefore believes".[31] In short, Greco-Roman culture impacted *oneiric content itself* and Greco-Roman culture impacted *one's perception of oneiric content*. Over time, a cultural pattern, then, could become responsible for a certain kind of dream. Dodds' explanation is preferable to that of Edelstein.

Concluding Remarks

Dreams as they evolved in religious incubation were directly influenced by the view of dreams, sketched in the introduction to Part I, that was prevalent in early Archaic Greece. Similar to the general view of divine dreams of Archaic times, the medical dreams of religious incubation involved an appearance of some (healing) deity (or representative of such a god) in sleep for the purpose of conveying important information in a relatively straightforward manner. In incubation, however, the information concerned convalescence, and dreamers did not have to be aristocrats: The god appears to all that are willing to travel. Allegorical dreams, the focus of the oneirocritical art and important tools for secular medical detection of illness, were seldom employed by a god for healing in temples.

By the second century (and here I use Aristides' *Sacred Tales* as a base for tentative generalizations), the actual presence of a healing deity becomes less essential than it was centuries earlier. A healing god is now believed to work through a multiplicity of elements in dreams. When a god does appear, he does little himself to effect cure. He functions mostly to prescribe remedies that are consistent with the remedies of secular medicine. Overall, the miraculous cures that occur within dreams are entirely absent in Aristides' dreams.

---

[1] The cult of Asclepius was introduced in Athens after the plague in 429 B.C. Portico and temple were situated on the Acropolis between the theater of Dionysus and the precinct of Themis (LiDonnici 1989, 36 & Scully 1979, 204).
[2] Dodds 1951, 111 and Edelstein 1967 (vol. ii), 143.
[3] Scully 1979, 204-213 and Tomlinson 1976, 97.
[4] He was generally accommodated near or at other Greek sanctuaries, since he was a new arrival to the Greek Pantheon (Scully 1979, 205 & Tomlinson 1976, 96).
[5] These were actual prohibitions for the sake of maintaining the purity of the sanctuary. Testimonies 423.i & ii (Edelstein's numbering) attest to this. To help keep out the defiled, Burkert states that sanctuaries generally had only one entrance, defined by large stone walls (Burkert 1985, 86).
[6] It measures only 38' 7" by 75' 8".
[7] Essentially a Stoa with a length of 116 feet (in pre-Roman times), this was to the north of the temple and separated from it by only a narrow passage-way, perhaps to allow the god ready access to the ill in sleep (Tomlinson 1976, 101).
[8] These *stelae* are rougly 5'7" tall by 2 1/2' wide. Two have survived in relatively complete form, along with fragments of another two. In all, we have 70 tales of cures at Epidaurus. LiDonnici gives a fine description of these *stelae* in her dissertation (LiDonnici 1989, vi-vii, 9, & esp. 36-44; see also Miller 1994, 111).
[9] In the dreams of Aristides, bathing is often part of the prescriptive regimen for cure given by the god to Aristides (Behr 1968, e.g., 206, 209, & 227).
[10] I use Edelstein's (1945) numbering throughout.
[11] As T.423.xx indicates, a dream was not an essential element of cure. Here a blind boy, while awake, had his eyes licked by a dog in the temple. His sight was thereby restored.
[12] The range of votive offerings was great. It would be no exaggeration to say that anything of value could have been and was left behind in honor of the greatness of Asclepius (LiDonnici 1989, 2 & 136-142).
[13] An exception to this is T. 448 (Hippocrates, *Ep.* XV).
[14] Literally, "ripe", "mature", or "in due season", when used to describe produce, or "in the prime of life" or "beautiful", when applied to people.
[15] Linguistic style and thematic arrangement indicate that these *stelae* are drawn from a variety of sources (votive inscriptions and an oral tradition regarding these and the sanctuary itself) and that they betray a "long history of collection, arrangement and redaction" that strongly suggests that certain

testimonies have a longer history than others (DiLonnici 1989, 134-135). This, however, does not affect the argument that I am presenting.

[16] It is often the beauty, size, and brightness of the appearance in sleep that convinces sleepers of its divinity.

[17] When the Epidaurean tablets were inscribed all-at-once or over time is a matter of some debate. Stylistic differences among the tablets suggest the latter, but these differences are not so keen as to intimate any extended length of time. LiDonnici suggests that these *stelae* may have been "votive overloads", where votive offerings and the tales concerning them would be inscribed every few years on to the stones. She thinks that *Stela* A, for instance, contains three such groups of inscriptions (1989, 258-272).

[18] The testimonies of Lebena probably date some 200 years later than those of Epidaurus (c. second century B. C.) and are engraved upon the walls of the Stoa itself, not on tablets. The cures, in general, are less miraculous and more in keeping with the prescriptions of secular medicine at the time (Ibid, 147-151), which suggests either local variation or, more plausibly, a change in just how these sanctuaries operated over time.

[19] And so we have reason to be suspicious of Edelstein's (1945 vol. ii, 150-151) claim, "Everything in his (i.e., Asclepius) appearance announced his divinity".

[20] Miller 1994, 186.

[21] I use Behr's own translation of the *Sacred Tales* throughout.

[22] Not all of the visitations were through dreams; sometimes Asclepius revealed things "openly in his own presence" (I.3). Yet, though Aristides would still rely on the advice of physicians, the god was to become his "true and proper doctor" (I.57).

[23] Whose title, Aristides says, came from the god himself, who called the former's diary of dreams "Sacred Tales" (Ἱεροὶ Λόγοι) (II.9).

[24] Behr notes that the text is corrupt here. It seems unlikely that the surgery had any lasting impact upon waking reality for Aristides, for in Aristides' oneiric records, unlike many of the testimonies at the sanctuaries, a god does not effect cure directly, but merely suggests an appropriate course of convalescence.

[25] Cf. Synesius' *Insomn.* (1308c-1309a, chapter nine).

[26] In general, lengthier dreams occur toward the end of sleep.

[27] Herzog 1931, 67.

[28] Edelstein 1945, 142-145.

[29] Ibid, 162-165.

[30] Dodds 1951, 103-104 & 112.

[31] Ibid 1951, 112.

Appendix A: Key Figures/Works

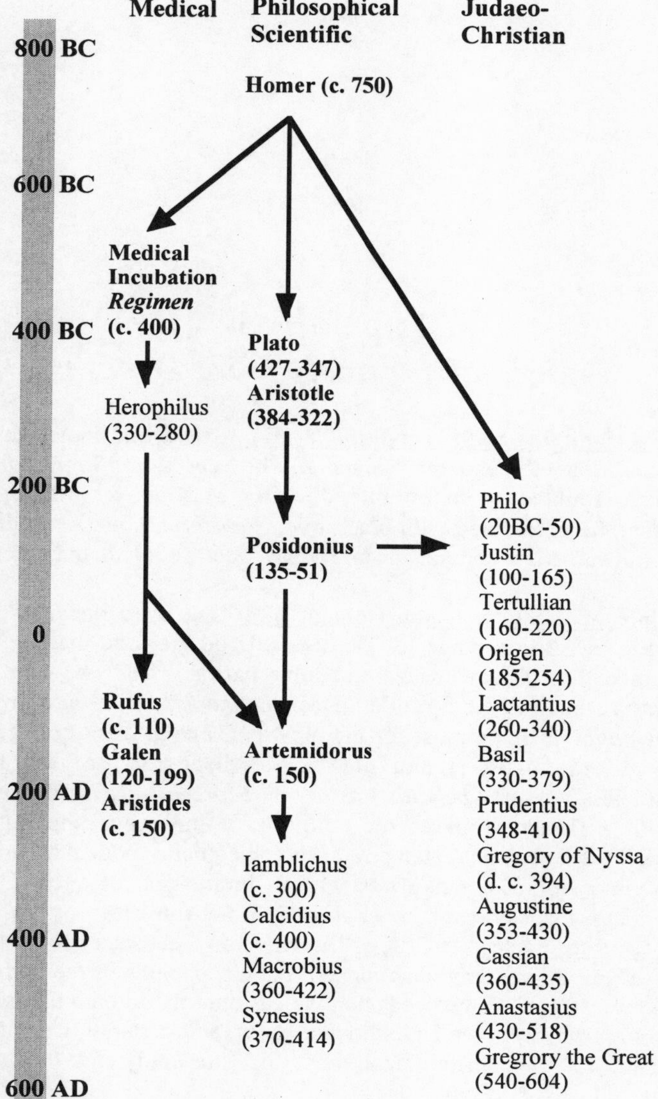

The Homeric Legacy. Some of the key figures and works in Greco-Roman oneirology. Arrows indicate approximate causal influence. Emboldened names/works are examined in this work.

Appendix B
Galen's *Diagnosis from Dreams*

Dreams signifying bodily condition (1-6K): "The dream indicates to us the condition of the body. Someone who sees a *conflagration* in a dream is troubled by yellow bile, but if he sees *smoke*, *mist*, or *deep darkness*, he is troubled with black bile. *Rainstorm*, however, indicates that cold moisture abounds, while *snow, ice*, and *hail* indicate cold phlegm."

Time of dream and nourishment (6-16K): "And one must also attend to the critical stage [of the disease] and the food that has been consumed. For if someone who dreams that *he is covered with snow* has this vision during onset of an attack and *he is shaking or shivering*, or *has chills,* then we must for the most part assign this to the critical stage [of the disease] and not to the disposition of the body. Nonetheless *one who beholds this dream near post-crisis* will furnish us with a firmer proof of the coldness of the prevailing humors, especially if he has not eaten any of the phlegmatic foods that, holding fast to the stomach, make possible an impression of such a kind, although the disposition in the whole body is not similar."

3 types of dreams (16-20K): "But since, in sleep, the soul not only brings about impressions that concern the dispositions of the body, but also [impressions] of the deeds that we customarily do on a daily basis, and some from what we have thought about, and certainly some things are made manifest prophetically by this [the soul] (for this too is witnessed by experience),..."

Problem of differentiation (20-27K): "the diagnosis of the body on the basis of dreams that are set in motion from the body becomes difficult. For were it necessary merely to distinguish [diagnostic dreams] from dreams of deeds and thoughts of the day, then it would not be difficult to suppose that all those dreams that are not from our deeds or thoughts seem to be set in motion from the body. But since, in addition, we acknowledge that some dreams are prophetic, it is not easy to say how these can be distinguished from dreams that are set in motion from the body."

Examples (27-39K): "At any rate, *someone dreamed that one of his legs had turned to stone*, and many skilled in such matters interpreted the dream as a reference to the man's slaves, but the man became paralyzed in that leg, though none of us expected that.

"For instance, we have demonstrated that the wrestler who dreamed he was *standing in a pool of blood and was scarcely able to stay above it* had an abundance of blood in him and was in need of blood-letting.

"And *some who are about to sweat at their crisis* have dreamed they are bathing and swimming in pools of hot water. So too the dream of *drinking without slake of thirst* occurs especially to those who are thirsty, just as a dream of *eating insatiably* occurs to those who are hungry, and a dream of *love-making* occurs to those filled with sperm."

Why such dreams (39-43K): "For the soul, in sleep, seeming to enter into the depths of the body and to withdraw from external perceptions, perceives the disposition of the body, and it receives an impression of all those things to which it reaches out as if these were then present."

Immobility, mobility in dreams (43-51K): "And if this is the case, then no one should be surprised that, whenever the psychic capacity is weighed down and troubled by a plethora of humors, *those moving themselves with difficulty form that impression in a dream and bear a certain burden*. Contrariwise, since the impressions of the soul are always similar to the dispositions of the body, whenever the disposition of the body is light and without excess, then those thus disposed see [themselves] *flying or running very quickly*, to the point of seeming to experience foul- and good-smelling things [in sleep]."

Correspondence of oneiric images and bodily conditions (51-56K): "For those who have impressions that *they are lingering in dung or mud*, certainly have bad, foul-smelling, and putrid humors in them, or an excess of dung clinging to their bowels. One must believe that those of the contrary disposition, who dream of *lingering in good-smelling places*, have the opposite condition in their body."

Conclusion (56-59K): "Therefore, whatever those who are ill see and seem to do in their dreams often indicates to us deficiency, excess, and quality of their humors."

Appendix C
Secular Medicine and Religious Incubation

In this appendix, I address the issue of the relationship between secular medicine and religious incubation.

It is generally admitted these days that secular medicine and religious incubation probably had more of a symbiotic relationship than one of antagonism. The reasons for this are as follows. First, it is clear that the secular attitude toward medical practice did not exclude divine causation. In Greco-Roman antiquity, divine influence in all things was the norm, since nature itself was perceived to be divinely imbued. At once, a natural explanation was also a divine explanation.[1] What most physicians refused to accept was the notion of a *direct* causal impact of a god. This, at least, allowed the practicing physician some justification for intervention in the course of events in the realm of human health. The Hippocratic author of *Dreams*, as we saw in chapter eight, even advocates prayer, though he cautions, "And while praying is a good thing, one himself must also be of help when calling on the gods."[2] Second, like oneirocriticism, secular medicine was not a wholly credible science in antiquity[3] and physicians could best secure a reputation for themselves and best justify their practice as science (τέχνη) by success in their craft. One way to maximize the likelihood for success was to avoid difficult or hopeless cases—a path, it seems, that many physicians selected.[4] If a physician refused a hopeless case, then this person may have had no recourse other than healing sanctuaries. This itself, as Edelstein notes, may be mostly responsible for the negative attitude that many physicians had toward certain, intractable diseases: "[T]he physician presupposes that the patient, if not treated by him, will go to the temple."[5] Of course, some physicians may have simply referred desperate clients to these temples,[6] but it is easy to see that too many referrals could undermine a physician's role as one who strives for "the complete removal of the distress of the sick,"[7] and perhaps foster the view that the success physicians have had against disease was due to chance and not art. Third, many noteworthy physicians and schools of thought acknowledged the efficacy of god-sent dreams at healing sanctuaries. The Hippocratic author of *Dreams* around the fourth century B. C. noted the prophetic function of dreams (IV.lxxxvii). So too did the prominent physician Herophilus[8] (330-280 B. C.). As we saw in the previous chapter, Galen himself, as reputable a physician as there was in antiquity, mentions divine visitations through dreams that have profoundly impacted his career and was certainly favorably disposed to medical incubation.[9] Galen, in *Outline of Empiricism*, also mentions that the Medical Empiricists were committed to divinely prophetic dreams.[10] In addition, one medical school at Athens sacrificed yearly to Asclepius as its patron saint.[11]

With this understood, the incredible popularity of such sanctuaries is easily explicated. Stated simply, for Greco-Roman people, the "physician" at healing sanctuaries was a god—one who possessed superhuman capacities as compared to the limited abilities of secular physicians.

---

[1] This is just what the author of *The Sacred Disease* means when he states that epilepsy is no more sacred than any other disease. Disease, or any other pollution of the body, is not the act of a god, for contamination cannot be caused by what is most pure (IV). Nevertheless, the divine element is present in all natural things.

[2] *Insomn.* lxxxvii (see also xc).

[3] The Hippocratic work *de Arte* is itself a spirited defense of medicine as science (τέχνη).

[4] E.g., *de Arte* III & *Prog*. I. The author of *On Joints*, in contrast, argues that difficult cases should be undertaken for the advancement of knowledge, the physician's reputation, and humanitarian reasons.

[5] Edelstein 1967, 243-246.

[6] Ibid, 245-246.

[7] *De Arte* II (Chadwick and Mann's trans.).

[8] Ps.-Plutarch's *Plac.* V.ii.3 and Galen's *Phil.Hist.* CVI.

[9] *Lib.Prop.* II.2, *Meth.Med.* IX.4, *UP* X.12, *San.Tuen.* I.8.19-21, & *Morb.Diff.* IX.

[10] *Sub.Emp.* X.

[11] Walton 1979, 58.

Bibliography

Ancient Sources

Aeschylus. (1972). *Aeschyli Tragoediae.* Denis Page (ed.). New York: Oxford University Press.

Aristides. (1968). *Aelius Aristides and the Sacred Tales.* C. A. Behr (trans. and comm.). Amsterdam: A. M. Hakkert.

Aristotle. (1955). *Parva Naturalia.* W. D. Ross (ed. and comm.). New York: Oxford University Press.

---------. (1961). *De Anima.* W. D. Ross (ed. and comm.). New York: Oxford University Press.

---------. (1981, [1935]). *The Eudemian Ethics. Aristotle XX.* H. Rackham (trans.). Loeb Classical Library. Cambridge: Harvard University Press.

---------. (1984). *The Complete Works of Aristotle*, Vols. I & II. Revised Oxford Translation. Jonathan Barnes (ed.). Princeton: Princeton University Press.

---------. (1986, [1936]). *Parva Naturalia. Aristotle VIII.* W. S. Hett (trans.). Loeb Classical Library. Cambridge: Harvard University Press.

Artemidorus. (1963). *Onirocriticon Libri V.* Roger Pack (Ed.). Leipzig: Teubner.

-----------. (1965). *Traumbuch.* Martin Kaiser (Trans. and comm.). Stuttgart: Schwabe & Co.

-----------. (1975). *The Interpretation of Dreams.* Robert J. White (Trans. and comm.). Torrance, CA: Original Books.

-----------. (1975). *La Clef des Songes.* A. J. Festugière (Trans. and comm.). Paris: J. Vrin.

Augustine. (1950). *The City of God. Saint Augustine, Vols. VI-VIII.* Demetrius B. Zema, S. J. and Gerald G. Walsh, S. J. (trans.). New York: Fathers of the Church, Inc.

---------. (1951). *Letters. Saint Augustine, Vols. IX & XI.* Sister Wilfrid Parsons, S.N.D. New York: Fathers of the Church, Inc.

Calcidius. (1962). *Timaeus: A Calcidio Translatus Commentarioque Instructus.* London: The Warburg Institute.

Cicero. (1920). *De Divinatione*, vols. i and ii. Arthur Stanley Pease (Comm. and ed.). Chicago: The University of Illinois.

------. (1992, [1927]). *De Divinatione. Cicero XX.* William Armistead Falconer (trans.). Loeb Classical Library. Cambridge: Harvard University Press.

------. (1979, [1933]). *Academica* and *de Natura Deorum. Cicero XIX.* H. Rackham (trans.). Loeb Classical Library. Cambridge: Harvard University Press.

---------. (1977, [1942]). *De Fato. Cicero IV.* H. Rackham (trans.). Loeb Classical Library. Cambridge: Harvard University Press.

---------. (1971, [1914]). *De Finibus. Cicero XVII.* H. Rackham (trans.). Loeb Classical Library. Cambridge: Harvard University Press.

Clement. (1903). *Miscellenies. The Ante-Nicene Fathers, Vol. II.* Alexander Roberts and James Donaldson (eds.). NY: Charles Scribner's Sons.

Diogenes Laertius. ([1925], 1991). *Diogenes Laertius: Lives of Eminent Philosophers*, vol. ii. R. D. Hicks (trans.). Loeb Classical Library. Cambridge: Harvard University Press.

Epicurus. (1966). *Epicurea.* Hermann Usener (ed.). Stuttgart: B. G. Teubner.

------------. (1975). *Epicurus: The Extant Fragments.* Cyril Bailey (ed. and comm.). New York: Georg Olms Verlag.

------------. (1993). *The Essential Epicurus: Letters, Principal Doctrines, Vatican Sayings, and Fragments.* Eugene O'Connor. Buffalo: Prometheus Books.

Galen. (1893). *De Sectis Ingredientibus. Galeni Pergameni Opera Minora*, vol. iii. G. Helmreich (ed.). Leipzig.

-----. (1930). *Subfiguratio Empirica. Die greichische Empirikerschule.* Berlin.

-----. (1944). *On Medical Experience.* R. Walzer (ed.) Oxford.

-----. (1965, [1821-1833]). *Opera Omnia.* C. G. Kühn (ed.). Hildesheim: Georg Olms Verlagsbuchhandlund.

-----. (1968). *On the Usefulness of the Parts of the Body*, vols. i & ii. Margaret Tallmadge May (trans.). Ithaca, NY: Cornell University Press.

-----. (1985). *Three Treatises on the Nature of Science: On the Sects for Beginners; An Outline of Empiricism; and On Medical Experience.* Richard Walzer and Michael Frede (trans.). Indianapolis: Hackett Publishing Company.

-----. *On Diagnosis in Dreams.* Lee T. Pearcy (trans.). 13 January 2000. http://www.ea.pvt.klz.pa.us/medant/dreams.htm.

Gregory of Nyssa. (1893). *On the Making of Man. A Select Library of Nicene and Post-Nicene Fathers of the Christian Church, Vol. V.* Philip Schaff and Henry Wace (eds.). NY: The Christian Literature Company.

Heraclitus. (1968, [1903]). *Die Fragmente der Vorsokratiker*, vol. i. H. Diels (ed.). Zurich: Weidmann, 139-109.

----------. (1986). *Heraclitus: Fragments.* T. M. Robinson (trans. & comm.). Toronto: University of Toronto Press.

Herodotus. (1991). *Historiae*, vols. i & ii. Carolus Hude (ed.). Oxford: Oxford University Press.

Hippocrates. (1923). *Hippocrates, Volumes I & II.* W. H. S. Jones (trans.). Loeb Classical Library. Cambridge: Harvard University Press.

-----------. (1928). *Hippocrates, Volume III.* E. T. Withington (trans.). Loeb Classical Library. Cambridge: Harvard University Press.

-----------. (1992, [1931]). *Hippocrates, Volume IV.* W. H. S. Jones (trans.). Loeb Classical Library. Cambridge: Harvard University Press.

-----------. (1988). *Hippocrates, Volumes V & VI.* Paul Potter (trans.). Loeb Classical Library. Cambridge: Harvard University Press.

-----------. (1994). *Hippocrates, Volume VII.* Wesley D. Smith (trans.). Loeb Classical Library. Cambridge: Harvard University Press.

-----------. (1962, [1849]). *Oeuvres Complètes D'Hippocrate.* E. Littré (trans.). Amsterdam: Adolf M. Hakkert.

-----------. (1967). *Hippocrate: Du Régime.* Robert Joly (trans. and comm.). Paris.

Homer. (1966, [1902]). *Iliadis*, vols. i & ii. David Monro and Thomas Allen (eds.). London: Oxford University Press.

-----. (1974, [1908]). *Odysseae*, vols. i & ii. Thomas Allen (ed.). London: Oxford University Press.

Iamblichus. (1989). *De Mysteriis Aegyptiorum.* Stephen Ronan (ed.). Thomas Taylor and Alexander Wilder (trans.). Chthonios Books.

Jerome. (1893). *Letters*, in *A Select Library of Nicene and Post-Nicene Fathers of the Christian Church, Vol. V: Dogmatic Treatises, Etc.* New York: The Christian Literature Company.

Lucretius. (1886, [1864]). *De Rerum Natura.* H. A. J. Munro (trans. and comm.). Cambridge: Deighton Bell and Co.

---------. (1916_1). *Lucrète: De Rerum Natura*, vols. i & ii. Alfred Ernout (trans. and comm.). Paris: Societe d'Édition "Les Belles Lettres".

---------. (1916_2). *Lucrète: De Rerum Natura: Livre Quatrième.* Alfred Ernout (trans. and comm.). Paris: Librairie C. Klincksieck.

---------. (1942). *De Rerum Natura.* William E. Leonard and Stanley B. Smith (eds. and comm.). Madison: University of Wisconsin Press.

---------. (1947). *De Rerum Natura*, vols. i-iii. Cyril Bailey (trans. and comm.). New York: Oxford University Press.

Macrobius. (1990). *Commentary on the Dream of Scipio.* William Harris Stahl (trans. and comm.). New York: Columbia University Press.

Pausanias. (1918). *Description of Greece*, vol. i (Books I and II). W. H. S. Jones (trans.) Loeb Classical Library. Cambridge: Harvard University Press.

Philo. (1958). *De Insomniis. Philo*, Vol. V. F. H. Colson and G. H. Whitaker (trans.). Loeb Classical Library. Cambridge: Harvard University Press.

Pindar. (1989). *The Odes of Pindar.* Sir John Sandys (trans.). Loeb Classical Library. Cambridge: Harvard University Press.

Plato. (1979, [1900-1907]). *Platonis Opera, Vols. I-V.* John Burnet (ed.). Oxford: Clarendon Press.

-----. (1937). *The Dialogues of Plato*, vols. i & ii. Benjamen Jowett (trans.). New York: Harcourt, Brace and Company.

-----. (1894). *Plato's Republic: The Greek Text*, vols i-iii. B. Jowett and L. Campbell (trans., comm., and essays). Oxford: Clarendon Press.

-----. (1965). *The Republic of Plato*, Vols. I & II. James Adam (ed. and comm.). Cambridge: Cambridge University Press.

-----. (1994). *Republic*, vols. i & ii. Paul Shorey (trans. and comm.). Loeb Classical Library. Cambridge: Harvard University Press.

-----. (1990). *Theaetetus*. M. J. Levett (trans.) and Myles Burnyeat (intro.). Indianapolis: Hackett Publishing Company.

-----. (1929). *Timaeus and Critias*. A. E. Taylor (comm.). London: Methuen & Co., Ltd.

-----. (1937). *Plato's Cosmology: The Timaeus of Plato*. Francis M. Cornford (trans. and comm.). Indianapolis: The Bobbs-Merrill Company, Inc.

-----. (1963, [1925]). *Timée. Oeuvres Complètes X*. Albert Rivaud (trans. and comm.). Paris: Société d'Edition <<Les Belles Lettres>>.

-----. (1976, [1841]). Études sur le Timée de Platon. Thomas Henri Martin (trans. and comm.). New York: Arno Press.

-----. (1973, [1888]). *The Timaeus of Plato*. R. D. Archer-Hind (ed. and comm.). New York: Arno Press.

-----. (1989, [1929]). *Timaeus. Plato IX*. R. G. Bury (trans. and comm.). Loeb Classical Library. Cambridge: Harvard University Press.

Plotinus. (1966-1988). *Enneads*, vols i-vii. A. H. Armstrong (trans.). Loeb Classical Library. Cambridge: Harvard University Press.

Plutarch. (1967). *Adversus Colotem. Moralia, Vol. XIV*. Benedict Einarson and Phillip H. DeLacy (trans.). Loeb Classical Library. Cambridge: Harvard University Press.

--------. (1972, [1929]). *De Pythiae Oraculus. Moralia*, vol. iii. W. R. Paton, M. Pohlenx, and W. Sieveking Ieds.). Liepzig: Teubner.

--------. (1971). *Placita Philosophorum. Plutarchi Moralia*, vol v.2,1. Jurgen Mau (ed.). Leipzig: Teubner.

--------. (1959). *Adversus Colotem. Moralia*, vol vi.2. M. Pohlenz (ed.). Liepzig: Teubner.

Porphyry. (1886). *De Antro Nympharum. Porphyrii Philosophi Platonici Opuscula Selecta*. A. Nauck (ed.). B. G. Teubner.

Rufus of Ephasus. (1970). *Quaestiones Medicinales*. Hans Gärtner (ed.). Leipzig: B. G. Teubner.

----------------. (1963, [1879]). *Oeuvres de Rufus d'Éphèse*. C. Daremberg and E. Ruelle (eds.). Amsterdam: Adolf M. Hakkert.

Sextus Empiricus. (1961, [1935]). *Adversus Mathemeticos, Vols. VII & VIII. Sextus Empiricus II*. Rev. R. G. Bury (trans.). Loeb Classical Library. Cambridge: Harvard University Press.

Soranus. (1956). *Gynecology*. Oswei Temkin (trans.). Baltimore: Johns Hopkins Press.

Statius. (1935). *Silves*. Henri Clouard (trans.). Paris: Garnier Frères.

Stoicorum Veterum Fragmentum, vols. i-iii. ([1905], 1978]). Hans Von Arnim (ed.). Stuttgart: Teubner.

Synesius. (1864). *De Insomniis. PG, Tomus LXVI*. J. -P. Migne (ed.). Paris.

--------. (1926). *The Letters of Synesius of Cyrene*. A. Fitzgerald (trans.). Oxford: Oxford University Press

--------. (1930). *The Essays and Hymns of Synesius of Cyrene*, vols. i & ii. A. Fitzgerald (trans.). Oxford: Oxford University Press.

--------. (1944). *Synesius Cyrenensis Opuscula*, vols. i & ii. N. Terzaghi (ed.). Rome.

Tertullian. (1947). *De Anima*. J. H. Waszink (ed. and comm.). Amsterdam: J. M. Muelenhoff.

Modern Sources

Annas, Julia. (1982). *Introduction to Plato's Republic.* Oxford: Oxford University Press.

Asmis, Elizabeth. (1984). *Epicurus' Scientific Method.* Ithaca: Cornell University Press.

Bailey, D. R. S. (1971). *Cicero.* London: Gerald Duckworth & Company Limited.

Beard, Mary. (1986). "Cicero and Divination: The Formation of a Latin Discourse." *JRS* LXXVI, 33-46.

Behr, C. A. (1968). *Aelius Aristides and the Sacred Tales.* Amsterdam: A. M. Hakkert.

Berve, Helmut and Gottfried Gruben. (1962). *Greek Temples, Theatres, and Shrines.* New York: Harry N. Abrams, Inc.

Bettmann, Otto L. (1956). *A Pictoral History of Medicine.* Springfield, IL: Charles C. Thomas.

Blum, Claes. (1936). *Studies in the Dream Book of Artemidorus.* Uppsala.

Bollack, Jean and André Laks (eds.). (1976). *Cahiers de Philologie, Vol. I: Études sur l'Epicurisme Antiqué.* Université de Lille III.

Bouché-LeClercq, A. (1963, [1879]). *Histoire de la Divination dans l'Antiquité.* Bruxelles: Culture et Civilisation.

Bregman, Jay. (1982). *Synesius of Cyrene: Philosopher-Bishop.* Berkeley: University of California Press.

Brill, Barbara Price. (1976). *Lucretius and the Diatribe against the Fear of Death.* E. J. Brill.

Brisson, Luc. (1974). *Le Même et L'Autre dans la Structure Ontologique de Timée de Platon.* Paris.

Brock, Arthur J (ed. and trans.). (1929). *Greek Medicine.* New York: E. P. Dutton & Co. Inc.

Brown, Peter. (1978). *The Making of Late Antiquity.* Cambridge: Harvard University Press.

Brown, Robert. (1987). *Lucretius on Love and Sex.* New York: E. J. Brill.

Buckley, Terry. (1996). *Aspects of Greek History: A Source-Based Approach.* New York: Routledge.

Burnyeat, Myles. (1970). "The Material and Sources of Plato's Dream." *Phronesis* 15, 101-122.

Chadwick, John and W. N. Mann. (1950). *The Medical Works of Hippocrates.* Oxford: Blackwell Scientific Publications.

Claus, David. (1981). *Toward the Soul: An Inquiry into the Meaning of θυψή before Plato.* New Haven: Yale University Press.

Clay, Diskin. (1983). *Lucretius and Epicurus.* Ithaca: Cornell University Press.

------------. (1980). "An Epicurean Interpretation of Dreams." *American Journal of Philology* 101, 342-365.

Colgan, Michael. (1993). *Optimum Sports Nutrition.* New York: Advanced Research Press.

Dämska, Isadore. (1961). "Le problème des songes dans la philosophie des anciens Grecs." *Revue Philosophique*, 11-024.

Demuth, G. (1972). *Ps-Galeni De dignotione ex insomniis. Ausgabe mit Ubersetzung und Kommentar*. Gottingen.

Diels, H. ([1879], 1976). *Doxographi Graeci*. Berlin: Walter De Gruyter.

Diels, H. and Walther Kranz. (1968, [1903]). *Die Fragmente der Vorsokratiker*. Zurich: Weidmann.

Diller, H. (1952). "Hippokratische Medizin und attische Philosophie." *Hermes* 80.

Dodds, E. R. (1951). *The Greeks and the Irrational*. Berkeley: University of California Press.

--------. (1970). *Pagan and Christian in an Age of Anxiety*. New York: W. W. Norton.

Dulaey, Martine. (1973). *Le Rêve dans la Vie et la Pensée de Saint Augustin*. Paris: Études augustiniennes.

Edelstein, Emma and Ludwig Edelstein. (1945). *Asclepius: A Collection and Interpretation of the Testimonies*, vols. i and ii. Baltimore: The Johns Hopkins Press.

Edelstein, Ludwig. (1967, [1937]). "Greek Medicine in its Relation to Religion and Magic." *Ancient Medicine: Selected Papers of Ludwig Edelstein*. O. Temkin and C. L. Temkin (Eds.). Baltimore: The Johns Hopkins Press.

Ellis, Havelock. (1976, [1922]). *The World of Dreams*. Detroit: Gale Research Company.

Esnoul, A. M. and P. Garelli (Eds.). (1959). *Les Songes: Sources Orientales II. Les songes et leur interpretation*. Paris.

Farrington, Benjamin. (1949). *Greek Science: Thales to Aristotle*. Middlesex: Penguin Books.

Ferrari, G. R. F. (1992). "Platonic Love." *The Cambridge Companion to Plato*. Richard Kraut (ed.). New York: Cambridge University Press, 248-276.

Frede, Michael. (1980). "The Orignal Notion of Cause." *Doubt and Dogmatism*. M. Schofeld, M. Burnyeat, and J. Barnes (eds.). Oxford: Oxford University Press, 217-249.

-------------. (1980). "Stoics and Skeptics on Clear and Distinct Impressions." *Doubt and Dogmatism*. M. Schofeld, M. Burnyeat, and J. Barnes (eds.). Oxford: Oxford University Press, 151-176.

-------------. (1986). "The Stoic Doctrine of the Affections of the Soul." *The Norms of Nature: Studies in Hellenistic Ethics*. Malcolm Schofield and Gisela Striker (eds.). Cambridge University Press, 93-110.

Fredrich, C. (1899). *Hippokratische Untersuchungen*. Berlin.

Freud, Sigmund. (1993, [1900]). *The Interpretation of Dreams*. James Strachey (trans.). NY: Harper-Collins.

Fromm, Erich. (1974). *The Forgotten Language: An Introduction to the Understanding of Dreams, Fairy-Tales, and Myths*. New York: Holt, Rinehart and Winston.

Furley, David. (1966). "Lucretius and the Stoics." *BICS* 13, 13-33.

-------------. (1977). "Lucretius the Epicurean." *Lucrèce: Huit Exposés*. Genève: Fondation Hardt.

Gain, D. B. (1969). "The Life and Death of Lucretius." *Latomus* 28, 545-553.

Gallop, David. (1972). "Dreaming and Waking in Plato." *Essays in Ancient Greek Philosophy*. John Anton and George Kustas (eds.). Albany: State University of New York Press.

---------------. (1988). "Aristotle on Sleep, Dreams, and Final Causes." *Proceedings of the Boston Area Colloquium in Ancient Philosophy*, Vol. IV. J.J. Cleary and D. C. Shartin (eds.) Lanham, 257-290.

---------------. (1990). *Aristotle on Sleep and Dreams*. Lewiston, NY: Broadview Press.

Geer, Russel M. (1927). "On the Theories of Dream Interpretation in Artemidorus." *The Classical Journal* XXII.8, 663-670.

Gill, Mary Louise. (1987). "Matter and Flux in Plato's Timaeus." *Phronesis*, Vol. XXXIII.

Glare, P. G. W. (ed.). (1982). *Oxford Latin Dictionary*. Oxford: Clarendon Press.

Gordon, Benjamin Lee. (1949). *Medicine Throughout Antiquity*. Philadelphia: F. A. Davis Company.

Halliday, W. R. (1913). *Greek Divination*. London: and Co., Limited.

Hatfield, J. A. (1954). *Dreams and Nightmares*. Middlesex: Penguin Books Ltd.

Hempel, Carl G. (1965). *Aspects in Scientific Explanation, and Other Essays in the Philosophy of Science*. New York: Free Press.

Herzog, Rudolf. (1931). *Die Wunderheilungen von Epidauros. Philogus*, suppl. 22, fasc. 3. Leipzig: Dieterich.

Holowchak, Mark A. (1996). "Aristotle on Dreaming: What Goes On in Sleep When the 'Big Fire' Goes Out. *Ancient Philosophy* 16, 405-423.

Hunt, Harry. (1991). The Multiplicity of Dreams: Memory, Imagination, and Consciousness. Yale University Press.

Jaeger, W. (1944). *Paideia: The Ideals of Greek Culture*, Vol. III. New York: Oxford University Press.

Joly, Robert. (1960). *Récherches sur le traité pseudo-hippocratique Du Régime*. Paris.

------------. (1966). *Le Niveau de la Science Hippocratique*. Paris: Societé d'Édition <<Les Belles Lettres>>.

Jones, Nicholas. (1997). *Ancient Greece: State and Society*. Upper Saddle River, NJ: Prentice Hall.

Kahn, Charles H. (1991). "Some Remarks on the Origins of Greek Science and Philosophy." *Science and Philosophy in Classical Greece*. Alan C. Bowen (ed.). New York: Garland Publishing Inc.

Kanter, Mitchell M. (1994). "Free Radicals, Exercise, and Antioxidant Supplementation." *International Journal of Sport Nutrition"* 4, 205-220.

Kany-Turpin, Jose and Pierre Pellegrin. (1989). "Cicero and the Aristotelian Theory of Divination by Dreams." *Cicero's Knowledge of the Peripatos*. W. W. Fortenbaugh and P. Steinmetz (eds.). New Brunswick: Transaction Pub.

Kelsey, Morton. (1968). *Dreams: The Dark Speech of the Spirit*. NY: Doubleday.

Kenney, E. J. (1977). *Lucretius*. Oxford: Clarendon Press.

Kessels, A. H. M. (1970). "Ancient Theories of Dream Classification." *Mnemosyne* XXIII, 389-424.

-----------------. (1978). *Studies on the Dream in Greek Literature.* Utrecht: HES Publishers.

Kirk, G. S. (1954). *Heraclitus: The Cosmic Fragments.* Cambridge.

Kirk, G. S.; J. E. Raven; and M. Schofield. (1983). *The Presocratic Philosophers.* Cambridge: Cambridge University Press.

Kissling, Robert C. (1922). "The OCHMA-PNEUMA of the Neo-Platonists and the De Insomniis of Synesius of Cyrene. *American Journal of Philology* 22, 318-330.

Kuhn, Thomas S. (1996). *The Structure of Scientific Revolutions.* University of Chicago Press.

Lang, W. (1926). *Das Traumbuch von Synesius von Kyrene.* Tubingen.

Langfeld, Herbert S. (1946). "The History of Dream Theory." *Psychological Review* 53, 225-233.

Lee, Edward N. (1978). "The Sense of an Object: Epicurus on Seeing and Hearing." *Studies in Perception.* Peter K. Machamer and Robert G. Turnbull (eds.). Columbus: Ohio State University Press, 27-59.

LeGoff, J. (1985). "Le Christianisme et les Rêves." *I Sognis nel Medioevo: Seminario Internazionale Roma, 2-4 Ottobre 1983.* Lessico Intellettuale Europeo, XXXV. Roma.

Lennox, James. (1983). "Plato's Unnatural Teleology." *Platonic Investigations.* Dominic J. O'Meara (ed.). Washington: The Catholic University of America Press.

Levine, Edwin Burton. 1971. *Hippocrates.* New York: Twayne Publishers.

Lewis, Naphtali. (1976). *The Interpretation of Dreams and Portents.* Toronto: Samuel Stevens, Hakkert & Company.

Liddel, Henry; Robert Scott, and Henry Stuart Jones. (1968, [1940]). *A Greek-English Lexicon.* Oxford: Clarendon Press.

LiDonnici, Lynn R. (1989). *Tale and Dream: The Text and Compositional History of the Corpus of Epidaurian Miracle Cures.* Ph. D. Dissertation: University of Pennsylvania.

Llyod, G. E. R. (1979). *Magic, Reason, and Experience.* Cambridge: Cambridge University Press.

-------------. (1991). "The Definition, Status, and Methods of the Medical Τέχνη in the Fifth and Fourth Centuries." *Science and Philosophy in Classical Greece.* Alan C. Bowen (ed.). New York: Garland Publishing Inc.

Long, A. A. (1986). *Hellenistic Philosophy.* London: Duckworth and Co.

Long, A. A. and Sedley, D. N. (1987). *The Hellenistic Philosophers,* vols. i & ii. Cambridge: Cambridge University Press.

Malcolm, Norman. (1959). *Dreaming.* London: Routledge & Kegan Paul.

McCurdy, Harold Grier. (1946). "The History of Dream Theory." *Psychological Review* 53, 225-233.

Meseguer, Pedro. (1961). *The Secret of Dreams.* Paul Burns (Trans.). Westminster, MD: The Newman Press.

Miller, Patricia Cox. (1994). *Dreams in Late Antiquity: Studies in the Imagination of a Culture.* Princeton: Princeton University Press.

Minyard, J. D. (1985). *Lucretius and the Late Republic.* Leiden: E. J. Brill.

Morgan, Michael. (1992). "Plato and Greek Religion." *The Cambridge Companion to Plato.* Richard Kraut (ed.). New York: Cambridge University Press.

Mourelatos, Alexander P. D. (1991). "Plato's Science—His View and Ours of His." *Science and Philosophy in Classical Greece.* Alan C. Bowen (ed.). New York: Garland Publishing Inc.

Oberhelman, Steven M. (1981). "The Interpretation of Prescriptive Dreams in Ancient Greek Medicine." *Journal of the History of Medicine and Allied Sciences* 36, 416-424.

--------------------. (1983). "Galen: On Diagnosis from Dreams." *Journal of the History of Medicine and Allied Sciences* 38, 36-47.

--------------------. (1991). *The Oneirocriticon of Achmet: A Medieval Greek and Arabic Treatise on the Interpretation of Dreams.* Lubbock: Texas Tech University Press.

--------------------. (1993). "Dreams in Graeco-Roman Medicine." *Aufstieg und Niedergang der Romischen Welt* 37.1. Wolfgang Haase (ed.). Berlin.

Oppenheim, A. Leo. (1956). "The Interpretation of Dreams in the Ancient Near East, with a Translation of an Assyrian Dreambook." *Transactions of the American Philosophical Society* 46.3, 179-373.

Osley, Arthur S. (1963). "Notes on Artemidorus' *Oneirocritica.*" *Classical Journal* 22, 65-70.

Owens, Joseph. (1991). "The Aristotelian Conception of Pure and Applied Sciences." *Science and Philosophy in Classical Greece.* Alan C. Bowen (ed.). New York: Garland Publishing Inc.

Pack, Roger A. (1941). "Artemidorus and the Physiognomists." *TAPA* 72, 321-334.

-------------. (1955). "Artemidorus and his Waking World." *TAPA* 86, 280-290.

-------------. (1957). "Textual Notes on Artemidorus Daldianus." *TAPA* 88, 189-196.

-------------. (1959). "Lexical and Textual Notes on Artemidorus." *TAPA* 90, 180-184.

-------------. (1960). "Further Notes on Artemidorus." *TAPA* 91, 146-151.

-------------. (1965). "Pascilis Romanus and the Text of Artemidorus." *TAPA* 96, 291-295.

Palm, A. (1933). Studien zur hipokratischen Schrift περὶ διαιτῆς.

Parman, Susan. (1991). *Dream and Culture: An Anthropological Study of the Western Intellectual Tradition.* New York: Praeger.

Pearcy, Lee T. (1985). "Galen's Pergamum." *Archeology* XXXVIII.6, 33-39.

Phillips, E. D. 1973. *Greek Medicine.* London: Thames and Hudson.

Price, S. R. F. (1986). "The Future of Dreams: From Freud to Artemidorus." *Past and Present* 113, 3-37.

Rankin, H. D. (1964). "Dream/Vision as Philosophical Modifier in Plato's Republic." *Erkenntniss* 62, 75-83.

Rehm, A. (1941). *Parapegmastudien. Mit einem Anhang Euktemon und das Buch de signis.* Munchen.

Rist, J. M. (1972). *Epicurus: An Introduction.* Cambridge: Cambridge University Press.

Robinson, Rachel Sargent. (1981). *Sources for the History of Greek Athletics.* Chicago: Ares Publishers Inc.

Sandbach, F. H. (1971). "Phantasia Kataleptike." *Problems in Stoicism.* A. A. Long (ed.). London, 9-21.

--------------. (1975). *The Stoics.* New York: W. W. Norton and Co.

Sarton, George. (1954). *Galen of Pergamon.* Lawrence, KS: University of Kansas Press.

----------------. (1977). "La Cassification des Rêves Selon Herophile." *Mnemosyne,* XXX, 13-27.

Scarborough, John. (1971). "Galen and the Gladiators." *Episteme* V, 98-111.

-----------------. (1988). "Galen Redivivus: An Essay Review." *Journal of the History of Medicine and Allied Sciences* XXXXIII, 313-321.

Schofield, Malcolm. (1986). "Cicero for and against Divination." *JRS* LXXVI, 47-65.

------------------. (1992). "Aristotle on the Imagination." *Essays on Aristotle's de Anima.* M. Nussbaum and Amélie Oksenberg Rorty (eds.). Oxford: Oxford University Press, 249-277.

Schrijvers, P. H. (1976). "La Pensée d'Épicure et de Lucrèce sur le Sommeil." *Cahiers de Philologie, Vol. I: Études sur l'Épicurisme antiqué.* Jean Bollack and André Laks (eds.). Université de Lille III, 229-259.

Scully, Vincent. (1979, [1962]). *The Earth, The Temple, and the Gods: Greek Sacred Architecture.* New Haven: Yale University Press.

Siegel, Rudolph E. (1973). *Galen on Psychology, Psychopathology, and Function and Diseases of the Nervous System.* New York: S. Karger.

Sigerist, Henry E. (1955). *A History of Medicine,* vols. i & ii. New York: Oxford University Press.

Smith, A. (1974). *Porphyry's Place in the Neoplatonic Tradition: A study in Post-Plotinian Neoplatonism.* Martinus Nijhoff: The Hague.

Smith, Jonathan. (1978). "Towards Interpreting Demonic Powers in Hellenistic and Roman Antiquity." *Aufstieg und Niedergang der Römischen Welt. Principat* 16.1. Wolfgang Haase (ed.). Berlin: Walter de Gruyter, 425-439.

Smith, Martin. (1970). "Fragments of Diogenes of Oenoanda Discovered and Rediscovered." *American Journal of Archaeology* 75, 357-389.

--------------------. (1977). "More New Fragments of Diogenes of Oenoanda." *Cahiers de Philologie, Vol. I.* Jean Bollack and André Laks (eds.). Université de Lille III.

Spriet, Lawrence L. (1995). "Caffeine and Performance." *International Journal of Sport Nutrition* 5-S, S84-S99.

Taylor, M. (1947). "Progress and Primitivism in Lucretius." *American Journal of Philology,* 180-194.

Temkin, Owsei. (1991). *Hippocrates in a World of Pagans and Christians.* Baltimore: The Johns Hopkins University Press.

Tomlinson, R. A. (1976). *Greek Sanctuaries.* New York: St. Martin's Press.

Turnbull, Robert G. (1991). "Platonic and Aristotelian Science." *Science and Philosophy in Classical Greece.* Alan C. Bowen (ed.). New York: Garland Publishing Inc.

Trice, Isaiah and Emily M. Haymes. (1995). "Effects of Caffeine Ingestion on Exercise-Induced Changes During High-Intensity, Intermittent Exercise." *International Journal of Sport Nutrition* 5.1, 37-44.

Usener, Hermann (ed.). (1966). *Epicurea.* Stuttgart: B. G. Teubner.

Van de Castle, Robert. (1994). *Our Dreaming Mind.* New York: Ballantine Books.

Van Lieshout, R. G. A. (1980). *Greeks on Dreams.* Utrecht: Hes Publishers.

Vlastos, Gregory. (1973). "Degrees of Reality in Plato." *Platonic Studies.* Princeton: Princeton University Press, 1-19.

Von Staden, Heinrich. (1978). "The Stoic Theory of Perception and Its 'Platonic' Critics." *Studies in Perception.* Peter K. Machamer and Robert Turnbull (eds.). Columbus: Ohio State University Press, 96-136.

--------------------. (1989). *Herophilus: The Art of Medicine in Early Alexandria.* Cambridge: Cambridge University Press.

Wallach, Barbara Price. (1976). *Lucretius and the Diatribe against the Fear of Death.* Leiden: E. J. Brill.

Walton, Alice. (1979). *Asklepios: The Cult of the Greek God of Medicine.* Chicago: Ares Publishers.

Waszink, J. H. (ed.). (1962). *Timaeus: A Calcidio Translatus Commentarioque Instructus.* London: The Warburg Institute.

White, Nicholas P. (1979). *A Companion to Plato's Republic.* Indianapolis: Hackett Publishing Company.

Winkler, John J. (1990). *The Constraints of Desire: The Anthropology of Sex and Gender in Ancient Greece.* New York: Routledge.

Index